SURVIVING
COLLEGE
SUCCESSFULLY

Other books by Gary DeMar

God and Government:
A Biblical and Historical Study, 1982

God and Government:
Issues in Biblical Perspective, 1984

God and Government:
The Restoration of the Republic, 1986

Ruler of the Nations:
Biblical Blueprints for Government, 1987

The Reduction of Christianity:
Dave Hunt's Theology of Cultural Surrender, 1988
(with Peter J. Leithart)

SURVIVING COLLEGE SUCCESSFULLY

A Complete Manual for the
Rigors of Academic Combat

Gary DeMar

Illustrations by Dan Riedel

Wolgemuth & Hyatt, Publishers, Inc.
Brentwood, Tennessee

Surviving College Successfully was produced by American Vision,
a Christian educational and communications organization.
American Vision publishes a monthly newsletter, *The Biblical
Worldview*, which is edited by Gary DeMar. For more information
about American Vision, write: American Vision, P.O. Box 720515,
Atlanta, Georgia 30328.

Published by Wolgemuth & Hyatt, Publishers, Inc.
P.O. Box 1941, Brentwood, Tennessee 37027.

Printed in the United States of America.

First printing, April, 1988
Second printing, August, 1988
Third printing, May, 1989

Library of Congress Cataloging-in-Publication Data

Demar, Gary.
    Surviving college successfully.

    Bibliography: p.
    1. College students—Religious life.   2. Study,
Method of. 3. Christian life—1950-   . I. Title.
BV4531.2.D46   1988   248.8'34   88-10613
ISBN 0-943497-24-8

To my parents

CONTENTS

ACKNOWLEDGMENTS

Surviving College Successfully began as an idea in 1985 after I read an unpublished manuscript by Dr. Gary North entitled *Christian Survival on the Secular Campus*. After reading through his work, I decided to try my hand at a manual that would deal more with the academic side of college education and also handle many of the philosophical issues all students encounter. Through Dr. North's encouragement, this book became a reality.

Dr. Greg L. Bahnsen made invaluable suggestions to the first five chapters. His clear thinking, unequaled grasp of philosophical systems and traditions, and precision of language greatly enhanced the usefulness and clarity of these chapters.

Peter Leithart, my associate at American Vision, filled in the gaps when last minute changes had to be made. He worked up to the last day of my deadline to get the needed material completed.

My parents deserve the most credit for the completion of this book. They worked hard to ensure that I received a college education in spite of the evaluation of my high school guidance counselors that I was not "college material."

INTRODUCTION

I can still see the expression on my mother's face after the guidance counselor told her that I was "not college material." An opportunity to get a free college education was just about to go down the drain because my grades were so bad. Now, I wasn't stupid. My high school transcripts always read: "Gary is not working up to his abilities." Anyway, school was boring. And to top it off, during the '60s, educators were "experimenting" with new teaching methods: programmed learning, split classes, modules, etc. Education became a free-for-all, and I was caught in the middle. It was a great excuse to pursue other interests.

I did just enough work to get by. Instead of studying, I pursued athletics and my own academic interests. During my senior year in high school I had thrown the shot put nearly 65 feet (64' 2½"), far enough to rank me fifth in the nation, far enough to break the Pennsylvania state record, and far enough to bring me nearly 50 scholarship offers. But my grades did not meet National Collegiate Athletic Association (NCAA) standards. What began as a way to get a free ride to the college of my choice became a nightmare for my parents. I was so close, yet still so very far away.

Good grades didn't concern me as I spent nearly four hours every day while school was in session training for an eventual spot on the Olympic team in either track and field or weightlifting. I increased my training to six hours each day during the summer months. I was waiting until I got to college to pursue good grades. To put a twist on a more familiar phrase, procrastination is the mother of bad grades.

Well, I made it to college, took advantage of my waning athletic prowess and graduated. I even went on to graduate school, and as of this writing, have authored six books. What happened after high school? What turned me around? The realization that my athletic abilities would not take me into the big time forced me to pursue other avenues. But my study skills were weak. All those years of "just getting by" took their toll.

1

Surviving College Successfully is the accumulation of over 20 years of experience of what works and what doesn't work in getting better grades. Some manuals tell you to "study harder." This manual shows you how to study smarter. You will not find a more helpful course on the market today. I've studied nearly 100 books dealing with how to get better grades. While all of them have some good things to say, not one of them includes all the practical advice you will find in this single volume. Some study guides to improve grades include a lot of needless information. I've sifted through all the data and included what I consider to be the best advice.

But this manual is unique in another way. Very few manuals on the market today show students how to deal effectively with the attacks they will encounter regarding their Christian beliefs. Since most of the study courses are not written by Christians, we should not be surprised at this omission. But even the Christian study manuals give scant attention to the development and defense of the Christian worldview. *Surviving College Successfully* fills this need. You will learn how to defend the faith, and you will gain expertise on how to evaluate contrary worldviews, spotting their presuppositional makeup and avoiding their pitfalls.

Surviving college is not enough. You want to be *successful*. You want to come out of college, not only with good grades and a good education, but with the ability to transform this world through the power of God's Spirit and in the name of the Lord Jesus Christ. This will mean putting your faith to work as you tackle academics and engage in spiritual warfare. *Surviving College Successfully* is designed to help you accomplish your goals.

Surviving College Successfully does not cover everything you will encounter in college. I've tried to touch on the more current worldviews. You will have to make the necessary adaptations to your specialized situation. You can make this a better book by sending me information on the latest campus trends. Copies of student newspapers, tapes of lectures, reproduced lecture notes handed out by your professor, and advertisements for special speakers are especially helpful. If you have ideas that will make *Surviving College Successfully* a better book, please send them to me at the following address:

Surviving College Successfully
American Vision
P.O. Box 720515
Atlanta, Georgia 30328

PART ONE

LEARNING HOW TO SURVIVE

1

PREPARING FOR BATTLE

PHILOSOPHY I: (Prerequisite—five
hours of sitting around doing nothing).

Philosophy I is where you learn how the
great thinkers of the past view man's
existence, such as Descartes who said,
"I think, therefore I am."

It turns out he was right because he
stopped thinking a while back, and now
he no longer is![1]

WHEN entering a battle, you had better be prepared for the opposition. The following story will set the stage for what you will be learning in *Surviving College Successfully.*

It's ten o'clock at night. You're just leaving the library building. This is the third night this week that you've had to work on your research paper. You begin to walk toward your dorm. Out of the shadows of the alley behind the library building a man appears. He attempts to block your path. He appears to be about six feet, four inches tall, and probably weighs nearly two hundred fifty pounds. He's holding a knife with a ten-inch blade. He starts to walk toward you. The campus is deserted. Screaming for help would be fruitless. You know he wants to run you through. He's not after money. He wants your life.

You panic for a moment. But you remember that you're armed with a .45 service automatic. The instructor at the survival school warned you there would be nights like this.

5

Your sweat-drenched hand reaches into your coat to grasp the handle of the gun. The campus menace is just a few feet away. You shout to him in a weakened but confident voice:

"Stop! If you take one more step, I'll shoot!"

He laughs. Your calm turns to panic. Fear descends on you like a thick cloud. He shouts back to you,

"I don't believe in guns. And I certainly don't believe in .45 service automatics."

Fear has now gripped you like a vise. You put the gun down and allow the brute to slash you to pieces.

Of course, this student's reaction is absurd. Nobody in his right mind would cease to believe in the effectiveness of his weapon just because some brute didn't believe in it. Let's repeat the scene, but with a different twist.

The mugger steps out from the shadows of the alley to block your path. His knife blade reflects the parking lot lights, and the reflection catches your eye. The knife looks huge! You realize that he wants to slash you to pieces. You remain calm. You pull out your .45 service automatic and point it at the attacker. You shout to him in a confident voice,

"Stop! If you take one more step, I'll shoot!"

He laughs. He shouts back to you,

"I don't believe in guns. And I certainly don't believe in .45 service automatics."

With that last word he lunges at you with death in his eye. You make a believer out of him by emptying the clip of bullets into his lunging body.

In the second scenario the student had confidence in his weapon. The mugger's beliefs about the reliability of the .45 service automatic were irrelevant. His lack of belief in the power of the gun did not change the gun's effectiveness. But the student's beliefs about the reliability of the service automatic were most relevant.

The student's life depended on his believing in the reliability of the weapon and the weapon's reliability to do what he was told it could do. The gun remained a gun, and the bullets remained bullets no matter what the mugger or student decided to believe. In order for the student to appropriate the potential of the gun, however, he had to unleash its power. The mugger was made epistemologically self-conscious* when the gun destroyed his unbelief.

> *Epistemology* is that part of philosophy which studies the nature, sources, and limits of human knowledge, as well as analyzing crucial concepts such as "truth," "belief," and "knowledge." To be *epistemologically self-conscious* means to become fully aware of the consistent implications and nature of your espoused position.

How many times have you been confronted by someone who said he didn't believe in God, the inerrancy and infallibility of the Bible, the divinity of Jesus Christ, miracles, the resurrection, and a whole host of other Bible doctrines? And when you were confronted with such unbelief, how many times were you cut to pieces because you acted as if the Bible were not true unless you could convince the skeptic of its truthfulness? How often do you in practice deny the faith or its power because a skeptic did not believe the Bible?

Let's take a final look at our mugging story. There is another methodology that a number of Christians use that is equally ineffective.

The mugger sees your gun, but he is not convinced of its effectiveness. You consider his words of doubt and seek to persuade him that your gun is indeed effective. You tell him about your gun's fire power and the latest ballistic tests. You inform him of your weapon's accuracy and its reliability under adverse conditions. You even recite a list of experts who agree with your position. In the meantime, however, your attacker runs you through. You see, he doesn't believe your sources of information or considers them irrelevant. In his mind, they're just not reliable. They have no bearing on the present moment. He says your facts are all wrong. The experts? Well, they're just biased. They don't like knives. They never have. Those in the "American Knife Throwers Association" have their own statistical data, and they refute the conclusions of the "National Gun Lovers of America."

DEFENDING THE FAITH

Your faith will be under constant attack by professors and fellow students. In the classroom, the assault will sometimes be overt. In the open attack, professors will spend considerable time trying to refute the basic doctrines that every Christian holds to be true. They will begin by going to the source of the Christian's authority: the Bible. Once the Bible is set aside as true and reliable, all other doctrines are easily refuted since their veracity and credibility rest upon the Bible's authority. Some professors and students will use ridicule to discredit the Bible, while others will engage in a reasoned attack, using their own worldview to debunk the Christian worldview* piece by piece.

> *Worldview*: A network of elementary assumptions which are not verified by the procedures of natural science but in terms of which every aspect of man's experience and knowledge is interrelated and interpreted.

It's possible that you have never had your faith attacked in such an open way. At the high school level, an open assault on the Christian faith is rare, although the occurrence of these hostilities is on the rise. You may be convinced of the skeptic's reasons for rejecting the Bible and the Christian faith because you have never been taught how to defend what the Bible teaches. You have always been taught that the Bible is true, Jesus is God, man is a sinner, and there is an afterlife. Few Christians really question these basic beliefs. In the college classroom, all beliefs are open to criticism. Any belief system that claims to be *the* true system is doubly suspicious.

Preparing for the Confrontation

Like the man with the knife who confronted the college student with the gun, rival faiths are at work in the world, especially in the university. Often these rival faiths are consciously designed to stamp out all things Christian. Sometimes it's more subtle than that. Many professors just ignore the Christian worldview. Because the Christian worldview is rarely discussed in the classroom (except to be ridiculed), students never consider it as a serious option as a viable worldview. Be on your guard. This is the most subtle and destructive tactic. If you can be convinced that you and your world can be defined and interpreted without reference to Jesus Christ and His Word, then Christianity has been rendered irrelevant, and you are on the road to skepticism or outright unbelief.

You may have tried to defend the faith, but found that the arguments were too difficult to handle. The next time your beliefs were attacked, you remained silent. You may have felt guilty after not standing up for Christ, but you really didn't know what to say. After hearing the same arguments leveled against Christianity time after time, the walls of your own belief system start to crumble. Skepticism begins to take over where faith once prevailed.

Maybe you have been taught that you should not defend the faith. You just "believe." Well, that doesn't work for long. It gets to you in time. Why believe in something if you cannot defend it? Anyway, the Bible tells us as Christians that we are responsible to defend the faith. Defending the faith is part of the Christian's life. It's not an option.

The best way to handle attacks by skeptics is to have worked out an apologetic* methodology. It's been said that the best defense is a good offense.

> *"*Apologetics* is the vindication of the Christian philosophy of life against the various forms of the non-Christian philosophy of life."[2]

Keep in mind that the Bible is like a loaded .45. The power to destroy all speculations raised up against the knowledge of God is inherent in God's Word.

> For though we walk in the flesh, we do not war according to the flesh, for the weapons of our warfare are not of the flesh, but divinely powerful for the destruction of fortresses. We are destroying speculations and every lofty thing raised up against the knowledge of God, and we are taking every thought captive to the obedience of Christ (2 Corinthians 10:3-5).

Yet many Christians either don't know how to use the Bible as a spiritual weapon or really don't believe it's very effective as a weapon. There are others who believe that the brutish worldviews of unbelief are valid if they simply deny the Bible and everything it stands for. However, a cogently presented, comprehensive, and consistent Christian worldview can stand up to any hostile belief system. But it takes work to understand how skeptics think, believe, and behave. And your job is not finished until you are always "ready to make a defense to every one who asks you to give a reason for the hope that is in you" (1 Peter 3:15). This is what apologetics is all about.

APOLOGETICS IN ACTION

Jesus and His disciples were constantly doing battle with opponents who were a lot meaner than today's college professors. There was more at stake than scoring points with students. Jesus was not passive in the face of hostility and opposition. He met his attackers and systematically demolished their arguments against Him. Jesus won every argument. He sent the antagonists away mumbling to themselves. When the religious leaders of the day couldn't answer His arguments, they worked to have Him crucified. That's a rather extreme way to "win" an argument. But it's not so far-fetched. Consider the creation/evolution and abortion controversies. Why isn't creation given a fair hearing in the public schools? Isn't the classroom the place where there is a free exchange of ideas? Aren't students exposed to *all* the options? Why do evolutionists work so hard to keep creationists out of the public school classrooms? Evolutionists are afraid of the competition. If they were really convinced that the arguments for their position are irrefutable, then they would welcome a defense by creationists just to show how wrong they are.

Why do pro-abortion groups fight to keep pro-life groups from showing what an abortion is really all about? Moreover, why is it that parents must be notified and permission must be sought for a minor to receive a flu shot, but parents are not told when their daughter is considering an abortion? If women knew the truth about abortion many of them would choose not to get one. This would jeopardize the multi-million dollar abortion business. Contrary positions are effectively silenced when those who hold the prevailing worldviews are allowed to regulate the discussion of evolution or abortion.

Jesus and the Skeptics

Jesus' defense of the faith against the skeptics, religious leaders, and legal profession had an effect on the people. After hearing Jesus the people began to question the bankrupt ideology of their leaders. First, Jesus' message began to turn the people away from the anti-supernatural worldview of the Sadducees. The Sadducees were the religious skeptics of the day. They didn't believe in the resurrection of the dead, for example. Upon hearing Jesus show the absurdity of the Sadducees' worldview, the people were "astonished at His teaching" (Matthew 22:33). Next up were leaders from the religious and legal professions: "But when the Pharisees heard that He had put the Sadducees to silence, they gathered themselves together. And one of them, a lawyer, asked Him a question, testing Him" (vv. 34-35). Jesus again defends the faith against unbelief. Their response? "And no one was able to answer Him a word, nor did anyone dare from that day on to ask Him another question" (v. 46).

Something had to be done with this troublemaker. It's no accident that Jesus was taken away to be tried secretly. The people would have turned on their leaders had they known what they had planned for Jesus. Jesus gave the people answers to life's most perplexing questions. Those in power were about to take it all away:

> Then the chief priests and the elders of the people were gathered together in the court of the high priest, named Caiaphas; and they plotted to seize Jesus by stealth, and kill Him. But they were saying, "Not during the festival, lest a riot occur among the people" (Matthew 26:3-5).

Jesus had challenged the perverted worldviews of both the Sadducees and Pharisees, and the people were on the verge of rejecting them, lock, stock, and barrel. In order to keep their public credibility intact and to hide the defects of their worldview, Jesus had to go.

NO APOLOGIES PLEASE

Instead of defending the faith against unbelief, many Christians actually apologize for what they believe. This is *not* Biblical apologetics. "Apologetics" does not mean saying you're sorry for being a Christian. "Apologetics" comes from a Greek word which means "to give or make a defense." It is closely related to the operations of a courtroom where defendants are called on to present their legal case against accusations of wrong-doing.

> The Greek word *apologia* (from which we derive the English word "apologetics") denotes a speech made in defense, a reply (especially in the legal context of a courtroom) made to an accusation. The word originated in the judicial operations of ancient Athens, but the word occurs several times in the New Testament as well. The difference between the Greek and Christian methods of apologetics can be illustrated by contrasting the *Apology* of Socrates (as Plato records it) with the approach of the apostle Paul, who described himself as "set for the defense (*apologia*) of the gospel."[3]

One of the earliest occurrences of the word is found when Socrates defended himself against the charge of atheism and corrupting the youth of Athens. For Socrates, "all of life and every thought had to be brought under obedience to the lordship of man's reason."[4] When Socrates dared to question the opinion of the gods, in effect he had dared to question the opinion of the State since the State had its own pantheon of recognized gods that no one could refuse to honor, not even the nation's philosopher *par excellence*. The Grecian State, as the modern secular State, was a religious institution. To espouse another god was more than treason; it was blasphemy. Exile or the death penalty was mandated for such an offense. Socrates, because of his belief in a divine calling, could not accept exile as an alternative to execution. Socrates' real sin was teaching that the individual, rather than man as a collective social whole, can be his own god, his own judge, determining for himself what is right, good, and true. This is what motivated his accusers to banish him. Instead of banishment, Socrates chose suicide.

Confronting Ignorance

The Apostle Paul found himself in a similar situation. Not only did he question the opinion of the gods, he called all men everywhere to repent and worship the one true God. Even reason* had to bow in submission before the God who created heaven and earth.

12

> *Reason* is man's intellectual ability, a tool for understanding ourselves and the world. Some people try to make it more than a tool, using man's independent intellect as a final authority or judge.

Paul went to the very heart of religious skepticism by confronting the Greek philosophers of Athens with their own ignorance. The Bible says that "his spirit was being provoked within him as he was beholding the city full of idols" (Acts 17:16). At this point, Paul went to work defending the faith, "reasoning in the synagogue with the Jews and the God-fearing Gentiles, and in the market place every day with those who happened to be present" (v. 17). Even "some of the Epicurean and Stoic philosophers were conversing with him" (v. 18). They, however, found that some of his views differed greatly from their own. He was accused of being a "proclaimer of strange demons" (v. 18). He was then brought to the Areopagus,[5] a public debating forum, so they could learn more about these new teachings. Here is a summary of Paul's defense in Acts 17:22-33:

1. He shows them that they are inherently religious, pointing out to them their objects of worship (v. 22).

Application: No person is without basic religious commitments. This point needs to be stressed throughout any defense of the faith. The issue is not between faith and reason, but between faith and faith. Since reason is only a *tool*, the issue is, Which faith-commitment (worldview) is employing the tool? The person who says that man's unaided "reason must be used to explain everything" has already made a faith commitment—to man's unaided ability to reason independent of God. He must believe that unaided reason can explain everything before he will use that same unaided reason to prove its ability.

2. He notes that even the Athenians admit that they do not have all the facts, pointing out an altar that they erected "TO AN UNKNOWN GOD" (v. 23).

Application: The skeptic wants to be the judge as to whether God exists and what kind of God exists. But how can he ever be sure that *his* God exists? How can he be sure that his *kind* of God exists? Not having all the facts limits the dogmatism of the unbeliever. Ultimately, when we do not have personal observations of all the facts, the argument will come down to a faith-commitment because all of us are forced to trust some other authority outside ourselves which interprets the observed facts and reveals what we do not observe. Paul's point is that God is that outside Observer.

3. He shows them a way out of their ignorance by describing the true God who is "Lord of heaven and earth" (v. 24).

Application: The Bible never leaves the skeptic in his ignorance. The skeptic is left with nothing if he can be shown that his entire belief system is based upon unknowns. He can't be sure of anything. But the Christian's position establishes that because God is "Lord of heaven and earth," we can make sense of the world. Randomness does not characterize the universe. "Christianity provides an explanation even for our ignorance. We may be ignorant because of our finiteness as human beings. Yet, we can be sure that if an answer is to be found it must be done by dependence on the revelation of God."[6] That revelation is reliable because it comes from a God who is "Lord of heaven and earth."

4. He shows them that the true God is in need of nothing, "since He Himself gives to all life and breath and all things" (v. 25).

Application: Trusting in the God of the Bible means trusting Someone who is able to sustain us in life and death. There is no assurance of this in the skeptic's worldview. He either depends on himself or he looks to other belief systems to satisfy his spiritual hunger. But there is no assurance that any of these can supply what man needs: purpose, love, hope, fulfillment, a sense of meaning and belonging, the relief of guilt, and life after death. Only an independent God who is in need of nothing can supply what others cannot supply for themselves.

5. He shows them that there is no way to escape the presence and government of God since He has "determined their appointed times, and the boundaries of their habitation" (v. 26). Neither can they escape the implications of God's providence, "For in *Him* we live and move and exist" (vv. 26-28).

Application: There is no escaping God. The breath that God gives man to enable him to speak is used to deny Him. A personal God who sees and judges what man does is banned by those who want to live independent, autonomous* lives, free from the restrictions of a holy God.

**Autonomous*: Characterized by self-sufficiency or independence from outside authority (especially God's authority). The word is derived from two Greek words, *autos* (self) and *nomos* (law).

God is defined or rationalized out of existence. When King David was confronted by Nathan with his sin, David's confession brought him back to reality: God sees and judges all things. There is no escape from the gaze of God: "Against Thee, Thee only, I have sinned, and done what is evil in Thy sight, so that Thou art justified when Thou dost speak, and blameless when Thou doest judge" (Psalm 51:4a).

Here David acknowledges the reality of that guilt and notes two very important factors. First he notes that the sin is *ever* before him. It hounds him and pursues him. He sees it wherever he goes. He cannot rid himself of the memory. Like Lady Macbeth, the spot is indelible. Second, he notes that he has done evil in the sight of God. Thus, David not only sees his sin but he realizes it has not escaped the notice of God.[7]

A Biblically transcendent* God—a God who sees, acts, and judges—cannot be allowed in the universe by those who deny an absolute law they must obey or a deity to whom they must submit.

> *Transcendent*: The quality of originating beyond, or exceeding, man's temporal experience. Biblical transcendence should not be confused with the notion that God has nothing to do with the world.

6. Paul shows the Athenians that God is no longer overlooking "the times of ignorance." He "is now declaring to men that all everywhere should repent" (v. 30), that is, change their *minds* about the God of the Bible, their sin, and Jesus Christ, their Redeemer.

Application: Ultimately, the defense of the faith is not about knowledge of the facts but about ethics, that is, how we act. The reason that man seeks to escape from God by rationalizing argumentation is that he has sins to hide and a Judge he doesn't want to face. Most arguments that seek to deny God or the validity of the Christian message are simply smoke screens to obscure the real issue: Man is a sinner who "suppresses the truth in unrighteousness" (Romans 1:18).

7. He shows them that God has "fixed a day in which He will judge the world in righteousness through a man He has appointed" (v. 31).

Application: The skeptic cannot remain neutral when he is confronted with the gospel. Refusal to decide for Christ with a wait-and-see attitude does not absolve him of his guilt and eventual judgment. Straddling the fence will not save him. Judgment is coming. Even if we do not "win" our argument with the skeptic, we must always warn him of the consequences of unbelief. When the arguments are laid aside, the question still remains: "What do you think of Jesus Christ?," and "What does He think of *you?*"

8. He shows them that God has furnished proof to all men that this is all true "by raising Him from the dead" (v. 31).

Application: The resurrection of Jesus from the dead is incredible but not in terms of the Christian worldview where God is Lord of heaven and earth and supplies to all life and breath, and all things. The resurrection is a confirmation of God's power and a vindication of His grace. The resurrection is taken for granted as a premise by Paul. It proves that Jesus is the final judge. Paul does not argue for the resurrection as a conclusion. He presents it as fact.

"Now when they heard of the resurrection of the dead, some began to sneer, but others said, 'We shall hear you again concerning this'" (v. 32). This is the essence of defending the faith. Some will reject the faith because what you tell them does not fit within the framework of their worldview. Those who rejected the faith at this point did so because their starting point was contrary to the Christian faith. Their worldview was constructed on a foundation of unknowns: unknown gods, unknown forces, unknown random facts, unjustifiable universal laws, and unverified claims to authority. Such ignorance God will no longer tolerate. Such a worldview is destined for judgment. It can only lead to skepticism, mysticism, or irrationality. The words to the youthful student Timothy are appropriate advice for any young college student:

> O Timothy, guard what has been entrusted to you, avoiding worldly and empty chatter and the opposing arguments of what is falsely called "knowledge"—which some have professed and thus gone astray from the faith. Grace be with you (2 Timothy 6:21).

Greg Bahnsen sums up the Christian's apologetic task.

> Until the Holy Spirit regenerates the sinner and brings him to repentance, his presuppositions will remain unaltered. And as long as the unbeliever's presuppositions are unchanged, a proper acceptance and understanding of the good news of Christ's historical resurrection will be impossible. The Athenian philoso-

phers had originally asked Paul for an account of his doctrine of resurrection. After his reasoned defense of the hope within him and his challenge to the philosophers' presuppositions, a few were turned around in their thinking. But many refused to correct their presuppositions, so that when Paul concluded with Christ's resurrection they ridiculed and mocked.

Acceptance of the facts is governed by one's most ultimate assumptions, as Paul was well aware. Paul began his apologetic with God and His revelation. The Athenian philosophers began their dispute with Paul in an attitude of cynical unbelief about Christ's resurrection. . . .

Paul knew that the explanation of their hostility to God's revelation (even though they evidenced an inability to escape its forcefulness) was to be found in their desire to exercise control over God (e.g., v. 29) and to avoid facing up to the fact of their deserved punishment before the judgment seat of God (v. 30). They secretly hoped that ignorance would be bliss, and so preferred darkness to light (John 3:19-20).[8]

RIVAL FAITHS AT WORK

The Biblical faith is dogmatic. It makes some absolute statements about fundamental doctrines: God exists, man was created, sin has infected this world, man is accountable to God, and Jesus Christ is our only hope in life and in death. This will not do in the typical college classroom. The university is not in the business of dealing in absolutes,* at least in absolutes that make man accountable to God.

> *An *absolute* is a statement whose truth is not conditioned by qualification or limitations (such as subjective bias or cultural trends and conditioning).

The goal of the university is to strip students of the absolute worldview they grew up with and to clothe them with the robe of criticism and relativism. No view of life is sacred. All views but one are equal in the eyes of the university. It has only one dogma: criticism. It has only one absolute: Nothing is absolute (all is relative).

17

What makes the university unique is the centrality of criticism and debate in every facet of its functioning. The discussion is open, and all the members of the community, i.e, the inquirers, are entitled, in fact obliged, to participate. All members of the community, but most importantly the leadership, are made accountable by the checks and balances of constant peer review. This is not some occasional occurrence; it is the way of life in the university. No claim, issue, or position is insulated from critical inquiry. The university certainly has other important goals, but they are all subordinate to this one.[9]

As Christians we do not want students to accept every new idea or every interpretation of reality without a degree of healthy skepticism. Questions should be asked. Mistrust of dogma is helpful, if put in the context of a reliable worldview in terms of which criticism has a foundation on which to stand. There must be standards for our criticism. But for the "open university" all absolutes are exposed to criticism. Are we to hold the existence of God up for criticism by "peer review"? What "checks and balances" govern the "community" engaged in the criticism? Consider what it means to maintain that "no claim, issue, or position is insulated from critical inquiry" and that all the goals of the university "are all subordinate to this one." The claim that God is the sovereign ruler of heaven and earth and that man is accountable to Him in thought, word, and deed "is subordinate" to critical inquiry. The men of Athens are still with us.

How did this happen? What went wrong in the university? There was a day when the university taught that all of life should be viewed through the interpretive and corrective lens of Scripture. God was considered to be the foundation of knowledge and final authority in life, not some spurious and seemingly neutral community of "critical inquirers." In actuality, the modern university still stands on that earlier foundation (since there is no other way to gain knowledge), although it rarely acknowledges it. The philosophical walls are crumbling, however, and it is only a matter of time until the entire edifice comes crashing down. The foundation will still be there, but it will take a new generation of Christians to rebuild the walls.

The only reason the university can do any positive work today is that it hasn't been consistent with its own bankrupt worldview. Consistency would send it into despair, ignorance, and social chaos. When the academic world wakes up one morning and fully comprehends what it means to live in a world without God, the university and life as we know it will no longer exist. The savage will replace man, the image-bearer of God. Of course, there is another avenue. The university might return to the One who originally gave it life.

But at the heart of the university's critical agenda there still remains a more fundamental problem: Man and the universe in which he lives have been reduced to machine-like status, to something less than what they were created to be. With God slowly pushed to the edge of the universe, man is no longer a "little lower than the angels" (Psalm 8:5); he is only a little higher than the apes.

BUILDING A SPIRITUAL ARSENAL

The importance of being prepared to succeed academically in a university environment is nothing new to the typical high school student. And I suspect that most Christians agree that some spiritual preparation must accompany academic preparation. But how do you prepare yourself spiritually for college? What is *spiritual* preparedness? Why must you be spiritually prepared? Isn't academic preparation enough? Besides, what does education have to do with religion anyway? Aren't they separate and distinct areas of life?

These fundamental questions must be answered. Religion, the fundamental belief system that all men and women use to interpret reality, cannot be separated from anything, let alone education. All men and women choose something outside themselves to interpret reality. This external standard is spiritual in nature. Keep in mind that when we talk about "spiritual," we do not mean only the world that exists beyond our senses. We are also talking about our relationship with God through Jesus Christ, which leads to complete devotion—heart, mind, soul, and body—to Him. When the Bible talks, for example, about "the spiritual man," it's usually talking about the guidance, direction, and regulation of a person's life. A Spiritual person is someone whose relationship with Jesus Christ shapes the way he or she believes, thinks, and acts—who is led by *God's* Spirit. Thus, the following questions test your "spirituality."

What *standard* is *guiding* your decisions?

What *principle* is *directing* your view of life?

What *laws* are *regulating* your behavior?

Spirituality is inseparable from first principles of ethical behavior. Ethics has to do with deciding what is right and wrong, good and evil, just and unjust. There are always unseen precepts that stand behind our thoughts and actions. They are always present, and they give meaning to our concept of reality. In Biblical language, to be Spiritual means "to be guided and motivated by the Holy Spirit. It means obeying His commandments as recorded in the Scriptures. The Spiritual man is not someone who floats in midair and hears eerie voices. The Spiritual man is the man who does what the Bible says (Romans 8:4-8)."[10]

Even those who deny the Christian faith are religious. They are just as much controlled by implicit internal principles as the most devout Christian. Their spiritual first principles, however, are contrary to the Bible's spiritual principles. This is why the Bible tells us not to "believe every spirit, but test the spirits to see whether they are from God" (1 John 4:1). There is a spirit behind every decision. Is it the spirit of man or the Spirit of God?

> Now we have received, not the spirit of the world, but the Spirit who is from God, that we might know the things freely given to us by God, which things we also speak, not in words taught by human wisdom, but in those taught by the Spirit, combining spiritual thoughts with spiritual words. But a natural man does not accept the things of the Spirit of God; for they are foolishness to him, and he cannot understand them, because they are spiritually appraised. But he who is spiritual appraises all things, yet he himself is appraised by no man. For who has known the mind of the Lord, that he should instruct Him? But we have the mind of Christ (1 Corinthians 2:12-16).

The religious commitments of those who reject the wisdom of God in Christ can go in two directions. At first, those who reject Biblical spiritual guidance deny that there is a spiritual reality beyond what they can observe. They say that there isn't anything more to life than eating, drinking, sleeping, dying, and then nothing more beyond the grave. For them there is nothing beyond what they experience with their senses. This very premise, however, is something which goes *beyond* what anybody can experience with his senses! How do they really *know*?

But this denial usually doesn't last very long. It is a transitional position. Eventually, they realize that this interpretation of reality cannot satisfy them. Then, if they don't turn to Christ and the guidance offered

20

through the Holy Spirit and His Word, they turn to any number of spiritual substitutes. Some become self-conscious, consistent humanists* or atheists, believing that man should be his own god.

> *Humanism* is the view that man is the highest value and authority in terms of knowledge or behavior (rejecting any transcendent reality or revelation).

Most don't go that far. Instead, they operate with an inconsistent, rough-and-ready view of the world that excludes God and exalts man. Though they are not very consistent, they are humanists in their basic orientation. Some become self-conscious Satanists. Between these two extremes there are all types of spiritual counterfeits.

Here is one striking example of an opposing and deeply religious faith that is designed to supplant Christianity. Notice that all the forms of religion are present:

> I am convinced that *the battle for humankind's future must be waged and won in the public school classroom* by teachers who correctly perceive their role as the proselytizers of a new faith: a religion of humanity that recognizes and respects the spark of what theologians call divinity in every human being. These teachers must embody the same selfless dedication as the most rabid fundamentalist preachers, for they will be ministers of another sort, utilizing a classroom instead of a pulpit to convey humanist values in whatever subject they teach, regardless of the educational level—preschool day care or large state university. *The classroom must and will become an arena of conflict between the old and the new — the rotting corpse of Christianity, together with all its adjacent evils and misery, and the new faith of humanism, resplendent in its promise of a world in which the never-realized Christian ideal of "love thy neighbor" will be finally achieved.*[11]

Therefore, the question is not: Are you religious and does your religion affect the way you think and act? Rather, the question ought to be: What is your religion and how is it governing the way you think and act? As the above quotation makes clear, education is one vehicle by which the new faith is implemented. The task is to exclude all contrary faiths, especially Christianity. Man-centered religious principles should be implemented to define and interpret the world.

A Man-Centered Substitute

A denial of the Christian faith,* therefore, does not mean a denial of faith itself.

Faith, contrary to common conceptions, does not mean abandoning intellect for feeling, experience, or intuition. To have "faith" is to believe something and live in terms of it.

Abandoning faith in the God of Scripture means choosing another faith-commitment. A shift takes place, from a God-centered, God-created, and God-interpreted universe to a man-centered, man-interpreted, man-controlled universe. All of life is explained in terms of man:

1. Man is the center of the new faith. *Conclusion*: Man defines what is real.

2. There is no will greater than man's will. *Conclusion*: Right and wrong are determined by man and man alone.

3. This world is all there is. *Conclusion*: There is no God to worship and obey, no heaven to consider, and no hell to fear. Even if these do exist, man can never know for sure.

4. There is no spiritual dimension to man's existence, nothing beyond the world of physical experience that can give meaning to life. By observing and drawing conclusions from what man hears, sees, and experiences, man gains all the "meaning" available in life. *Conclusion*: If it cannot be measured with scientific instruments, then it is not real.

5. If there is a spiritual dimension to life, man defines it, creates it, and lives in terms of his own definitions. *Conclusion*: All religions are valid except any religion that says that not all religions are valid; therefore, Christianity is banned because it is exclusive in what it claims to be true.

Christians tend to believe that a denial of the God of the Bible means a denial of religion altogether. This is never true. Even the most ardent atheist is religious.*

> *Religion* involves our ultimate commitments regarding the nature of reality and knowledge, about man's place in the universe, how we should live, and the meaning of life. A religious person does not have to believe in a personal god. Anything will do.

An atheist shifts his worship from the true God to himself or to some other man-made object of worship, such as power, money, or fame. Of course, he may not admit this. In fact, he may deny it by claiming that he is an atheist (*a* means no; *theos* means god). Yet, he lives by a new set of religious principles on a daily basis. It's not only what a man *says* he believes, but also how he acts which shows what his basic commitments (beliefs) are. But there are some who understand the implications of denying God, and how this denial shifts religious sentiment to autonomous man. Consider this letter from a self-professed atheist:

1. I am my own authority (my own god). You choose to follow another authority while I do not.

2. I firmly believe in moral anarchy (to determine my own morality and to deny you and your kind the authority to impose yours on me).

3. I deny the existence of any objective "god's law."

4. I don't have to justify my ethical rules to you or to anyone else, so long as my acts hurt no one but myself.[12]

You can't be much more specific than this. While this man denies the existence of one God, he considers himself to be an adequate substitute. He now makes the rules, and he will work to bring the world under the terms of his new law-order. This is an obvious inconsistency. The "rule" that "we must not hurt anyone else" is taken as an objective to be imposed on all of us!

CONCLUSION

The abandonment of God is never complete or comprehensive. When the God of Scripture is abandoned an idol is substituted, usually some man-made philosophy.[13] As G. K. Chesterton observed, when people cease to believe in God they do not stop believing. What is worse, they believe in anything, no matter how foolish.

We are experiencing the conflict of two rival faiths—Christianity that teaches God is Sovereign over all He has created, and the variety of worldviews that teaches that Man is sovereign over all that has evolved up to this moment. This was brought home to me as I was picketing with a group of pro-life activists at an Atlanta abortuary. We were singing a number of hymns in our march around the building. As we sang "A Mighty Fortress is our God," I could hear one of the staff members of the abortuary say, "I guess we ought to sing 'A Mighty Fortress is our Man.'" He understood the nature of the battle. The issue is God or Man. According to the man-centered faiths, man believes he is in control of the evolutionary process. Man works to determine the future.

> Through billions of years of blind mutation, pressing against the shifting walls of their environment, microbes finally emerged as man. We are no longer blind; at least we are beginning to be conscious of what has happened and of what may happen. From now on, evolution is what we make it.[14]

The man-centered views of life want every vestige of Christianity expunged from every nook and cranny of the universe. As history shows us, such worldviews breed totalitarianism, enslavement, and the wholesale slaughter of untold millions. The State becomes the new god.

When man is left to himself (without God) to be his own authority, this leads either to anarchy (every man is his own law) or Statism (collective man makes the laws). Since anarchy destroys civilizations (the individual's personal peace and affluence) the tendency in history is for anarchistic periods to give way to totalitarianism.

Is your faith strong enough to survive the attack from those who are hostile to everything the Bible stands for? You must be ready.

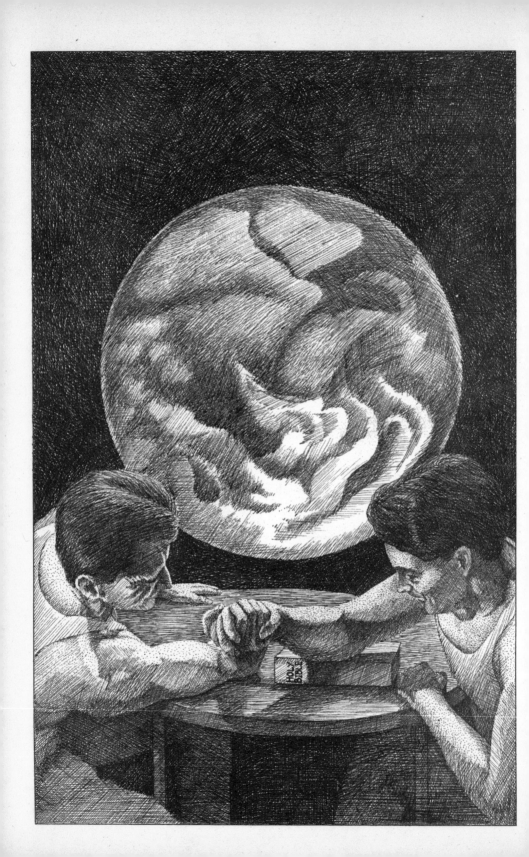

2
WORLDVIEWS IN CONFLICT

There is no longer a Christian mind.

It is commonplace that the mind of modern man has been secularized. For instance, it has been deprived of any orientation towards the supernatural. Tragic as this fact is, it would not be so desperately tragic had the Christian mind held out against the secular drift. But unfortunately the Christian mind has succumbed to the secular drift with a degree of weakness and nervelessness unmatched in Christian history. It is difficult to do justice in words to the complete loss of intellectual morale in the twentieth-century Church.[1]

THE college classroom is a spiritual and intellectual war zone. Few students expect to encounter outspoken hostility toward the Christian faith. At the high school level, most teachers who are hostile to the Christian worldview are somewhat restrained in their animosity because they must answer to parent/teacher groups and school boards. There is little accountability at the university level where "academic freedom" supposedly rules.

Many college students think of the classroom as an open forum for the honest exchange of ideas. The pursuit of knowledge is thought to be a neutral enterprise. Supposedly there is a give and take atmosphere where, given enough of the facts, any student can come to the correct conclusions about any subject.

But is this true in practice? Is the university free and open to all ideas? Consider recent events at Northwestern University near Chicago. In the September 1986 issue of *Commentary*, Joseph Epstein, editor of *The American Scholar*, described the case of Barbara Foley, an avowedly Marxist professor of English at Northwestern. Foley is a strong supporter of InCAR, the International Committee Against Racism, a student group with well-known Marxist sympathies. Foley and InCAR gained widespread attention during a visit by Adolfo Calero, a leader of the Nicaraguan resistance. Before Calero spoke, Foley took the stage, announced herself as a member of InCAR, and said that "Adolfo Calero was a monster" and that "Calero had the blood of thousands on his hands and no respect for the rights to life and free speech of the people he helped slaughter with the CIA's help," and therefore that "He had no right to speak that night." She concluded, "We are not going to let him speak" and he "should feel lucky to get out alive."

Foley's lies and rhetoric aroused the students. Epstein writes:

> When Adolfo Calero arrived there was a great deal of chanting and shouting in opposition to his presence. His talk was delayed some ten or fifteen minutes. Before he could begin someone– not Barbara Foley–rushed to the stage and threw a red liquid on him. The liquid had been variously described as paint and as animal blood. At this point, with a good deal of shouting in the hall, Adolfo Calero, his suit coat bespattered with the red liquid, was led from the hall by security men and did not speak that evening. Barbara Foley acknowledges joining in the chanting during the tumult. A witness claims that she also shouted "the only way to get anything done would be to kill him [Calero]," though she and another witness, a graduate student who is also a member of InCAR, deny that she said this.[2]

The modern "free" university rarely tolerates contrary opinion. Other worldviews? "Well, we discuss them all here." The Christian world view? "That's not really an option anymore. It's more in the area of superstition." The creation-evolution debate? "What debate? Evolution has been proven to be true."

At Tennessee Tech in Cookeville, Josh McDowell, a popular speaker at Christian and non-Christian colleges and universities, was barred from campus because of the religious content of his message.[3] Some state colleges and universities now prohibit the use of its campus facilities for any meeting where religious worship takes place. A number of colleges have a ban on outside religious speakers.

The reason for the bans? Religion is a *private* affair. As soon as religion is involved in *public* life, the State must enforce the infamous and mythological constitutional "church/state separation"[4] doctrine. Religious expression, according to the prevailing view, is restricted to the mind and designated areas like churches and homes. You are within the law as long as you only *think* religious thoughts.

The Jigsaw Worldview

Modern educational philosophy sees life as a gigantic jigsaw puzzle. Man's job is to find all the pieces and put the puzzle together. But there's a catch. Man can never gather all the facts. And even if he could, what pattern would he follow to put all the pieces in the right places? Professors will tell you that they do not interpret the facts; they only discover them and make them known. The facts, students are told, speak for themselves. Students are equally told that they can have no confidence that there is a "pattern" to the facts (a grand scheme of things). All meaning is therefore imposed by man's mind. Meaning is man's creation.

This is like expecting that after an hour of shaking a box of jigsaw puzzle pieces, the puzzle would be put together. But, of course, it can never happen. Someone must show you how the pieces fit. An already-established design must be followed. Your professors' worldview will be the determining factor in all that is said and done in the classroom. They will show you how the pieces fit. And if the pieces don't fit, you will be told that they either belong to some other puzzle, or they don't exist.

YOU AND YOUR WORLDVIEW

What is a worldview? A worldview is the way a person looks at and evaluates the world in which he or she lives. This evaluation includes what a person sees, feels, and believes. Questions concerning values and ultimate reality are answered through worldviews. Worldviews embrace the daily operations of life, whether recognized or not:

The intellectual life (what they believe is true about themselves and their place in history); *the physical* (how they treat or mistreat their bodies by eating, sleeping, and exercising); *the social* (how they interact with friends and enemies, the rich and

29

the poor, the strong and the weak); *the economic* (why they work and how they spend their wages); and *the moral* (what ethical guidelines and obligations direct their thinking about justice and issues such as abortion and euthanasia).[5]

Worldviews consist of presuppositions* that give us a refocused picture of the world. Because of sin, man and his world are distorted. "As we study God's Word we can progressively gain a clearer understanding of what the world is like, and how we can serve God more effectively in it."[6]

---

*A *presupposition* is an elementary assumption, basic commitment, or foundational perspective in terms of which particular experiences and events are interpreted.

A WORLDVIEW FRAMEWORK

While there are many worldviews, there are certain characteristics that form a framework for all of them. You can determine a professor's worldview by asking certain questions:

1. What is he using to interpret the facts? What is he using as his worldview? What are his fundamental beliefs about life?

2. How consistent is his worldview? How consistent, for example, is a professor who says that God does not exist? Are there *any* absolutes? Why? Are there any right or wrong answers? If so, why? Does this include tests? Mathematical formulas? The rules of logic?

3. What are the practical implications of believing a certain worldview? What will it mean for me personally and the world in general?

These questions and many more reveal what constitutes a professor's operating worldview. Let's look at these characteristics in detail.

I. Worldviews Consist of Presuppositions

Have you ever gotten into an argument with someone over a political, ethical, or religious question and found that you just could not come to an agreement? Maybe you saw a movie together and could not agree on what it was all about. You saw the same movie. Then why the disagreement? The disagreement could be the result of two things. First, the difference could be one of perspective. Everyone sees things in a unique way, because of his experiences and interests. One of you might have watched the movie with an eye to the symbolism. Another might have watched looking for philosophical ideas in the movie. Someone might have evaluated it in terms of its story line. These are differences of perspective. There is nothing wrong with having different perspectives. At this level, every perspective would give a part of the whole. They could all be correct. A discussion would help you see different dimensions of the movie and enrich your understanding of it.

Second, your disagreement could be more fundamental. Your disagreement about the movie could be a disagreement about *presuppositions*, those fundamental values that we use to interpret life. For example, you might have watched *Tender Mercies*, a movie about how the grace of God transforms the life of an aging country singer. If you are a Christian, you would be able to understand and identify with the movie's themes. You would conclude that it gives a true picture of reality. An unbeliever, on the other hand, might see it as a naive fairy tale about something that can never happen in the real world. More likely, he will see nothing but despair. The man's daughter died in a senseless automobile accident. For him, there are no answers in life. Believing in a sovereign God is absurd. If this is the kind of disagreement you have, your disagreement really comes down to presuppositions about what life is all about. While you saw the same movie, and you discussed the same questions, you saw things differently. But these differences of opinion affect eternal things.

In other words, disagreements about issues often result from a more fundamental disagreement about the evaluating principles each of you used to see the facts. Now, if this type of disagreement is present in personal relationships where in many cases the issues being discussed are not very significant, what will happen when you enter the classroom where life's most perplexing issues are discussed? Conflict.

Presuppositions, our basic commitments, influence all our thinking. They are the building blocks of a worldview. Presuppositions are the spectacles through which you, your friends, and your professors will view the facts. They are, by definition, more basic than our particular judgments and applied interpretations. Presuppositions govern the way all of us think and act, and they have significant personal and cultural ramifications. They determine the *ultimate* standards and so cannot be proved by anything else "more ultimate." An ultimate presupposition is "a belief over which no other takes precedence."[7] They are "proved" by the impossibility of the contrary. There are no answers to life's most fundamental questions if the God of the Bible is left out of the thinking process. We could not think or live without thinking presuppositionally.

> Human existence is structured by ideas. [Sets of] presuppositions and ideas [make up] worldviews—the grid through which we view the world. More importantly, a person's presuppositions are the basis upon which he or she acts.
>
> People are more than a mere product of their environment. Men and women project their inward thoughts out into the external world where, in fact, their thoughts affect their environment. Ideas, thus, have consequences, which can be productive or destructive—depending upon their basis or foundation.
>
> Ideas are, then, not neutral. Their mere existence implies impact.[8]

But it's not enough to have presuppositions. You must have the correct presuppositions. If you are wrong about your fundamental values—your presuppositions, the grid through which you evaluate life—then all your facts will be out of alignment. What you believe to be real could in fact be an illusion or a distortion. So then, presuppositions must be more than mere opinion. They cannot be arbitrary or subjective. For example, the ultimate "sin" of a "scholar" is inconsistency and arbitrariness. Yet this is precisely what the modern university condones and encourages regarding ultimate commitments: There are no fixed rules or standards, yet a professor will demand rules and standards be followed in scholarly research.

Without presuppositions, thinking is impossible. For example, if you do not begin with the presupposition that the God of the Bible exists, then some other presupposition will replace it. Without the God of the Bible, however, the explanation for the origin and maintenance of the universe degenerates into chaos, chance, unpredictability, and impersonalism. Without God, all things are possible and permissible including theft, slavery, rape, murder, and genocide. And there is no one to tell us that these things are evil. At the same time, there is no way to study science because the scientific method requires predictability in experimentation. Only an orderly universe designed by a God of law can effectively work for the scientist.

The Bible assumes God's existence. There is no attempt to prove His existence. No other type of world can be imagined without the existence of the Triune God of Scripture: "In the beginning, God created the heavens and the earth" (Genesis 1:1). Creation testifies to the reality of God.

Presuppositions, or worldviews, influence and shape all other convictions and are the prime interpreters of the facts. This bears repeating because most students rarely get beyond the facts to the belief system that is being used to interpret those "facts."

2. Worldviews Claim to be Unified

Worldviews work to unify thinking and the many new experiences that confront you daily. Without a predetermined system of evaluation for new information, facts would float unrelated to anything and be without meaning. If you did not think in terms of presuppositions, every new fact would have to be studied and examined as if no other fact had ever existed. All new facts would be independent facts. Your outlook would be fragmented. You would not have confidence that any single fact could ever be related to other facts. The Bible presents a unified view of reality that is consistent, rational, logical, and coherent.

There is a reason why schools of higher learning were first described as *uni*versities. Knowledge was thought to be unified. There was an attempt to have basic presuppositions govern all fields of knowledge. As a student moved from science to mathematics to political science to theology, he took with him a set of presuppositions which unified life and experience. There was little tension between the various disciplines. Such a view no longer governs educational pursuits at the university level. All is possible and permissible, except, of course, the Christian worldview. Rushdoony writes:

> In the 20th century, educators have spoken of the university at times as a *multiversity,* having room for a variety of ideas and faiths. The teaching of witchcraft, astrology, and related concepts by some schools is related to this concept of the multiversity. High schools in a major city have introduced yoga and palmistry. If the world is a multiverse, then all things are permissible except a sovereign God and a universal law-order. Hence our polytheistic world is tolerant of almost every kind of belief except orthodox Christianity. A universal law-order and a sovereign God rule out the possibility of a polytheistic multiverse. But, because the sovereign and triune God of Scripture rules, there is no multiverse but rather a universe and a unified law-order.[9]

When evaluating worldviews, you must evaluate them in terms of their inner consistency and cogency. Do the various aspects of the worldview and practices associated with it agree with each other? One would expect those who believe in saving the whales to support the issue of the sanctity of the unborn. If they believe that a whale or baby seal is important, then we have a right to ask them why they should not also emphasize the protection of defenseless *human* life.

If someone says *all* human laws and generalizations are relative, he will have to explain the absolutism and the universality of the laws of logic. If someone says there are no ethical absolutes, he will have to explain why falsifying lab reports in scientific research is forbidden or why cheating on exams is unacceptable to him.

3. Worldviews are Constructed to be Coherent

Worldviews aim to make the facts of experience fit together. New ideas often disturb entrenched worldviews. Observations or claims that do not fit a person's adopted worldview are often discarded as non-facts or determined to be irrelevant to the discussion. For example, when Jesus was raised from the dead, the chief priests realized that they could explain the event away by claiming that the whole story was fabricated by Jesus' disciples. The soldiers who reported the resurrection were given large sums of money to say, "His disciples came by night and stole Him away while we were asleep" (Matthew 28:13).

What about those who knew the truth about the resurrection? Did they become believers in light of the resurrection evidence? Not all of them. Many were content to dismiss the obvious testimony of eyewitnesses to keep their anti-supernatural worldview intact. No amount of evidence which you will present will convince someone who does not like the implications of the evidence:

This is true of even the most "convincing" Christian argument—a cogent case for the historicity of the resurrection. Upon hearing such an argument, one listener may reply, "Aha, this *is* ultimately a chance universe in which even the most unexpected of things can happen once. A man rising from the dead, can you imagine that?" Or another may say, "Erik Von Daniken must be right. Jesus must have been one of those men from outer space, evidently from a planet where men are so constituted that they come back to life after dying." In neither case has the data been seen to confirm that claim which it was intended to confirm—that Jesus is divine, the Son of God.[10]

How can this be? Why doesn't evidence always convince? In the case of evidence relating to Jesus Christ, once a person acknowledges that Jesus is indeed the Son of God, then a change of life is in order. Repentance from sin and trusting in His finished work on the cross is the necessary response in light of the evidence. In order to avoid submission to Christ, many people are willing to dismiss the facts or reinterpret them to be absolved of having to face the risen Christ. The naturalist must find ways to explain away the apparently *super*natural; when an explanation is not readily available, he asks for more time—rather than abandoning his naturalism as a philosophy.

4. Worldviews are Exclusive

The Christian worldview cannot exist in the same arena of thought with contrary worldviews at the same time. Non-Christian worldviews often work together to displace the Christian worldview. Of course, the Christian worldview should be working to displace the non-Christian worldviews. In principle, there is never any room for compromise. (In practice, however, both a believer and an unbeliever can work together to stop abortion, help the poor, or build a hospital. Why? The unbeliever is working within the Christian's worldview.) Communism's goal, for example, is to eradicate any vestige of God from the universe.

> The Communist vision is the vision of Man without God. It is the vision of man's mind displacing God as the creative intelligence of the world. It is the vision of man's liberated mind, by the sole force of his rational intelligence, redirecting man's destiny and reorganizing man's life and the world. It is the vision of man, once more the central figure of the Creation, not because God made man in His image, but because man's mind makes him the most intelligent of the animals. Copernicus and his successors displaced man as the central fact of the universe by proving that the earth was not the central star of the universe. Communism restores man to his sovereignty by the simple method of denying God.[11]

Non-Christian belief systems cannot afford to allow competition. As long as people believe in a higher law or another sovereign, then the new ideology can never completely win over the people.

Nazism is a classic expression of the exclusive nature of worldviews. Nazi Germany brings to mind the extermination of the Jews in what has been called the Holocaust. Adolf Hitler's disenfranchisement of the Jews in Germany in the 1930s and 1940s is a prominent theme in any study of World War II, Germany, or political tyranny. The Jews were slowly and efficiently barred from economic, educational, and political participation. Eventually they were driven from the nation. What many people do not know is that the Christian church was put on notice to either follow the Nazi Party line or be closed down. William Shirer, author of *The Rise and Fall of the Third Reich*, writes that under the leadership of Alfred Rosenberg, an outspoken pagan, "the Nazi regime intended eventually to destroy Christianity in Germany, if it could, and substitute the old paganism of the early tribal Germanic gods and the new paganism of the Nazi extremists. As Bormann, one of the men closest to Hitler, said publicly in 1941, 'National Socialism and Christianity are irreconcilable.'"[12] Shirer in *The Nightmare Years*, writes: "We know now what Hitler envisioned for the German Christians: the utter suppression of their religion."[13] The internal intelligence agency of the Nazi SS "regarded organized Christianity as one of the major obstacles to the establishment of a truly totalitarian state."[14] Why? Christians believe that there is another King, Jesus (Acts 17:7).

In *Mein Kampf* Hitler stressed "the importance of winning over and then training the youth in the service 'of a new national state.'"[15] Shirer continues by showing how Hitler used education as a device to direct the future of the nation:

> "When an opponent declares, 'I will not come over to your side,'" he said in a speech on November 6, 1933, "I calmly say, 'Your child belongs to us already, . . . What are you? You will pass on. Your descendants, however, now stand in the new camp. In a short time they will know nothing else but this new community.'" And on May 1, 1937, he declared, "This new Reich will give its youth to no one, but will itself take youth and give to youth its own education and its own upbringing."[16]

All the German schools "were quickly Nazified." Control was taken away from the parents and local authorities and "[e]very person in the teaching profession, from kindergarten through the universities, was compelled to join the National Socialist Teachers' League which, by law, was held 'responsible for the execution of the ideological and political coordination of all the teachers in accordance with the National Socialist doctrine.'"[17] Only the Nazi worldview was permitted.

Of course, this is an extreme example. But our nation's public schools are bastions of intolerance. In Greenville, Tennessee some Christian parents wanted alternative textbooks for their children. Here's what a syndicated columnist had to say about the incident:

> These poor children are being denied the most basic of childhood's freedoms, the right to imagine and learn. Someone should remind their parents the law of this land still requires we educate our children in qualified schools with qualified teachers. That a sound education involves free exploration of ideas and fact. That they may rant and rave against humanism and feminism and any other "ism" on Sunday, but come Monday the children belong in school.[18]

The Christian worldview is relegated to the church. You can have your religious views but keep them private. According to a recent radio editorial, "a man's religion and the strength of his conviction are his own personal matter. Religion should not interfere with politics."[19] I wonder what he would say about the abolition of the slave trade in England and the civil rights movement in the United States? These movements were headed by religious leaders who were motivated out of religious conviction.

5. Worldviews are Transformational

Worldviews are seen as vehicles for cultural transformation. Many in the entertainment field, for example, believe that they are the nation's conscience and the only guiding light. In an interview with film director and producer Francis Ford Coppola, the aggressive nature and comprehensive effects of worldviews come to light:

> My dream is that the artist class—people who have proven through their work that they are humanists and wish to push for what Aldous Huxley called the desirable human potentialities of intelligence, creativity and friendliness—will seize the instrument of technology and try to take humanity into a period of history in which we can reach for a utopia. Of course, it is possible for the technology to be misused—we could end up with a Big Brother—but we could also have a balanced society, with an

37

artist class leading the culture toward something approximating a happy family or tribe.

At the moment, the nation is in a fog, and we've got to put our headlights on. Artists–those who rely on their intuition–can be the nation's headlights.[20]

Coppola believes that an "artist class" is the only group that can establish a consistent and workable worldview. But he goes even further. He wants us to believe that an artist class should be in the position of worldview leadership. Apparently, no other group or combination of groups is capable of articulating a worldview without their innate expertise. An artist's "intuition" is the basic presupposed authority for Coppola. Nearly every discipline maintains the same exclusivity. We could substitute "lawyer class," "economic class," "education class," "science class," or "medical class" for "artist class."

THE RADICALIZATION PROCESS

Some professors believe that they must break down every traditional belief you hold. In other words, they want to "radicalize" you so that you will adopt a secularized, man-centered, naturalistic worldview by presenting new facts that will force you to give up your presuppositions. Their techniques are similar to indoctrination and brainwashing methods used by the Chinese Communists. The following is written by a professor who understands the necessity of a solid worldview based on firm convictions. His worldview is radically opposed to a Biblical worldview; therefore, his advice is valuable. Through his words you will understand how the skeptic thinks:

Your feelings of insecurity may be greatly increased by our ruthlessly ripping away the myths which have supported your faith in yourself and America. This faith has been one of the basic sources of security, and learning the truth about the Pilgrims, the Indians, and the Philippines, and so on can make you feel terribly alone and insecure.

The social necessities for telling you the truth have already been discussed, but you should also realize that the truth may hurt, but you can be secure without it–one prick of the truth and you'll explode. The Chinese Communists proved that by using selective versions of American history as a brainwashing technique. They told American prisoners part of the truth about our history, and the men just folded up.

However, the Chinese Communists also realized that this technique would not work on people with a solid understanding of the truth. They therefore *didn't even try* to brainwash most officers and college-educated men. The experiences in the Korean prisoners-of-war camps are one of the most dramatic illustrations of a principle we college professors never tire of pointing out: *knowledge, real knowledge, not myths, or propaganda, is the firmest and surest foundation for psychological security.*[21]

You would like to believe that college is the place where more facts are added to your already growing reservoir of knowledge, and that by this enterprise you will grow in your understanding of the real world. To a certain extent, you will gain a better understanding of the world. But at the same time you may not realize that a great deal of propaganda and indoctrination will accompany the facts. The impression you will get at the university level is that truth is imparted from men and women who just have a better grasp of the facts. Allegedly, they are not filtering the facts through any preconceived worldview. Why, they wouldn't be teaching at the university level unless they really knew the impartial, unbiased truth. This is what they want you to believe. The sad thing is that most professors believe this, and many students fall for it.

This is not a true portrait of college life. In fact, life in general does not operate like this. Some philosophy of life guides an instructor as he or she teaches. In all probability, you will encounter tension because of competition between competing philosophies or worldviews. And the worldview most at risk in the classroom is the Christian worldview because it is well aware that no claim to truth (factuality) is neutral. Non-Christians believe in a philosophical "pluralism" where all worldviews must be considered valid except any worldview which insists that its way is the only way. The Christian realizes that portrayals of reality are interpreted "reality." Everybody has primary commitments (not based on observation) that he uses to organize and interpret the facts. Therefore all worldviews, if their starting points differ, are at war with one another. And all non-Christian worldviews are together at war with the Christian worldview.

Regulating Reality

The facts that support a position are chosen and interpreted in terms of religiously held presuppositions. Apparent "facts" that do not fit the presuppositions may be discarded as non-facts. At times, people recognize that there are many, many facts that cannot fit into their interpretive framework. Sometimes, an investigation of these facts will lead the person to change a previous opinion. In many cases, though, the facts that don't fit are thrown out. The instructor may decide to leave out certain facts because he is committed to an opposing worldview.

Some professors might tell you that man is the "determiner of all things": A woman has a right to do what she wants with her own body; those in political control can use the power of the State to "create" a "just" society; all sexual choices are proper and good choices, etc. This is a religious law that regulates his interpretation of the facts that he presents to you. It's a religious declaration, and it gives meaning to everything he or she might say. If he is an evolutionist, then he will see things in terms of an evolutionary worldview.

Atheism might be another instructor's starting point in evaluating the world. All the facts he encounters will be squeezed through this antitheistic grid. If a study of the design of the human body seems to demonstrate the necessity of a designer, then that fact must either be discarded as a non-fact, and therefore never considered for discussion, or the design of an organism must be interpreted in terms of a nontheistic conception of reality. For example, "the *wisdom* of DNA." In other words, "Nature" might be personified to take the place of a personal God. The random choices of Nature brought about design. Of course, it is rarely explained how this could be. Just as it's never explained how matter came into existence in the first place. What, after all, "caused" the universe to come into existence so that we even have "Nature"?

What exactly is "Nature" except a summary expression for the way things happen. In that case, "Nature" does not explain the way things happen. But atheists prefer empty references to "Nature" over guilt-inducing references to a Creator God who judges man in his sin.

There can be no room in the atheist's world for any fact that might point to a Creator, a God who stands over man in judgment and evaluation. Any evidence that seems to point to a Creator somehow must be explained away or ignored.

A LITTLE LOWER THAN THE ANGELS

What determines how we think and act? Are our actions nothing more than a series of chemical reactions and nerve responses? Should man be defined solely in terms of his biochemical makeup or is there more to us than meets the eye? For some modern thinkers, science has redefined man, not in terms of special creation, but in terms of biology:

> [The] sciences owe their spectacular progress to the assumption that all the processes of life can be interpreted finally as simply physical and chemical ones. Many of them have been imitated in the laboratory test-tube. The actions of enzymes, hormones, nucleic acids, complex proteins, and other substances concerned with the processes of life in general, so far as science can analyze them, follow the same laws that govern all the lifeless universe. To many the conclusion is now obvious that man, like every other living thing, is only a material mechanism, extraordinarily complex but no different in his basic nature from any other piece of machinery. This conception readily solves the dilemma of man's dual nature by denying that the intangible mental and spiritual side of him really exists at all.[22]

We are all religious beings with a spiritual nature. We are created this way. Biology does not make us unique. The scientist will not find the human spirit under a microscope. Man as a biological unit means we are nothing more than "naked apes." Describing man in mechanistic terms will transform humanity into an organic machine. Consider what can happen to man when he is no longer afforded the dignity of previous generations. What's to stop the powerful from using the weak for their own unjust ends? Totalitarian regimes around the world are noted for their inhumanity to man. Why should man be treated in any way different from the animals when the belief prevails that man is nothing more than a highly complex evolving animal? Why not experiment on man to see what makes him tick? Maybe we can accelerate the process of evolution and create supermen.

> With the philosophy of modern science, what is to stop genetic transfers of animal genes into humans? There is no secular ethic that can effectively argue against such things. Once the concept of man's uniqueness as being created in the image of God is lost, then all logical defenses against fusing man and animal are, at

41

best, spurious. This obviously calls into question the worth of human beings in the man-animal-machine complex once the distinctions are blurred.[23]

In time man will rebel against this dehumanization. Man is more than ape, more than a mechanism. We cannot escape this fact, although there are many who want us to try. But to deny our spiritual nature is to deny what makes us uniquely human. All that we hold valuable, good, and true are lost when men deny their essential spiritual nature. The loss of a Biblical view of man where God is sovereign over all the affairs of men tends to elevate some other sovereign to the place of God. In the classroom, this is usually the "expert." In society, this usually means the State. When a civil government adopts the view that man is less than what the Bible says, you can expect the dignity of man to be stripped from him. "Historically Western society has derived its belief in the dignity of man from its Judeo-Christian belief that man is the glory of God, made in His image. According to this view, human rights depend upon the creator who made man with dignity, not upon the state. In the American formulation, 'men . . . are endowed by their creator with certain inalienable rights.' "[24]

CONCLUSION

In the twentieth century, Biblical Christianity has fallen on hard times, especially in the university. This is not entirely the fault of the university. The Christian worldview has not been well articulated. In fact, many Christians have seen no need to apply the Bible beyond the limits of personal salvation and the life to come. In a word, the Bible has little or nothing to say to this world. The university, therefore, has adopted other worldviews to replace the once-prevailing worldview of Biblical Christianity. The results have been less than encouraging.

In the past sixty years there has been more brutality and obscurantism, more senseless conflicts, more of the past's heritage destroyed, more crass idolatry, more lies and hoaxes perpetuated, more people murdered or cast adrift as undesirable elements than in any other time in history; most of this in purportedly just causes for the advancement of mankind in general.[25]

When the former darling of the media, Aleksandr Solzhenitsyn, said, "Man has forgotten God, that is why this has happened," the intelligentsia aimed "their barbs of 'simplistic' at the author of *The Gulag Archipelago*."[26] But it is that simple.

3
THE CHRISTIAN WORLDVIEW

> Just as old or bleary-eyed men and those
> with weak vision, if you thrust before
> them a most beautiful volume, even if
> they recognize it to be some sort of writ-
> ing, yet can scarcely construe two words,
> but with the aid of spectacles will begin
> to read distinctly; so Scripture, gathering
> up the otherwise confused knowledge of
> God in our minds, having dispersed our
> dullness, clearly shows us the true God.[1]

WHAT makes up the Christian worldview? The foundation of a proper study of God, the universe, and man is God and His revelation, not man and his ideas about God. God gives meaning to the universe and to man. Now, there are all types of descriptions of "God": from Aristotle's Prime Mover to Shirley MacLaine's belief that God is a part of all of us and we are a part of God. Our description of God, therefore, must go beyond the mere belief in *a* god; we must consider the one *true* God. Our foundation then is the God of the Bible, because it is in Scripture that God reveals Himself. All other descriptions of God must be evaluated in terms of the Bible's witness.

1. *God is the Creator.* While the universe had a beginning, the God of the Bible is eternally self-existent in three Persons—Father, Son, and Holy Spirit. God made the created order, what is commonly referred to as "Nature," out of nothing. This is called creation *ex nihilo*. This doctrine is unique to Christianity. God did not create out of His own being (*ex deo*) or out of pre-existing material (*ex materia*).

2. *God is Personal and Triune.* God is not a "thing" like a tree or a "force" like electricity. He is a person. One question about the creation

45

of man that a child often asks is, Why did God create man? Many parents have given this simple answer: Because He was lonely. But this is not what the Bible teaches. The Persons of the Godhead—what the Church has called "the Trinity"[2]—communicated with one another before man was created. They could communicate because they are persons. Each Person of the Godhead thinks, wills, and acts, never in opposition, always in unity. Since communication takes place between the Persons of the Godhead, as creatures created in the image of this Triune God, we too can communicate with Him and with one another.

3. *God is both Lord and Father.* In many pagan worldview philosophies, the gods are either so exalted, transcendent, and "otherly" that they do not identify with men, or they are so much like men that they are unpredictable and at times helpless and even sinful. The Bible describes God as Lord and Father, two terms that express God's transcendence and immanence. *

> * *Immanence* is the quality of being near at hand or involved in man's temporal experience.

As our Lord, God is sovereign, ruler, and teacher. He is mighty, mysterious, exalted, and powerful so that He's able to do all things. As our Father, God is tender in mercy, compassionate, loving, patient, forgiving, and always willing to listen even to our most feeble prayers. He meets with us in our creaturehood and identifies with us in our weakness. Yet, these two ways of looking at God are not mutually exclusive. The transcendence (God is *distinct from* us) and immanence (God is *near to* us) of God are not contradictory concepts. John Frame writes:

> These two attributes do not conflict with one another. God is close *because* he is Lord. He is Lord, and thus free to make his power felt everywhere we go. He is Lord, and thus able to reveal himself clearly to us, distinguishing himself from all mere creatures. He is Lord, and therefore the most central fact of our experience, the least avoidable, the most verifiable.[3]

God can be our Father because He is our Lord. Because God is all-powerful, He can do what He pleases. He can help us. God has chosen to love rebellious sinners who want nothing of His love. Because He is the all-powerful Lord of all things, He can love those who do not deserve to be loved. What non-Christian worldview has this to offer you?

4. *God knows everything.* God knows intuitively. He does not have to search for more information to make a decision. All the knowledge in the universe is at His disposal. His knowledge makes the universe what it is. There is no new knowledge for God. God's thoughts are thus "original" and "independent." While ours are always "derivative" and "dependent." This means that God can never be mistaken about anything; therefore, what God tells us is true. If there is any misunderstanding or misapplication of God's Word, the fault lies with us. God has not chosen to reveal to us all that He knows. Much of what God knows is described as "secret things" (Deuteronomy 29:29). But He has revealed to us all we need to know.

5. *God is good, holy, and just.* One of the first attributes that a child learns about God is that He is good. God's goodness tells us what God *is* and how He *acts*. Goodness is not above God as an abstract idea. *God is goodness,* and He always acts in terms of His goodness. This means that He cares for all of His creation, from the plants and animals to men and women, even rebellious men and women. But God's goodness is not cheap and sentimental, because God is also holy. "Who is like Thee among the gods, O Lord? Who is like Thee, majestic in holiness, awesome in praises, working wonders?" (Exodus 15:11). The holiness of God is one of the most awesome themes in the Bible. Holiness has a very rich meaning in Scripture, but part of God's holiness is His perfect sinlessness. He is light, and there is no darkness in Him. To be in the presence of a thrice-holy God is disturbing, especially to rebel sinners. Isaiah described it as being "ruined" (Isaiah 6:5).

God's justice is the working out of His holy nature and will. This means that there are ethical absolutes that have God's character as their reference point. God's "work is perfect, for all His ways are just; a God of faithfulness and without injustice, righteousness and upright is He" (Deuteronomy 32:4). God's law then is a reflection of God's perfect character of holiness, goodness, and justice. There can be no ethical relativism in God or in His law.

Created in God's Image

God personalized His creation by creating man in His own image. This means that man reflects the attributes of God in a way that no other creature does. Animals have not been created in God's image. Man has a personality because God has a personality. Man is rational because God is rational. Man is self-conscious because God is self-conscious; that is, man can think about and judge himself. But there remains a fundamental Creator/creature distinction. Man does not possess these and other attributes of God in the same degree as God possesses them. For example, while God knows everything, as creatures we know only some things, and what we do know, we do not know in a comprehensive way. What we do know, however, we know truly. While we might not understand all the implications of what the Bible means when it says that God created the world out of nothing, we do know something of what is involved in that assertion. The idealist philosophers imply that knowledge is impossible until *all* the facts are known. The Creator/creature distinction means that we will never become more than creatures. We will not evolve into gods or even angels.

There is a fundamental distinction between God's being and man's being. First, God is uncreated (self-existent), independent, infinite, eternal, and unchangeable, while man is created (derivative), dependent, finite, temporal, and changeable. What does this mean in practical terms? When the creature denies God, he works to take on God's attributes for himself. But if every man decides that he is god in an absolute sense, we end up with moral anarchy. So, what happens? Some *institution* takes on the divine attributes, usually civil government, the State. The State then acts as if it were god—a tyrannical and capricious god: controlling lives, confiscating property, closing the borders of the country in order to keep its "subjects" from going to what the State perceives to be another god, and imprisoning those who defy the new god-State. Conde Pallen's utopian novel depicts what happens when the true God is rejected. Man looks for a suitable substitute:

Q. By whom were you begotten?

A. By the sovereign State.

Q. Why were you begotten?

A. That I might know, love, and serve the Sovereign State always.

Q. What is the sovereign State?

A. The sovereign State is humanity in composite and perfect being.

Q. Why is the State supreme?

A. The State is supreme because it is my Creator and Conserver in which I am and move and have my being and without which I am nothing.

Q. What is the individual?

A. The individual is only a part of the whole, and made for the whole, and finds his complete and perfect expression in the sovereign State. Individuals are made for cooperation only, like feet, like hands, like eyelids, like the rows of the upper and lower teeth.[4]

He Is There and He Is Not Silent[5]

One of the most controversial doctrines of the Christian worldview is the belief that God can and does reveal Himself so men can really know Him: First, in general revelation; second, in written, special revelation; and third, in the Person of Jesus Christ.

In general revelation God speaks to man through the created order. "The heavens are telling of the glory of God; and their expanse is declaring the works of His hands. Day to day pours forth speech. And night to night reveals knowledge" (Psalm 19:1-2). If the creation could speak as a man, it would pour forth words day in and day out that God is the one who created the world. The creation is His handiwork. This is why the Apostle Paul could write of how inexcusable it is to deny God when you look at the created order. "For since the creation of the world His invisible attributes, His eternal power and divine nature, have been clearly seen, being understood through what has been made, *so they are without excuse*" (Romans 1:20). Something has to account for what exists. The humanist opts for evolution: time, plus chance, plus pre-existent and impersonal matter.

While general revelation tells us that God exists, it also shows us what kind of God exists. Romans 1:21 says unbelievers know "*the* God." They *know* "what kind" of God He is through

- His invisible attributes (v. 20).
- His everlasting power (v. 20).
- His divine status (v. 20).
- His deserving of thanks (v. 21).
- His glory (v. 23).
- His moral character (vv. 24-32).

They know so much that they are "completely without excuse" for their pagan ideas and behavior (v. 20). They "suppress the truth" (v. 18).

Although we can learn from the created order that God is powerful and glorious, general revelation does not reveal *everything* we need to   49 know about God. So God has not left us without a *special* revelation of Himself. Special revelation comes to man in four ways: (1) in displays of power (the pillar of fire and the cloud of smoke that accompanied Israel in the wilderness); (2) specific one-time appearances (to Moses at the burning bush); (3) direct verbal communication (to prophets); (4) written, propositional revelation (as in the Bible). These types of revelation are called "special" because they are outside the normal workings of creation or general revelation. In each of the four methods of communication, God enters history to communicate directly with His people.

Of course, God went even beyond this by becoming man and entering history in the Person of Jesus Christ. Jesus' words were the very words of God. We have many of them recorded in the Bible, our only depository of God's revelation. The significant point here is that the Biblical worldview maintains that God can and does clearly communicate with man. This means that we can know God intimately. We can know who and what He is, and we can know His will. No other philosophy of life can make such a claim. This is why Christianity is exclusive. All other supposed revelations must be judged by God's special revelation, the Bible.

Man Lives in the Midst of a Fallen World

Not only must a worldview explain why something exists; it must also explain why it exists the *way* it does. God created the world and proclaimed it to be "very good" (Genesis 1:31). God's standards of righteousness were exhibited in the created order. There was neither death nor decay. But man chose to ignore God's commands and decided to live by his own rules. After the Fall, the world could no longer be described as "very good." Adam and Eve were cast out of paradise, and entered a world where the ground brought forth thorns and thistles (Genesis 3:18). Adam and Eve's rebellion brought about death, not only in the created order but for man himself:

> In *personality*, man lost his capacity to know himself accurately and to determine his own course of action freely in response to his intelligence. His *self-transcendence* was impaired by the alienation he experienced in relation to God, for as man turned from God, God let him go. And as man slipped from close fellowship with the ultimately transcendent one, so he lost his ability to

stand over against the external universe, understand it, judge it accurately and thus make truly "free" decisions. Rather, he became more a servant to nature than to God. And his status as God's vice-regent over nature (an aspect of the image of God) was reversed.

Man's *intelligence* also became impaired. Now he can no longer gain a fully accurate knowledge of the world around him, nor is he able to reason without constantly falling into error. *Morally*, man became less able to discern good and evil. *Socially*, he began to exploit his fellow men. *Creatively*, his imagination became separated from reality; imagination became illusion, and artists who created gods in their own image led man further and further from their origin. The vacuum in man created by this string of consequences is ominous indeed. (The fullest Biblical expression of these ideas is Romans 1-2).

Theologians have summed it up this way: Man has become alienated from God, from others, from nature and even from himself. This is the essence of man *fallen*.[6]

This explains why the world is in a mess. Man is not a mere product of his environment. Man has turned against God, and in turn, against other men, himself, and his world. Man's rebellion has twisted the created order and man; they can no longer be described as "very good." Only the Bible can adequately explain injustice, poverty, death, war, famine, and man's inhumanity toward other men.

Only in the Biblical worldview is there any hope of change, any chance of redemption. The Bible tells us why the world is in a mess, and the Bible shows us how to clean it up. This brings us back to the special revelation of the Lord Jesus Christ. Through His perfect life and His redeeming work, man can be changed; the image of God can be restored. "Man *redeemed* is man on the way to restoration of the defaced image—in other words, substantial healing in every area—personality, self-transcendence, intelligence, morality, social capacity and creativity."[7] And if man can be changed, so can the world. Even in death, there is hope. The Bible shows in vivid terms what lies beyond the grave. Only in Christ is the sting of death removed. No other worldview can offer such comfort and assurance.

THE DOMINO EFFECT OF DISBELIEF

You might have seen the TV show that aired a number of years ago called "That's Incredible," in which the good, the bad, and the unusual were paraded before the television viewing audience each week. One of the most ingenious feats ever performed was a world record domino extravaganza. Thousands of dominos were placed in intricate designs on a gymnasium floor by a "domino technician" who had to be careful not to allow even one domino to fall prematurely. The fall of the first domino would bring the entire exhibition to a less than incredible climax.

Ideas, like those dominos, are interdependent. If the first domino in a worldview begins to fall, you can expect the rest to follow eventually. The Christian worldview begins with the belief in a personal God who created and upholds all things. But the Christian worldview does not stop with creation and providence. God communicates with those whom He created in His own image through a written revelation that has come to be called the Bible. But what if one of these essential beliefs is denied? Can we expect that in time they all might be denied? Deny a personal God, and man becomes his own god. Deny that a personal God created and now sustains the universe, and you end up with a chance universe where anything is possible. Deny the reality of a written revelation, and all truth seems to be relative. Such denials set off a series of dominos of unbelief.

Domino One: Deism

Deism is the weakened bridge between Biblical Christianity and naturalism. In Biblical Christianity, the universe is dependent on God for its existence as well as its maintenance. These are the doctrines of *creation* and *providence*. In deism the Biblical doctrine of providence is denied. The Bible says that God "*upholds all things* by the word of His power" (Hebrews 1:3). The worldview of deism proposes that a "*transcendent God, as a First Cause, created the universe but then left it to run on its own. God is thus not immanent, not fully personal, not sovereign over the affairs of men, not providential.*"[8] The Christian worldview is therefore opposed to deism. While deism is formally "theistic," it is not Biblical; it does not have a doctrine of providence.

Deism was a prominent and self-conscious worldview during the post-revolutionary war period. Some of our nation's most famous founders have been classified as deists.[9] While deism is not an articulated worldview, today many religious people subscribe to it unknowingly. For them, God exists, but He does not concern Himself intimately with His creation. Some go so far as to maintain that God is powerless to work in the world. The reason bad things happen to good people, (as the book by a similar name insists), is that God is unable to intervene in people's lives or the affairs of this world. God is finite and thus unable to alleviate the suffering of men and women.

As you can probably tell, it is not very difficult for the first domino of the Christian worldview to fall with the presuppositions of deism. Deism maintains a transcendent God and a created universe. But it also postulates a God who is virtually impotent, and a worldview of "Nature" that has assumed His power. A person can be very religious and still be a deist. But once someone accepts the presuppositions of deism, he is ripe for the worldview of naturalism.

Domino Two: Naturalism

The next domino to fall is the presupposition that there is nothing more than the observable world or the world of man's temporal experience. Even naturalists insist that we have experiences that are not of "observable" things. Magnetic fields? God is put outside the world in deism. In naturalism, God is banished from the universe altogether, either as a force or as an explanation. We live in a world in which the Spiritual dimension of reality has been expunged from the universe. Carl Sagan of *Cosmos* fame expressed the fundamental presupposition of naturalism well: "The Cosmos is all that is or ever was or ever will be."[10] But of course Sagan did not *observe* that the Cosmos is all there is! It is his faith assumption. Science is inherently unable to tell us its own limits. All of life must be explained in terms of what can be observed and scientifically tested. There is no Spiritual dimension to the universe. Naturalism is Flatland country.

In 1884 Edwin Abbot published the story of "Flatland." Flatland is an imaginary country where everyone lives in only two dimensions. The people are circles, triangles and squares, and they live in pentagons. A line to them is like a wall to us. They do not know up or down, only north, south, east and west.

One day a sphere came to visit Flatland. At first the Flatlanders could not see him because the sphere remained outside their plane. They were confused by a voice that was not associated with a line, and they did not understand when he told them that he was "above" them. . . . So the sphere entered Flatland. Of course, to the Flatlanders he appeared to be a circle. But he talked to them about a three-dimensional world that was beyond their experiences.[11]

For the most part, the university is Flatland country. Biblical revelation remains outside the plane of those who believe as Carl Sagan believes. Their presuppositions cannot accommodate God, and if God were ever to enter history personally, as He did in the person of Jesus Christ, or propositionally as He speaks to man in the Bible, there would be no way for a Flatlander to recognize Him. A Flatlander's explanation would go something like this: There are no spheres (God speaking to man in special revelation), only circles (the world that we see around us and nothing more). A three-dimensional world is inconceivable and therefore can never be observed.

The tests that would be given to certify the claims of a personal God entering history or a written revelation that is God's very word would not be adequate to measure them. The surveyors would continue to come up with circles instead of spheres. Their naturalistic presuppositions would get in the way of the actual facts. The idea of a personal God entering history would be only the imaginary aspirations of a Flatlander who wanted to escape a two-dimensional world for a three-dimensional world that does not exist. Special revelation would be nothing more than the writings of some Flatlanders that simply *depicted* a fictional three-dimensional world. That three-dimensional world certainly does not exist.

Naturalism* teaches that nature is the whole of reality. The worldview of naturalism shuts man inside a closed universe. Naturalism is similar to the worldview of those who believed in a flat earth. Explorers were afraid to sail to the "ends" of the earth. Their false worldview limited their knowledge.

Naturalism as a philosophical worldview should not be confused with "naturalism" as a study of wildlife.

Since what is studied by the techniques of natural science is all that there is, there is no need for exploration that goes beyond the universe.

Nature is defined in terms of the material realm, broadly defined. The universe has its "origin" in pre-existent matter and thus has no real existence apart from it; therefore, the universe cannot be explained in any other terms. There is no "mind," for example. Thought is reduced to the chemical processes of brain tissue. Values are culturally determined and are therefore always in flux. Religion and the idea of God are the projections of people who want to believe in something beyond what they can see. A worldview that is synonymous with naturalism is secular* humanism.

Secular comes from the Latin *saeculum*, which means "time" or "age." Today, to describe someone as secular means he is completely bound to time with no vision of eternity. This means when you are dead, you are dead. Nothing is beyond the grave since man is nothing more than a complex combination of matter. Man has no Spiritual dimension. Of course, this also means that matter is eternal. Nothing existed before matter, certainly not a god. The secularist cannot and will not believe that God exists or acts in human affairs.

The following proposition is fundamental to the naturalistic or secular system of thought:

As non-theists, we begin with humans, not God, nature not deity. Nature may indeed be broader and deeper than we now know; and new discoveries, however, will but enlarge our knowledge of the natural.[12]

What presuppositions make up the worldview of naturalism?

1. *The universe is self-existent.* There can be no other explanation for what exists. The universe either came into existence out of nothing (the Christian position), or the universe in some form always existed.

2. *The universe consists solely of matter.* Since there is no personal God beyond the universe who controls the universe, then matter is all there is. There is no "spirit" or "soul" that can reside in man.

3. *The universe is evolving.* What we see today may not be here tomorrow. Chance dictates the direction the universe will take. In fact, man may not be the highest of evolved animals in another million years. *The Planet of the Apes* is a real possibility with naturalism.

4. *Man is nothing more than a highly evolved animal.* Man is nothing more than a reflection of the universe. He is the universe in microcosm; therefore, he can have no "soul" or "mind." (When naturalists speak as if man has a mind or can make free choices, they are being inconsistent with their worldview. Man is not greater than his "creator.")

5. *The end of man is extinction.* There is no God. There can be no judgment, no heaven, no hell. Life after death, while it may be a possibility, is still left to chance and ignorance. No one can know with naturalism. (The best naturalism can offer is extinction and scant reports of "bright lights" as people near death's door and soon return with stories of "peacefulness" and "tranquility." With naturalism, why does it matter? Man is nothing more than matter: simply a conglomeration of atoms.)

6. *There can be no certainty.* The naturalist can never be certain that what he believes is true. Given the fact (as naturalism teaches) that everything is evolving, "truth" itself must be in flux. What is "true" today may be "false" tomorrow. "One could well ask: 'If the mind, like all else in nature, is still evolving, how can we be sure that its present structure and operation guarantee any truth?' For example, did the Law of Contradiction, which is necessary for truth, evolve like the rest of the body? How can we be sure that there's not some new mental law, now struggling to be born, a law which will enable us to get even closer to the truth about reality? Would this new law confirm or contradict evolution and naturalism?"[13] With naturalism, we would never know. Charles Darwin understood the implications of his own evolutionary theory: "With me the horrid doubt always arises whether the convictions of man's mind, which has been developed from the mind of the lower animals, are of any value or at all trustworthy. Would anyone trust in the convictions of a monkey's mind, if there are any convictions in such a mind?"[14]

7. *Naturalism is committed to miracles.* The naturalist would have us believe that: "Everything came from nothing. Order came from chaos. Harmony came from discord. Life came from nonlife. Reason came from irrationality. Personality came from nonpersonality. Morality came from amorality."[15]

8. *History has no purpose.* Why should the naturalist expect history to "go anywhere" or to "mean" anything? The naturalist cannot predict future events based on past events, because there is no regularity in history. Henry Ford's words that "history is more or less bunk" becomes a truism while George Santayana's dictum that "those who cannot remember the past are condemned to repeat it" turns into nonsense.

9. *Man's purpose in life is self-actualization, hedonism, and narcissism.* Pleasure may often be the only goal of the naturalist, since for him man is nothing more than an animal. Sense perceptions are the only important considerations. The "good" is relative to the time, place, and tastes of particular persons. The pain of others can be "self-actualizing" for some hedonists. A Marquis de Sade is at home with a naturalistic worldview. For the naturalist it is "Let us eat and drink, for tomorrow we may die" (Isaiah 22:13). The Apostle links a belief in the resurrection with this verse: "If the dead are not raised, 'Let us eat and drink, for tomorrow we die'" (1 Corinthians 15:32).

10. *Man "saves" himself through education, law, science, technology, and politics.* One of the doctrinal pillars of the *Humanist Manifesto II* is, "No deity will save us; we must save ourselves."[16] And how does the naturalist propose that man will save us?: "Using technology wisely, we can control our environment, conquer poverty, markedly reduce disease, extend our life-span, significantly modify our behavior, alter the course of human evolution and cultural development, unlock vast new powers, and provide humankind with unparalleled opportunity for achieving an abundant and meaningful life."[17]

11. *Values are relative and subjective.* What type of ethical norms should we expect from a self-existent universe, an evolving order, and a biological component called man? Values evolve along with man and his world. Ethical considerations are tied to whatever works for maximizing the pleasure of the greatest number. (But then why is *that* ethically obligatory?) Joseph Fletcher sums up this avenue of the naturalistic worldview on ethics with this declaration: "I think there are no normative moral principles whatsoever which are intrinsically valid or universally obliging."[18]

12. *Human life is expendable.* We kill animals for food. Man is only a highly evolved animal. Therefore man can be killed for any number of "socially acceptable reasons": over-population, high medical costs for the terminally ill, and the inconveniences of too many children. After a debate on the abortion issue, a lawyer who had participated in the debate had the opportunity to speak with some of the other participants: "[M]ost of the students *already* recognized that the unborn child is a human life. Nevertheless, certain social reasons are considered 'high enough' to justify ending that life. According to some of the women, examples of 'high enough' reasons include protecting pregnant teenagers from the psychological distress of bearing a child, helping poor women who aren't able to care adequately for a child, and preventing children

57

from coming into the world 'unwanted.' Many charged that pro-life philosophies are not 'socially acceptable' because they fail to deal realistically with these problems."[19]

13. *All lifestyles are permissible while the family is considered obsolete.* Once ethical norms become arbitrary, we can expect the dismantling of long-standing Christian familial relationships like marriage and heterosexuality. Social relationships have to evolve along with nature. For example, in Marxist theory, which is nothing more than the political side of philosophical naturalism, the family is viewed as simply a development in the evolutionary process that will pass away in time. Engels remarked that "human society arose out of a troupe of tree-climbing monkeys."[20] A book on lesbianism, reviewed in the *New York Times*, attempts to help in overcoming traditional, that is, Christian, attitudes regarding "the nuclear family, that cradle of evil."[21] Biblical norms regarding heterosexual marriage relationships have been abandoned in favor of all types of "legitimate" lifestyles: homosexuality, bestiality, and paedophilia.

14. *Government is a creation of man and is usually centralized in the State.* As with the origin of the family, civil government is also a creature of the evolutionary process. The individual is of no consequence. Those with the greatest power control. All totalitarian regimes begin with the fallacies of naturalism and degenerate into perpetrators of unspeakable atrocities. Nazi Germany was no exception: "It is thus necessary that the individual should finally come to realize that his own ego is of no importance in comparison with the existence of his nation; that the position of the individual ego is conditioned solely by the interests of the nation as a whole . . . that above all the unity of a nation's spirit and will are worth far more than the freedom of the spirit and will of an individual."[22]

15. *Human rights are subjective, transient, and created by the State.* Why should we expect the protection of fundamental rights when man is nothing more than an animal? Why should the weak be protected by the strong? With naturalism there is no reason. All talk about human rights comes from those nations that have had a Christian base. The most familiar philosophy of human rights is found in the Declaration of Independence (1776). "All men," it states, "are endowed by their Creator with certain unalienable Rights, that among these are Life, Liberty and the pursuit of Happiness."

The philosophy of rights is intimately tied to the reality of the Creator who alone grants rights. No God, no rights. The Declaration makes it clear that these inalienable rights are not granted by governments; rather, they are an *endowment*, a gift, of the Creator of the universe.[23]

On the other hand, there are the French Declaration of the Rights of Man (1789) and the more recent United Nations' Declaration of Human Rights (1948), which are indicative of *governments* as the grantors of rights. If governments can give rights they can just as easily revoke them. "The State giveth. The State taketh away. Blessed be the name of the State."

The Declaration of Independence says that "among" the many rights God has bestowed, "Life, Liberty, and the pursuit of happiness" are just three of them. The assumption is that there are more rights, but to list them would be to limit them. On the other hand, the French Declaration of the Rights of Man enumerates the rights of citizens and, thus, limits "rights" to the seventeen listed. What happens when the State decides a certain right is no longer a right?

16. *Man's environment accounts for all the "evil" in the world.* Of course, there really is no evil for the naturalist. "Good" and "evil" are nothing more than subjective categories of what people like and dislike at a given time. But the designation exists even for the naturalist, so we have to deal with it. For the naturalist, evil itself (unpleasant acts) must have a physical cause. Man's environment, the world in which he lives, is at fault. Famine, death, and man's cruelty to man can all be explained environmentally. Change a person's environment and the man will change. Give the thief enough food to eat and he will stop stealing. For the environmentalist[24] "*salvation is escape from an evil environment to a good one.* In the good environment, man will develop his physical and mental abilities in all directions."[25] In a naturalistic worldview there can be no other explanation for "evil" except the world. Sin never enters the picture.

Domino Three: Relativism

How many times have you been in a heated debate with someone over some controversial issue only to have it end with, "Well, everything is relative." End of discussion. Nothing you say can make any difference because your opponent does not believe in absolutes. (Of course, maintaining that everything is relative is an absolute statement.) Most of America's youth have been raised on the relativism doctrine.

There is one thing a professor can be absolutely certain of: almost every student entering the university believes, or says he believes, that truth is relative. . . . The students' backgrounds are as various as America can provide. Some are religious, some atheists; some are to the Left, some to the Right; some intend to be scientists, some humanists or professionals or business-men; some are poor, some rich. They are unified only in their relativism and their allegiance to equality.[26]

Relativism is the offspring of naturalism. The relativistic worldview postulates that absolutes are impossible. What is wrong today can be right tomorrow. For example, prior to 1973 abortion was considered im-moral and illegal, although attitudes and laws were beginning to change as far back as the mid-1960s.

Prior to 1973 the Hippocratic Oath expressed the views of most doc-tors. But with *Roe v. Wade* anyone who practices abortion must repudiate the statement from the Oath which prohibits a doctor from giving a pregnant woman any "deadly drug, [or] . . . a pessary [suppository] to produce an abortion." Now doctors take an oath not to "do anything il-legal." How is this different from the Nazi atrocities that were perfectly "legal" according to Nazi law? The Declaration of Geneva (adopted in September 1948 by the General Assembly of the World Medical Organization), which was modeled after the Hippocratic Oath, was also used by medical school graduates. It included: "I will maintain the ut-most respect for human life from the time of conception." Subsequent editions show a modified Declaration of Geneva with the removal of "from the time of conception." After the *Roe v. Wade* pro-abortion deci-sion, abortion became moral and legal.

Fixed standards do not exist in a relativistic world. Of course, once naturalism wins the day through a relativistic philosophy, things remain fixed. The pro-abortionists would never want to admit that sometime in the future abortion could once again be made illegal. Relativism only seems to operate against a worldview that maintains absolutes. Once the old worldview is disposed of (in this case, the Christian worldview), the advocates of the new worldview do not allow others to tamper with the new order. All things are indeed relative, even the doctrine of relativism. And the college campus is not immune.

At Harvard University in November [1986], there was yet another of those meetings where university folk discuss how to "reform" higher education. There, Cornell University President Frank H. T. Rhodes suggested it was time for universities to pay "real and sustained attention to students' intellectual and moral well-being."

This elicited gasps and even catcalls from the audience of professors and students. One indignant student rose to challenge Rhodes. "Who is going to do the moral instructing?" he demanded. "Whose morality are we going to follow?" The audience applauded thunderously, believing that the student had settled the issue and shut Rhodes up simply by posing these unanswerable questions.[27]

Relativism thrives within the evolutionary worldview. Since for the naturalist nothing "governs" the universe except chance, why should we expect to find absolutes for moral decisions? And yet these same scientists will insist on absolutes when it comes to scientific experimentation and documentation of archeological specimens to support their evolutionary claims.

We see a related development in constitutional law. In an evolutionary and naturalistic universe, nothing is fixed and definite. Nothing endures over time. This includes language. We're told that there is no definite meaning in the language, for example, of the United States Constitution.[28] Thus, law becomes whatever the Supreme Court says it is.

[This shift] began with the application of Darwinism to law—all law. Julian Huxley once noted that the evolutionary belief system encompasses the disciplines such as "law and religion . . . until we are enabled to see evolution as a universal, all pervading process. . . . Our present knowledge indeed forces us to view that the world of reality is evolution—a single process of self-transformation."[29]

What does relativism do to the college student? The student remains an observer. He can study different cultures, for example, but he cannot make a value judgment that one culture is any better than another. In the study of religion there are similar pitfalls.

CONCLUSION

Who will set the standards for determining what is real and what is illusion? Modern science has its limits. It can only discover what the scientist can see. Science may not arbitrarily dismiss what it cannot see. This is outside the bounds of science. Naturalism is a faith because it postulates in absolute terms what it cannot measure. There is a difference between what cannot be measured and what someone determines is not there to be measured.

> The naturalist's argument is no more than a sophisticated version of the anti-theistic argument of Yuri Gagarin. Emblazoned on the walls of the anti-God museum in Leningrad are Gagarin's stirring words proclaimed upon re-entry from space, roughly translated: "I have been out in space and didn't see God; therefore there is no God." Such reasoning is foolish, but it illuminates an ancient insight: A viewpoint is important because it determines what one sees, not necessarily what there is to be seen.[30]

Science can only exist when it assumes that the world is not in chaos—that there is unity, order, law—that it is intelligible, logical, and consistent. But what made it so? Did order evolve out of chaos? Did what is random become law-like and predictable?

4
SHOPPING FOR A GOD

> When we speak of the whole man, we
> know that he is more than a skeleton
> with meat on it. Man, created in the
> image of God, is a whole entity
> comprised of body, mind, and soul.
> People are spiritual beings as well as
> material entities. We could say that this
> goes without saying, but it does not.
> We no longer operate from the same
> philosophical base as earlier generations.[1]

THE physical world abhors a vacuum. Remove the water from a glass and air will rush in to take its place. You can actually hear this principle at work as you open a vacuum-packed can of coffee. The rush of air is almost immediate. Once the lid is off, the vacuum is filled with the surrounding atmosphere.

The same principle is true for man. Remove the Triune God of Scripture from his life, and you can be sure that some other god will rush in to take His place. Herbert Schlossberg, in his foundational study of contemporary idol worship, said it this way: "Western society, in turning away from the Christian faith, has turned to other things. This process is commonly called *secularization*, but that conveys only the negative aspect. The word connotes the turning away from the worship of God while ignoring the fact that something is being turned *to* in its place."[2]

Keep in mind that you are a spiritual creation. You must nourish the part of you that the Bible describes as your "spirit." Just as there are all types of food for the body, there is food for the soul or spirit, "spiritual food" (1 Corinthians 10:3). But not just any food will meet the nutritional demands required by your spirit. Just as there is "junk food" that can rob your body of essential nutrients and can turn a healthy body into an anemic one, there are all types of spiritual junk foods that can wreck your spiritual health. If you don't eat the right spiritual food, you will starve to death or you will seek any nourishment that promises to satisfy your hunger.

The American public has sensed that something has been missing from discussions when man and his needs are discussed. In a recent survey of eighty thousand of its readers, *Better Homes and Gardens* learned some startling things about the belief patterns of its subscribers. But what was most notable was the recognition that the media, our nation's largest source of speedy and seemingly accurate information, are ignoring man's spiritual needs. This comment is representative:

> I am answering your questionnaire because I believe you have
> hit upon a part of our nature that too often is neglected in secular
> magazines. The physical and mental faculties are discussed in
> depth, but, in essence, they depend on our spiritual well-being.
> I think religion plays a far more important role in many families
> than most of the media realize.[3]

The spiritual spectrum of the survey varies widely: from "New Age" Spiritualists to Christian "Fundamentalists." Most believe in eternal life (eighty-nine percent), heaven (eighty-seven percent), miracles (eighty-six percent), and hell (seventy-six percent). But some believe in non-Christian doctrines like a spiritual/astral realm (thirty percent), channeling messages/lessons from spirits (thirteen percent), and reincarnation (eleven percent).[4] The survey showed that people crave spiritual things. For some, almost any type of spirituality will do. As one respondent wrote, "Faith is what you believe in."[5] But what is that "what"?

In this chapter we will look at what conditions make it easy for people to be seduced by spiritual counterfeits and what you can do to avoid being seduced by false prophets, promises, and messiahs.

THE SMORGASBORD MENTALITY

People are so confused about what is true that they tend to believe *anything* and *everything*. Students today are given "options," with no consideration that one of the many options under study could be correct. In fact, it seems to be an unwritten law among teachers not to say "this is right" or "this is wrong." It's fashionable to have an open mind. Like an open sewer, you never know what will drain there. Our society has moved from absolutism to an undiscerning openness. "Openness—and the relativism that makes it the only plausible stance in the face of various claims to truth and various ways of life and kinds of human beings—is the great insight of our times. The true believer is the real danger."[6]

The true believer is the outcast. A belief in norms, absolutes, and certainty is undemocratic. The student who enters college with an uncritical open mind will find himself swept away by every wind of doctrine, every appealing opinion, and every spiritual counterfeit to fill the spiritual vacuum. The doctrine of pluralism is the key that will be used to open your vacuum-packed mind.

> Pluralism refers to a diversity of religions, worldviews, and ideologies existing at one time in the same society. We are socially heterogeneous. One religion or philosophy doesn't command and control the culture. Instead, many viewpoints exist. We have Buddhists and Baptists, Christian Reformed and Christian Scientist—all on the same block, or at least in the same city. This can have a leveling effect on religious faith.[7]

Our nation is steeped in pluralism, tolerance, diversity, freedom, and the "democratic spirit."[8] All lifestyles are permitted. Homosexuality is tolerated because we live in a "diverse society." Abortion is legal because "you cannot impose your morality on someone else who has a different set of moral standards." The only view that is not tolerated is the view that does not tolerate all views. Christianity came on the scene with Jesus saying, "I am *the* way and *the* truth and *the* life; *no one comes to the Father but by Me*" (John 14:6). How intolerant of Him to exclude Mayan spirits, the Buddha, Mohammed, and just plain decent folk!

> Modern pluralism presents one prevailing opinion about Jesus Christ. Like all great religious leaders, he is special but not unique; and he is certainly not exclusive. That would be closed- and narrow-minded. He is classed with the multitude of masters, grouped with the gurus, but not exalted as supreme. He is tucked into a comfortable corner of the religious pantheon so as to disturb no one.

> The assumption is that Jesus just couldn't have claimed to be the only way; that's undemocratic! So instead of facing Christ's challenge as it stands, the whole idea is dismissed as anti-pluralistic, and closed-minded.[9]

There can be no true religion over against all false religions. Christianity is *a* religion but not *the* religion. The Bible can *sometimes* be taught as fictional literature like Shakespeare, but it cannot be taught as the Word of God. This would offend Moslems, Buddhists, Mormons,[10] and most certainly atheists. Unsuspecting students are then open to any and all philosophical gurus who are ready, willing, and seemingly able to lead the way to a new vision of reality. New worldviews are a dime a dozen. Those best able to express their views get the greatest following.

FROM RATIONALISM TO IRRATIONALITY

Christianity is rational.* Surprised? Well, you shouldn't be. The Christian faith offers the most rational explanation of why man and the universe operate the way they do.

> *Rational*: What pertains to and satisfies man's intellect. This should be distinguished from "rationalism" (the view that man's autonomous reason is his final authority).

As Christians we do not take a leap into the void of irrationality when we decide to believe in God and the authority of His Word although there are people who believe that religion, any religion, is simply one way to make people feel good and to give them a sense of security and meaning. The skeptic might say something like this: "Some people turn to drugs and alcohol, others 'get religion.'" The sad thing is, many people do turn to religion, all types of religions, to make them feel good. For the religious experimenters, there is no real understanding of Biblical Christianity. One religion is as good as any other. Jonestown taught us otherwise.

The Lesson of Jonestown

Why would nine hundred men, women, and children voluntarily take a lethal dose of cyanide-laced Kool-Aid? In November 1978 the nation viewed the horror of nine hundred bloated bodies lying peacefully in the remote jungle of Guyana, South America. There was no sign of a struggle. For these people and the families they left behind, it does matter "what" one believes. But what led these people to so unite with a religious leader like Jim Jones that they were willing to go with him to their deaths? A letter left behind by one of the suicide victims tells it all.

> For my part—I am more than tired of this wretched, merciless planet and the hell it holds for so many masses of beautiful people—thank you [Jim Jones] for the only life I've known.[11]

These desperate people saw something in Jim Jones that for a time filled a spiritual void. When it seemed the only hope they had ever had was going to be ripped from their very beings, they ended it all. Death was better than facing life with a spiritual void that could not be filled. For them, religion was nothing more than a personal harbor from a mounting storm.

Christianity is not a crutch or simply a haven for the restless. The Christian faith brings rebellious and hell-bound sinners into a right relationship with the Creator of the universe. Christianity works in the real world just because it is true. It explains why things are the way they are and what can be done to change man and creation for the better. Therefore, the Christian faith can be put to the test in the real world. Of course, this should be distinguished from unprincipled "pragmatism," where something is tried with little or no regard to absolutes. There is no guarantee that anything will work in the worldview of pragmatism.

The presuppositions that we hold regarding God, the Bible, and our ultimate destiny will work in the real world. Deep in his heart, Jim Jones knew that his religion could not weather the storms of life. His unprincipled pragmatic program, "Jonestown," lost. His only way out was in death.

How does the rationalist know for certain that his worldview is the right one? What will happen to the rationalist after death? Is the grave the end? Or is there a hell? He can never know outside of Christ and His Word. A worldview whose foundation is pure unaided rationality can never offer certainty. C. S. Lewis, in an address to the Oxford Socratic Club (1944), shows that the naturalistic worldview invariably reduces itself to skepticism:

> If . . . I swallow the scientific cosmology as a whole, then not only can I not fit in Christianity, but I cannot even fit in science. If minds are wholly dependent on brains and brains on bio-chemistry, and bio-chemistry (in the long run) on the meaningless flux of the atoms, I cannot understand how the thought of those minds should have any more significance than the sound of the wind in the trees.[12]

There is no certainty for the finite creature who attempts to interpret the world from his limited perspective. And there were no answers in the irrational world of Jim Jones. The irrational act of suicide proved little and offered nothing for those who so much wanted to hope and believe that everything would be all right.

DEFINING OUR TERMS

We should, at this point, define and contrast the terms *rationality*, *rationalism*, and *irrationality*. There are many irrational people who believe they are quite rational within the context of their worldview. Jim Jones was "rationally" carrying out the implications of his worldview. Suicide was the most "rational" thing to do, seeing that his world was about to be destroyed. In this use of rational, it is synonymous with "consistency." Jones followed the implications of his worldview to its "consistent" end. Those who reject the Christian faith also believe that they are doing so on purely "rational" grounds. But within the context of the Christian worldview, their actions are completely irrational as we will demonstrate. The following definitions are formulated within the bounds of the Christian worldview.

Rationality: Thinking God's Thoughts After Him

Rationality, the ability to think and reason, is a gift from God. The rational person makes accurate assessments of his world based on the facts at hand. A burner on a stove cannot be hot and cold at the same time. It can be warm, but this is neither hot nor cold. A rational person would not test his hypothesis every time the burner was turned on. If it did not turn red, he would assume that it was not turned up high enough to glow or that there might be a malfunction. He would test his reasoning by placing his hand over the burner at a safe distance. This is the process of rationality in action. It is not guesswork.

To state this more formally, the rational man applies the law of non-contradiction on a consistent basis; that is, "Nothing can be both A and not-A *at the same time and in the same respect*."[13] Refusal to live in terms of this principle will lead to skepticism. God cannot lie, so logical consistency is necessary for God's reasoning creature, man.

Let's go back to our burner. It can be hot, warm, or cold. But it cannot be hot, warm, and cold *at the same time*. To think that it can be all three at the same time can lead to a badly burned hand if a bright red burner is not seen as an indicator of high temperature.

Now, there may be things that cannot be *explained* rationally; that is, man's intellect cannot understand or explain all that is true (known by God). But this does not necessarily mean that these unexplainables are not true. There are scientists who work with theories without having all the facts to support the theory conclusively. Scientists are being rational even though they can't determine why something works the way it does. They would be abandoning rationality, however, if a theory did not work but they continued to use it as if it did. All of us work in terms of some ignorance. We don't know everything. "Ideas are everywhere, but knowledge is rare. Even a so-called 'knowledgeable' person usually has solid knowledge only within some special area, representing a tiny fraction of the whole spectrum of human concerns. Humorist Will Rogers said, 'Everybody is ignorant, only on different subjects.'"[14]

A rational person is someone who works on the basis of available evidence. If I know that I have $200.00 in my checking account, and yet operate in terms of having $300.00 in my account, I am being irrational (and sinful). Of course, I could be operating in terms of inaccurate evidence. I could be acting rational, that is, in terms of the available evidence I have, but I could be wrong. Therefore,

> . . . a rational belief is not necessarily a true one. When a jury finds someone guilty in light of the evidence, it is still possible that the person is innocent, even if the more reasonable view (on the basis of the evidence) is that he is guilty. . . . Truth does not change. Something either is or is not true. A rational belief can be changed when new evidence comes in.[15]

Rationality is the characteristic of man by which he uses his intellect to explain, predict, or control the world around and within him. A cook must presuppose that a bright red burner means "very hot," and he must believe that it will be so tomorrow. He places his confidence, faith if you will, in such predictability. Try studying for a test without a belief in a predictable (cause-effect) universe. A poor performance on a test will *cause* you to get a poor grade. You can *predict* that if you don't know the answers to the test, you will not do well. These presuppositions, controlling the use of reason as a tool, get you through life. Reason, then, is a God-given tool to discover how the world works. It is not the unaided criterion for truth itself; that is, reason serves the court, but it is not the final judge.

Rationalism: Thinking Man's Thoughts After Him

Rationalism takes an extreme position regarding man's ability to think and reason logically. For the rationalist, *autonomous* reason is considered the only criterion for real knowledge and understanding. Reason supposedly explains everything that can be explained. The rationalist does not consider revelation as a source or a vehicle of knowledge. Revelation is outside the bounds of "rational" discussion since it is not based on the authority of man's mind. Even if revelation existed, we could not understand or apply any of its propositions.

Anti-Christian worldviews have boasted in the presupposition that the world can be explained in terms of autonomous reason alone. In the minds of the rationalists, there is always a "rational" explanation for all that happens; that is, one acceptable to man's mind. There is no need to postulate, for example, that God created the universe and man. The origin of man can be explained adequately in terms of evolution. But can it? Can evolution explain love, compassion, grief, and hope? Is it any wonder that drug and shock therapy (and at one time lobotomies) have been used to treat "mental illness"? You see, there must be some "organic" reason for a person's problems. In a purely materialistic, naturalistic, and rationalistic worldview these emotions and mental disturbances cannot exist.

But experience teaches every man, woman, and child that these feelings do exist. We base our lives on the belief that *love* is real and unique to humans. Our halls of justice cry out to have *compassion* on the poor. As a nation we *grieve* as we visit the Vietnam Memorial in Washington, D.C. where the names of tens of thousands of dead soldiers are chiseled in granite for all the world to see. We *hope* that in the future the names of our children will not be immortalized in a similar way.

Basically, rationalism assumes that man is the final court of appeal when declaring what is true or false. If it cannot be explained by man and his reasoning abilities, then it cannot be true or it does not exist. For the rationalist, reason is the criterion for truth. But there are some things that the instruments of science just cannot measure.

THE MANY FACES OF IRRATIONALISM

There must be a way to account for all the "unexplainables," those things that just don't fit within the context of a materialistic, naturalistic, and rationalistic worldviews. The rationalist, if he is consistent with his reason-alone premise, has no ultimate answers to life's basic questions:

How did the world get here?

Who am I?

Is there any meaning to life?

What will happen to me when I die?

Are there any moral absolutes?

Is there any meaning to history?

How can the rationalist answer these questions with any certainty? Humanistic rationalism has forsaken the Christian worldview that has answers to all these questions. The rationalist can guess at an answer, but he can never know for sure. And if he is consistent with his rationalism, he really has no answers. In fact, it doesn't really matter if he asks the questions at all.

But few people are satisfied with rationalistic and naturalistic answers. There is more to man than the explanation that he is a highly evolved amalgamation of atoms. A better explanation must be sought from something greater than man. If the God of the Bible is not chosen, then rationalistic man drifts into the realm of the irrational. The rationalist throws reason to the wind for just enough time to salvage his rationalistic worldview. Two polar opposites—rationalism and irrationalism—join forces to solve the mysteries of the universe. They are surely an unlikely pair. The rationalist believes that all things can be explained and defined in terms of reason alone. But reason cannot explain all things. Leaps of irrationality become necessary to keep rationalism from disintegrating.

There is a "secret treaty" between rationalism and irrationalism in which the reason-alone worldview accepts irrational explanations of how the world might work to explain what scientism and naturalism cannot.[16]

Looking for ET

Consider this bit of irrationality from the minds of the rationalists. For over a hundred years—at least since the publication of Darwin's *Origin of Species* in 1859—scientists and skeptics in general have worked to shove God out of the universe. But in the past few decades, the theistic skeptics have once again turned their eyes and ears toward the heavens—not to seek for God, but to hope for a message from outer space, from a higher life form, for some "explanation" for the way the universe works. They are hoping there is something out there to give our existence meaning. Some have gone so far as to assert that our earth was visited by extraterrestrials thousands of years ago. In these visitations, primitive earthlings were given highly advanced medical, technical, and architectural skills, and, thus, mankind made tremendous leaps in evolutionary development. Eric Von Daniken argues this thesis in several books that have sold millions of copies: *In Search of Ancient Gods*, *Chariots of the Gods?*, *The Gold of the Gods*, and *Gods from Outer Space*.

Some scientists are going to great lengths to search for more highly evolved extraterrestrial life forms. The *Pioneer* and *Voyager* space probes were designed to search for life after the *Viking* mission to Mars turned up a dead planet. If *Viking* had found life on Mars it would have given the naturalists and rationalists the evidence they needed to push the idea of God further out of the universe and support for their unfounded faith in evolution. "It would have brought the question of the origin of life fully into the domain of science. . . . Believers in evolution in the fall of 1976 could only wish for one message from *Viking*—the demonstration of life on Mars."[17] They didn't get it.

The *Pioneer 10* and *11* and *Voyager 1* and *2* flights did not test the possibility of life on other planets. Instead, each of the crafts "carr[ied] long-playing records that contain[ed] electronically encoded pictures of Earth, as well as spoken greetings, sound effects, and a selection of music from around the world."[18] So much is done to prove that extraterrestrial intelligence (ETI) exists, while nothing is done with the insurmountable evidence of God's existence. Carl Sagan, for example, has dismissed God in spite of his own admission that "the size and age of the Cosmos are beyond ordinary human understanding."[19] How can insignificant man on an insignificant planet in an insignificant galaxy make a dogmatic statement about the non-existence of God? His dogmatism in the light of his own insignificance still leads him to proclaim the following in the opening line to his multimillion-selling *Cosmos*: "The Cosmos is all that is or ever was or ever will be."[20] Even so, he speculates wildly about the possibility, not of God, but of extraterrestrial intelligence.

In the Milky Way Galaxy there must be many planets millions of years older than Earth, and some that are billions of years older. Should we not have been visited? In all the billions of years since the origin of our planet, has there not been even once a strange craft from a distant civilization surveying our world from above, and slowly settling down to the surface to be observed by iridescent dragonflies, incurious reptiles, screeching primates or wondering humans?[21]

In spite of Sagan's admission that there are "no compelling cases of extraterrestrial visitation,"[22] he still probes the cosmos for evidence. Rational thought is discarded for a cosmic seance. He ends *Cosmos* with this: "*We* speak for earth. Our obligation to survive is owed not just to ourselves but also to that Cosmos, ancient and vast, from which we spring."[23] But he doesn't dare ask the next most rational question: From whence sprang the cosmos? Sagan is satisfied with the fact that it just is.

Earlier in *Cosmos*, Sagan attempts to dismiss the need to postulate God. With a bit of semantic sleight of hand he tries to convince his readers that the idea of God creating the universe is no more significant than a belief in Santa Claus or the Tooth Fairy. It's all right to discuss the question, but there really is no need for His existence. Sagan approvingly quotes a ninth-century Indian philosopher: "Some foolish men declare that a Creator made the world. The doctrine that the world was created is ill-advised, and should be rejected. If God created the world, where was He before creation? . . . How could God have made the world without any raw material? If you say He made this first, and then the world, you are faced with an endless regression. . . . Know that the world is uncreated, as time itself, without beginning and end."[24]

The belief that God created the world out of nothing and the belief that the world is uncreated are faith propositions. Neither can be proved scientifically because no one was there when it happened, except God, of course. In Sagan's worldview–God's testimony does not count. Rather, the views of a ninth-century Indian philosopher and the conclusions of twentieth-century minds that cannot come up with a cure for the common cold are considered definitive in their assertions. Sagan is certain that "ten or twenty billion years ago, something happened." But he doesn't know "why it happened."[25]

So what does Sagan do to resolve the "greatest mystery we know"?[26] He junks scientific rationalism and jumps into the universe of irrationalism.

> In many cultures it is customary to answer that God created the universe out of nothing. But this is mere temporizing. If we wish courageously to pursue the question, we must of course ask next where God comes from. And if we decide this to be unanswerable, why not save a step and decide that the origin of the universe is an unanswerable question. Or, if we say that God always existed, why not save a step and conclude that the universe has always existed?[27]

75

Is this science? Why not "save a step" in a scientific experiment? No scientist would dare suggest such a thing. Why not have your surgeon "save a step" in the operating room, or your mechanic "save a step" on your brake job. No one would ever suggest saving a step in these little things—little in terms of the vastness of the cosmos and the question of its origin—but not little in terms of losing your life. Without God nothing in science counts as an explanation or proof. Stop with the universe and you don't have *it* understood either.

The origin of the universe is one of the most important questions one can ask, especially if the answer is found in a personal God who holds man accountable for his sin. But Carl Sagan is willing to adopt irrationalism at this most crucial point. He is willing to dismiss Pascal's "Wager":

> If God exists and punishes unbelief, you will be punished in the hereafter if you do not believe.
>
> If God does not exist, there is no reward for belief but neither is there a penalty.

Of course, Pascal's "Wager" is not a very satisfying argument for belief in God. But Sagan has bet his soul on the unproven assumption that there is no need to postulate God. Without belief in God, one cannot justify acting or thinking in terms of this as a "Cosmos" (orderly and predictable), thus one cannot justify science. God is "needed" for science's methodology to be cogent. Sagan is willing to adopt irrationalism rather than to believe the most rational proposition of them all: "In the beginning God created the heavens and the earth" (Genesis 1:1). With Sagan's worldview, we are left with non-life giving birth to life, an impersonal universe giving rise to personality, chaos spawning order, and randomness generating predictability.

Where does the leap into irrationality take us? The answer is clear. With God shoved out of the universe man becomes the new god. Man now gives meaning to the evolutionary designs of the cosmos.

> Through billions of years of blind mutation, pressing against the shifting walls of their environment, microbes finally emerged as man. We are no longer blind; at least we are beginning to be conscious of what has happened and of what may happen. From now on, evolution is what we make it.[28]

At one time it was reasonable to believe without contradicting true science that an omnipotent and personal God created the universe. Now it's reasonable to believe that finite and fallible man, a mere compound of atoms, will one day control the direction of the universe. Irrationality has replaced rationality with a vengeance.

Save the Whales But Not the Babies

Irrationality is not unique to science. Irrational leaps work themselves out in the day-to-day thinking of ethicists and special interest groups as well. The radical environmental group "Greenpeace," for example, will work for legislation to save the whales and baby seals, but will not take a stand on abortion. The eggs of the nearly extinct American bald eagle have more legal protection than an unborn baby. When man wants to play god, all ethical norms are thrown out the window, except those that support, say, a political agenda or a deviant lifestyle. But it's irrational to believe that the eggs of a bald eagle are worthy of protection under the law, but the fertilized egg of a woman is not. The worldview of rationalism needs the leaps of irrationality to "explain" the unexplainable. Thus, the rationalistic worldview is willing to kill some human beings

> for their own good or that of others and is even able to place some of them below the status of animals. While stressing the special worth of human beings, it says they must not be kept alive if that would cost too much. Deeming people worthy of support and help when they are needy, humanism reduces their actions to automatic responses to the environment, like those of animals and machines.[29]

If AIDS were Only a Brand of Cigarette

Such irrationality is always current. Take the AIDS epidemic. Compare the advertisements to get the word out that people should stop smoking cigarettes, dipping snuff, chewing tobacco, and taking drugs because of their *potentially* lethal effects and that of the *always* lethal AIDS virus. What are young people told to do as they face the lure of alcohol, tobacco products, and drugs?: "Just say No!" But this won't do with the lethal AIDS virus. Why? Because AIDS is a disease most often transmitted by sodomy, and sodomy is practiced by men who reject God, especially a God who mandates laws against sodomy. So then it is best to act irrationally than to admit that AIDS kills.

CONCLUSION

Some men will go to great lengths to escape their Creator. But there's no place to hide. No one gets out of this world alive. Death is the great equalizer. Even in life there is no escape from God's world. The Psalmist writes:

Where can I go from Thy Spirit? Or where can I flee from Thy presence? If I ascend to heaven, Thou art there; if I make my bed in Sheol, behold, Thou art there. If I take the wings of the dawn, if I dwell in the remotest part of the sea, even there Thy hand will lead me, and Thy right hand will lay hold of me, and the light around me will be night (Psalm 139:7-10).

Rebels against God hope to create a world in which God is not needed. Carl Sagan has concluded: "As we learn more and more about the universe, there seems less and less for God to do."[30] Can this be? Or is it true that without God, man is nothing?

5
LEAPING INTO THE VOID

Because of the prestige of science as
a source of power, and because of the
general neglect of philosophy, the popular
[world-and-life view] of our times contains
a large element of what may be called
"nothing-but" thinking. Human beings,
it is more or less tacitly assumed, are
nothing but bodies, animals, even
machines. . . . Values are nothing but
illusions that somehow got themselves
mixed up with our experience of
the world.[1]

OUR culture grew up with the belief that reason, science, and technology would solve all of man's problems. When time revealed however, that these God-given tools, which had themselves been turned into gods, would not perform as gods, the disenchanted turned on them in an irrational fit of rage. The disenchanted became more and more consistent with the worldview handed down to them by the rationalists: There is no real meaning to life, the brain cannot be trusted, there is no help in science and technology, because man is "nothing but" an animal, and all values are mere illusions.

The beginning of the twentieth century brought with it the hope for unchallenged optimism. H. G. Wells, the author of the popular science fiction thrillers *The Time Machine* and *War of the Worlds*, described in his *Outline of History* (1920) a period of "evolutionary idealism, faith in progress, and complete optimism."[2] But it wasn't long before this optimism turned to despair. Shortly before his death, Wells "wrote an aptly-titled book, *The Mind at the End of Its Tether* (1945) in which he concluded that 'there is no way out, or around, or through the impasse. It is the end.'"³

World War I was to be the war to end all wars. The dream was never realized. The machinery of war was heard again less than twenty years later. The sons of World War I veterans fought again in desperation to realize the dream that this would be the war to end all wars. But World War II brought with it a weapon that could end all life. Technology, it seemed, was not enough. Science was not the savior it was thought to be. Something was wrong with *man*. This "defect" could not be corrected by an appeal to reason or continued advances in science and technology. What some men designed for good, other men intended for evil.

> Nuclear energy can be used to light cities or reduce them to ashes. Chemistry can improve nutrition or make nerve gas. Biology can make vaccinations or germ weapons. Science furnishes neither truth nor moral values.⁴

Man had put his trust in technology and the Darwinian worldview. But man was becoming less than man through the entire process. The atrocities of Stalin and Hitler revealed in stark detail how despotic and cruel the impersonal worldview of naturalism could be. It is no accident that Communism and Nazism claim Darwin as their patron saint. Darwin's naturalistic and mechanistic approach to origins found an immediate response in Karl Marx (1818-1883) and his successors, Lenin and Stalin. Darwin's *Origin of Species* "is the book," Marx wrote to his disciple Engels in 1866, "which contains the basis in natural history for our view."⁵ There are no absolutes, man is nothing, and the State is everything. For Communism, the advancement of the State is the march of god through the world. Communism insures this through raw power, the Gulag, and the "necessary" extinction of millions to bring the "ideals" of Communism to the masses. It is significant to note that "after 1949 when the communists took control of China, the first new text introduced to all the schools was neither Marxist or Leninist, but Darwinian."⁶ With Darwin, all things are permissible.

In a *Time* magazine cover of April 8, 1966, this question was asked: "Is God Dead?" In the minds of the naturalists, He had been dead a long time. It seemed that all the failed ideologies of naturalism, rationalism, and materialism had come home to roost. Those who denied the supernatural were ecstatic. But it took only three-and-a-half years for *Time* to ask another question: "Is God coming back to life?" (December 26,

1969). Religious man could not live for long in the shadow of the God-is-Dead "theology." He had to escape the world of cold rationalism. One way was to leap into the void of irrationalism. Man needed a god. Some god. Any god.

> Theodore Roszak has described the irrationalism of the youth counter culture of the 1960s in *The Making of a Counter Culture*. The "flower generation" staged a neo-romantic revolt against science, technology, and reason in favor of feeling, sexuality, drugs, rock music, fantasy, and Eastern Mysticism. The new heaven of peace, love, and freedom failed to materialize as expected, but the arational experientalism of these years lingers on in a younger generation of Americans.[7]

After so many years of having a naturalistic worldview dominate our culture, the results have been, ironically, just the opposite of what the rationalists expected. The rebellion of the youth on the college campus in the past few decades was a revolt against the impersonal treatment of man. The counter culture's depiction of reality as "plastic" was an accurate one. A rationalistic universe ruled solely by impersonal and non-purposed physical forces does not generate feeling, compassion, or moral restraint. Without God, everything human succumbs to the random control of impersonal mechanisms.

But, the rejection of one god brings with it the choking embrace of another. What did the disenchanted adopt after their rationalistic worldview failed to meet their God-implanted needs? The craving was not fulfilled by the insistence that the universe is all there is or ever will be. Some substitute had to be found. Irrationalism seemed to open the door to a vast new world that unveiled countless possibilities and innumerable pitfalls. It was a leap into the void.

THE ANTI-PHILOSOPHIES

Rationalism failed to give meaning to man in naturalism. (There is no mind or thought. Man is machine-like.) Rationalism is a leap of faith. How can we trust a brain that evolved by chance? Subjectivism failed to give meaning to man in existentialism. (With subjectivism there are no absolutes. Man can only authenticate *himself*.) Subjectivism is also a leap of faith. Who's to say that "authentication" is authentic? What is man to do?

Rationality and logic must be done away with. They are of no use to man now. The nonrational and nonlogical become the goal of the leap of faith. In the world of rationalism, "on the basis of all reason, man as man is dead. You have simply mathematics, particulars, mechanics. Man has no meaning, no purpose, no significance. There is only pessimism concerning man as man. But up above, on the basis of a nonrational, nonreasonable leap, there is nonreasonable faith which gives optimism."[8]

Eastern Mysticism

Man must take a leap of "nonreasonable faith" in the monistic worldview of eastern mysticism. What makes eastern mysticism the choice of a new generation of religious seekers, and how does it fulfill man's spiritual hunger?

1. *Eastern mysticism is nonrational and borders on the irrational.* In Zen Buddhism, for example, one's intuition is pitted against one's reason. The Hindus consider the mind to have all the stability and perception of a "drunken monkey" while the Hare Krishnas refer to the mind as a "garbage pail." All this might seem contradictory to the Western mind, and it is. But remember that the West has given up on rational explanations for the way the world works. Maybe East is best. If man is nothing more than a machine, why should we hold rationality in such high regard anyway? Western rationalism has failed.

> Perhaps another reason behind the popular abandonment of rationalism in the West is its inability to provide spiritual satisfaction. As Zen master D. T. Suzuki explains, "Zen has come to the definite conclusion that the ordinary logical process of reasoning is powerless to give final satisfaction to our deepest spiritual needs."[9]

We are often confused by the incessant chanting and the intellectual void associated with meditation on a mandala or some other fixed image. But these are simply the ways of the East. Much of Eastern thought is without intellectual content and meaning. The goal is to transcend the world of things and to reach a spiritual world beyond. The point is not to understand but only to do. This is the appeal of the East. The Western reliance on rationalism has failed. In the West, the law of non-contradiction reigned (A is not non-A). The East knows nothing of such distinctions. In Western rationalist terms, "to know reality is to distinguish one thing from another, label it, catalog it, recognize its subtle relation to other objects in the cosmos. In the East to 'know' reality is to pass beyond distinction, to 'realize' the oneness of all being one with the all."[10]

2. *Eastern mysticism is monistic.* The Christian believes in a *personal* God who is separate from His creation. We have called this the Creator/creature distinction. God did not create the world out of Himself, using the "stuff" of His own being to bring the universe and man into existence.[11] "By faith we understand that the worlds were prepared by the *word of God*, so that what is seen *was not made out of the things which are visible*" (Hebrews 11:3; cf. Genesis 1:1-2).

Eastern thought makes no distinction between man and cosmos. The name for this is *monism*. Monism "is the belief that all that is, is one. All is interrelated, interdependent and interpenetrating. Ultimately there is no difference between God, a person, a carrot or a rock."[12] Consider the ethical implications of such a view. The way you treat a person and the way you treat an animal are to be no different. This is why many advocates of monism are vegetarian. An animal is sacred; therefore, it cannot be killed for food. All is one. God and evil transcend the world of forms and plurality. God does not overcome evil. There is no value judgment in "good" and "evil." Ultimate reality is beyond good and evil. These rational and Christian concepts must be jettisoned in favor of an undifferentiated oneness.

The entertainment business has been quick to pick up on monism. In the *Star Wars* series, monism is quite evident in "the Force," a benign entity that neither condones the good nor suppresses the evil. The music industry was invaded in the early sixties by the Beatles who held a monistic worldview.

> In 1967, the Beatles made their now-famous link-up with a then-unknown guru, Maharishi Yogi and his occult-sounding product, Transcendental Meditation. In that same year Paul McCartney and John Lennon wrote "I am the Walrus" which opened with the pantheistic declaration: "I am he as you are he as you are me and we are all together." "Instant Karma" followed in 1970 and the next year saw the release of George Harrison's "My Sweet Lord" with its alternating chorus of "Hallelujah" and "Hare Krishna."[13]

Charles Manson adopted the monistic worldview of the Beatles, and at the LaBianca murder scene in 1969, he scrawled in blood on the refrigerator door the misspelled "He[a]lter Skelter," a song title from the Beatles' *White Album*. The ambiguity of right and wrong became a reality for Manson. In Manson's words, "If God is One, what is bad?"

3. *All is god*. It follows from monism that if there is god, then all is god. Pantheism (*pan* means all; *theos* means god) is the theology of the East. There is no personal God who stands above creation. In fact, there is no creation as such. To speak of a creation would mean to postulate a Creator, someone distinct from the cosmos. Thus, the pantheist agrees with the naturalist that there is just one level of reality, although the naturalist would not consider it to be "spiritual" or "divine." In pantheism, there is no God who is "out there." God and the material world are one and the same. The word god should be used to refer to the sum total of reality rather than to some being distinct from the rest of reality.

In Christianity, God is distinct from creation. God is certainly present *with* His creation, but He is in no way a *part of* creation. To destroy the created order would in no way affect God. "The Creator God is not an impersonal force, energy or consciousness, but a living, personal Being of infinite intelligence, power and purity. God is not an amoral entity, but a moral agent who says 'Thou shalt not' and calls people to repentance and faith."[14]

4. *We are god*. The consistency of monism brings us to one of its most bizarre features. If all is god, then man is god in some form. "Swami Muktananda—a great influence on Werner Erhard, founder of est and Forum—pulls no pantheistic punches when he says: 'Kneel to your own self. Honor and worship your own being. God dwells within you as You!' "[15]

Eastern mysticism teaches some form of "chain of being" or "continuity of being,"[16] the idea that man and God are one essence, and that in time, through an evolutionary process or a series of reincarnations, man becomes divine. Ray Sutton writes:

> Life according to this system is a *continuum*. At the top is the purest form of deity. At the very bottom is the least pure. They only differ in *degree*, not in kind. God is a *part of* creation. Man, who is somewhere in the middle of the continuum, is god in another "form." In other words, god is just a "super" man, and man is not a god . . . yet![17]

Of course, Christianity teaches that there is only one God: "And you are My witnesses. Is there any God besides Me, or is there any other Rock? I know of none" (Isaiah 44:8). Man's first sin was the attempt to "be like God," determining good and evil for himself (Genesis 3:5).

5. *There is no death*. Eastern mysticism makes its "leap of being" from mere man to god through raising the state of consciousness, evolu-

tionary development, reincarnation, or some combination of the three. Death is simply the final stage of growth; it is an illusion. Human beings, because they are of a "divine essence," are immortal. Ultimately, death does not exist. For death to exist would mean the extinction of part of the One.

Reincarnation is a fundamental pillar of New Age thinking. It "solves" the puzzle of death. Reincarnation has been popularized over the years through the writings of Edgar Cayce[18] and most recently, Shirley MacLaine. The Eastern variety of reincarnation would have never been accepted in the Christian West if it had not been stripped of the hideous concept of the "transmigration of the soul."

Reincarnation, as it is usually understood in Hinduism, states that all life is essentially one (monism): plant, animal, and human life are so interrelated that souls are capable of "transmigrating" from one form of life to another. A person could have been an animal, plant, or mineral in some previous existence. However, this version is unpalatable to American tastes, so in the newer version the movement of human souls is limited to human bodies.[19]

Modern proponents of reincarnation have cleaned up the Eastern variety. You don't hear Shirley MacLaine telling people that she was a rock or a slug in a former life. The typical reincarnationist usually believes that he was once some exotic personality. This is not true reincarnationism. This is "I've always been a star" reincarnationism.

6. *Monism has spawned the New Age movement.* John Naisbitt of *Megatrends*[20] fame sees a new age dawning at the corporation level. Old industrial structures must be dismantled to compete in the information society of the future. "Look at how far we have already come. The industrial society transformed workers into consumers; the information society is transforming employees into capitalists. But remember this: Both capitalism and socialism were industrial structures. And the companies re-inventing themselves are already evolving toward that new reality."[21] But there's more!

Mark Satin has described a *New Age Politics*[22] that will "heal self and society."

Fritjof Capra, author of *The Turning Point*,[23] sees changes in science that will affect society and culture.

Marilyn Ferguson, whose *The Aquarian Conspiracy*[24] is considered by many to be the manifesto of the New Age movement, describes "a new mind–a turnabout in consciousness, a network powerful enough to bring about radical change in our culture."

Much of this literature is rooted in Eastern and occult philosophy, which emphasize oneness (monism): the unity and interdependence of all things. There is a clever mix between Eastern religious philosophy and Western religious forms. The sixties counter culture brought the esoteric music and religious ideology of the East into the West. The Beatles made Eastern music popular on their *Rubber Soul* album when George Harrison introduced the Indian sitar music of Ravi Shankar.[25] Transcendental Meditation was also popularized by the Beatles. Some of those in the ecology movement base their concern for the environment on the inherent "oneness" of the universe.[26] Man and nature are one in essence. Man is not much different from the animals. He is only higher on the great scale of being. The environment should be protected, not as a stewardship under God, but because we are all god, nature included.

The advance of Eastern thought was gradual, but layer by layer it gained acceptance. As Christianity steadily lost its hold on the heart and mind of the nation, softer forms of religious beliefs were more easily embraced. Christianity's drift into an emphasis on experience over objective, written revelation has made it easy prey for the pure subjectivism of Eastern thought. Robert J. L. Burrows, publications editor of the evangelical Spiritual Counterfeits Project in Berkeley, California, writes:

> Humans are essentially religious creatures, and they don't rest until they have some sort of answer to the fundamental questions. Rationalism and secularism don't answer those questions. But you can see the rise of the New Age as a barometer of the disintegration of American culture. Dostoevsky said anything is permissible if there is no God. But anything is also permissible if everything is God. There is no way of making any distinction between good and evil.[27]

Os Guinness wrote about the meeting of East and West in 1973, in what has become a standard Christian critique of the decline of secular humanism, *The Dust of Death*. He tells us that the "swing to the East has come at a time when Christianity is weak at just those points where it would need to be strong to withstand the East."[28] He goes on to show the three basic weaknesses within the Church that open it up to Eastern influences.

The first is its compromised, deficient understanding of revelation. Without biblical historicity and veracity behind the Word of God, theology can only grow closer to Hinduism. Second, the modern Christian is drastically weak in an unmediated, personal, experiential knowledge of God. Often what passes for religious experience is a communal emotion felt in church services, in meetings, in singing or contrived fellowship. Few Christians would know God on their own. Third, the modern church is often pathetically feeble in the expression of its focal principle of community. It has become the local social club, preaching shop or minister-dominated group. With these weaknesses, modern Christianity cannot hope to understand why people have turned to the East, let alone stand against the trend and offer an alternative.[29]

Western Christians have a faith that is "extremely blurred at the edges."[30] This opens them up to any and all spiritual counterfeits.

New Age humanism is anti-Christian to the core. It is a utopian dream built on a flawed understanding of man's nature and a devotion to a westernized Eastern philosophy in which God is nothing more than a cosmic Idea. The copy on the dust jacket to Ferguson's *The Aquarian Conspiracy* shows that the Christian's fears are justified: "A Leaderless but powerful network is working to bring about radical change in the United States. Its members have broken with certain key elements of Western thought, and they may even have broken with history." With all its seemingly "good" emphases, the New Age movement is at heart humanistic (man is the center of the universe), materialistic (self-actualization is all-important), and anti-God (the God of the Bible is dismissed in favor of self-deification). The American public, with its inability to distinguish Biblical truth from anti-Christian religious subtleties, is easily sucked in by the seemingly harmless religious and cultural goals of New Age humanism.

The college campus is a breeding ground for New Age concepts. New Age ideas are upbeat, optimistic, and seemingly life-transforming. At a time when you are most susceptible to change and influence, the New Age movement can be a dangerous "friend." Keep far from it.[31]

REBELLION IN THE UNIVERSITY

The 1960s are known for the great campus rebellion. Today's campus is somewhat more calm when compared to that tumultuous decade. The rebellion has moved back indoors. The classroom is where revolutionary ideas are formed. The following worldviews are a sample of what you will most certainly encounter as you take your seat in the academic university.

Marxism

Perhaps you've heard the joke: There are no Marxists in the Soviet Union because they all found professorships in American Universities. Some joke! And it is not far from the truth. Though universities are not centers of revolutionary violence today as they were in the 1960s, Marxism is still alive and well on the university campus. Marxist scholarship is commonplace in literary studies, sociology, anthropology, and history. In some fields, Marxism and feminism are the *dominant* worldviews of scholars. Between 1970 and 1982, four Marxist textbooks in American government were published. In the 1960s, only a few universities taught courses on Marxism; today there are over 400 such courses at universities around the country.[32]

The Marxist professor is not always a raving lunatic revolutionary. Many sociologists and economists, for example, employ "Marxist analysis" without adopting wholesale its revolutionary agenda. But there are raving lunatics too. Harvard biologist Richard Lewontin has written in *New Political Science* that Marxism

> can do nothing *for* the university; the real question is what can Marxists do *to* and *in* the university. . . . For the natural and social scientist the answer is very clear. The university is a factory that makes weapons—ideological weapons—for class struggle, for class warfare, and trains people in their use. It has no other leading and important function in the social organization.[33]

In other words, some Marxist professors at least are at the university to train students to be revolutionaries. No wonder Secretary of Education William Bennett has warned about the prominence of antidemocratic opinion on the college campus.[34]

As mentioned above, Marxism has permeated many different areas of study. Don't think you will be safe from Marxist influence by majoring in English literature. Marxist professors and concepts have infiltrated virtually every area of study.

What is the worldview of Marxism? It would be impossible to discuss every facet of Marxist thought in these few pages. So, we will look at a few concepts that are especially important to the Christian student.

1. *Marx viewed all religions, including Christianity, as illusions.* Despite recent efforts to reconcile Christianity with Marxism, atheism is a basic premise of the Marxist system of thought. Marx himself said that "man makes religion; religion does not make man," and concluded that religion is the "opium of the people," providing an illusion of happiness without true happiness.[35] Marxism, in short, is a materialistic worldview; the consistent Marxist believes that the material world is the ultimate reality, that there is no God beyond the forces of history and nature.

Significantly, Marx's main attack was not on the idea of God's existence as such, but on God's sovereign dominion over all things. He rejected the Christian doctrine of creation, because he realized that a Creator-God is also a Sovereign God. Marx's philosophical hero was the mythical character, Prometheus, whose battle cry was, "I hate all gods."[36]

2. *Marx's view of history, which has come to be known as "dialectical materialism," is consistent with his rejection of Christianity.* History is not the story of God's dealings with men, but the progress of man from one social arrangement to another, from feudalism to capitalism for example. This progress takes place through changes in technology that lead to changes in the way that people are organized for production. Changes in the organization for production in turn lead to ideological and political conflicts between those classes which want to conserve the old order and those which seek to make drastic changes. Revolutionary class conflict, whether peaceful or violent, produces social change.

In the history of the West, this process has caused the change from feudalism to capitalism, and will, Marx believed, cause the change from capitalism to "scientific" socialism. In the last stage of history, after a transitional stage of the "dictatorship of the proletariat" (lower urban classes), the State will wither and a classless society will emerge. The details are not as important here as the basic point that Marx viewed history as the unfolding of completely materialistic forces.

3. *Another key presupposition of Marx was his view of man.* As a materialist, Marx denied that each man is a creature made in the image of a sovereign God. Rather, man is an essentially social being, with no individual human nature. His whole life is bound up with his social relations. This did not mean for Marx that man has no control over his destiny, and in fact Marxism wavers between a deterministic view that socialism is inevitable, and the call to action. Man is determined by the social forces of history, but he can act to hasten the revolutionary change. This apparent contradiction is resolved by Marxism's ethical imperative for men to act in ways that correspond with the direction of history. The

91

ethical foundation of Marxism, in short, is to jump on the bandwagon that is moving in the direction of the revolution. The one ethical imperative in Marx is to "overthrow all relations in which man is a debased, enslaved, forsaken, despicable being," with the ultimate end being to restore man to his true humanity from which he is alienated by capitalist society. In other words, Marx sees his purpose as teaching that "man is the highest being for man."[37] The revolutionary social transformation from capitalism to socialism will produce a new man and a new human nature, no longer alienated from himself and nature.

What makes Marxism so appealing on the college campus today? First, it provides a comprehensive, positive vision of human life and history. Once Christianity is rejected, some other worldview will fill the void, and Marxism is a total worldview. Second, Marxism is particularly appealing because it offers an alternative to Christianity that is very similar in structure to Christianity. Like Christianity, Marxism teaches that history has meaning and direction. Like Christianity, Marxism teaches that man can be saved from his present condition of alienation. Like Christianity, Marxism looks forward to a complete transformation of society. Third, Marxism, in a simplified form, can easily be used as a weapon to attack your opponents. Marx's claim that ideas are products of class has been used to undermine any and all philosophies. The Marxist radical can debunk a Christian's claim that God blesses His people by saying that the Christian view is just a product of a particular social class.

Liberation Theology

We have seen that Marxism is opposed to Christianity at several key points. It may surprise you, then, to discover that many Christians in this country and around the world believe that Christianity and Marxism are compatible. These "liberation theologians" advocate revolutionary social change as a legitimate goal of the church.

According to theologian Emilio A. Núñez, liberation theology is heavily indebted to Marxism.

No one can fail to notice that Marxist thought exerts a powerful influence on liberation theology. And the exponents of liberation theology do not try to hide that influence. On the contrary, they seem to pride themselves on the use they make of Marxism both for social analysis and for the action they propose to transform the structures of Latin American society. Some of the prominent ideas of liberation theology reveal Marxist influence: economics as a determining factor in the historical process, Marxist notions of work and class struggle, the liberating praxis of the oppressed by the oppressed themselves, man as a protagonist of his own history, the new man and the new society resulting from the proletarian revolution, as well as the ideological criticism of capitalism.[38]

What are the main features of liberation theology? Núñez lists several.

1. *Liberation theology says that an evangelical must be committed to overturning an unjust social system.* Sin is not merely a personal reality, but a social reality as well. The Christian helps to overturn an oppressive order by radically identifying himself with the poor and oppressed classes.

2. *Liberation theology's view of salvation is unbiblical in several key respects.* Núñez writes that "sin enters the picture, but the emphasis does not fall on individual sin but on social sin. Sin is characterized as an offense to one's neighbor, to the oppressed. There is no reference to the eternal consequences of sin, nor to the responsibility of the oppressed before the justice of God." Moreover, "not enough attention is given to the redemptive significance of the sacrifice of Christ, nor to the ministry of the Holy Spirit and the Word of God in the salvation of the sinner." Liberation theology does not stress the importance of repentance and faith, which are central to the biblical idea of salvation.[39]

3. *Liberation theologians often deny basic Christian doctrines, on such central issues as the person of Christ.* "Jesus of Nazareth, [liberation theology] claims, slowly became the Son of God; and the idea of the preexistent, eternal Word who came down from the Father to become a man in order to be the mediator between God and man is the product of theological development that took place after the resurrection of Christ."[40] In the writings he studied, Núñez found "no clear-cut, unambiguous confession that Jesus is God."[41]

4. *Liberation theology teaches that the mission of the church is not, as Jesus said, to "disciple the nations," but to "opt for the cause of the poor, to denounce the injustice of the oppressors, to announce the kingdom of God in order to 'conscientize' and 'politicize' the oppressed, and to participate directly in liberating praxis with a view toward establishing a socialist society that is 'more just, free, and human.' "[42]

5. *Liberation theology, by making the feelings and experience of the oppressed masses the highest standard of theology and Christian practice,[43] replaces Scripture with the oppressed poor as the standard for action.*

There is no denying that the people of Latin America have been oppressed for centuries. But there are better solutions than the baptized Marxism of liberation theology. Marxism has never freed the poor from oppressors, and it will not do so in Latin America. Moreover, in many areas, as we have noted, liberation theology is at odds with orthodox Christianity. Because it uses Christian and biblical language, however, it is often difficult to see through the rhetoric. Also, liberation theology often plays on the guilt that many middle class Christians feel when they are confronted with the awful realities of Third World poverty and oppression. Liberation theology has made significant inroads into the evangelical world, so the Christian student must be on guard.

Feminism

Several years ago, a constitutional Amendment was proposed to equalize the relations between men and women. Known as the Equal Rights Amendment (ERA), it circulated throughout the United States for several years, with each state having an opportunity to vote for or against it. The ERA failed to get enough votes to become a constitutional amendment, but many writers have since noted that feminism has not been stopped by the defeat of the ERA. Instead, many of the main proposals of the radical feminists have been adopted as law. Feminism, in short, has triumphed, even as the ERA was being defeated. The feminist movement has been equally victorious in America's college classrooms.

A reporter at a recent meeting of the Modern Language Association in San Francisco observes that

> so prominent a part of the academic literary scene has feminism become that during one afternoon time slot at the convention no fewer than nine sessions on feminist topics from lesbian writing to "feminist dialogics" were droning on concurrently. Feminism has gone from being a special and rather narrow interest to having become one of the large clumsy categories by which literary study is organized in the university.[44]

Feminists have also infiltrated other areas of study, such as history, sociology, anthropology, and even theology.

Even some evangelical professors claim to be "biblical feminists." Virginia Ramey Mollenkott, who teaches English at William Paterson

College, calls herself an evangelical, but has co-authored a book advo-cating "covenantal homosexuality." At a meeting of the Evangelical Roundtable, she defended abortion, saying, "It is our right . . . it is our body . . . it is our choice."[45]

Within many mainline Christian denominations, a separate "feminist theology" has developed. One of the leading Roman Catholic feminists, Rosemary Radford Reuther, has proposed new liturgies for her "woman-church," including liturgies for healing after an abortion, covenanting of lesbian couples, and a Summer Solstice Party. Mary Jo Weaver, another Catholic feminist, asks what feminists can do about the traditional patri-archal church. She sees two possible alternatives: "to reject the tradition and search for new alternatives (usually focused on the Goddess and a revival of witchcraft) or to reinterpret the tradition in order to change its direction and open it to the influences and lives of women."[46] Some churches have changed their hymnals and Bibles to avoid masculine references to God, and some have gone so far as to place crucifixes in the church sanctuary with female Christs!

Some "feminist" historians are interested only in studying the place of women in history, and some "feminist" biblical scholars are only inter-ested in understanding how the Bible addresses the problems of modern women. These are worthy exercises, and can be very fruitful. A study of President's wives, for example, can reveal a lot about American politics. But in addition to this relatively mild form of "feminism," there is a group of hard-core, self-conscious feminists whose main goal is to destroy the traditional family and Western "patriarchal" culture. At an extreme, there is a relatively small group of feminist witches. Though often scorned by other feminists, whose goals are mainly political, feminist witchcraft is the fastest growing segment of witchcraft in America today.[47]

What are the presuppositions of the feminist ideology?

1. *Radical feminists are virulently anti-Christian.* Some advocate a return to the ancient mythologies because the ancient pantheon of gods included female deities. Others do not go quite so far, but in the end, they have replaced the Christian God with woman. For the feminists, Woman is God. At a conference on woman's spirituality in 1976, the ad-vent of the goddess was proclaimed. One feminist writer noted that "proclaiming that the 'Goddess is Alive' in a traditional church setting is proclaiming that . . . being female is divine."[48]

2. *Feminists seek equality for men and women.* Some seek more than this, desiring feminine dominance over men. But, even equality between men and women is not a legitimate goal for a Christian move-

ment. The Bible teaches that every institution in society has a structure of authority. There are elders in the church to rule the church; there are magistrates in the State to rule the citizens; and there are husbands who are to rule their families. Though the Bible does not teach men to tyrannize their wives, the Bible clearly states that men are to be heads of the home, and women are to submit to them (Ephesians 5:22-33). In seeking to overthrow this God-ordained order, radical feminists are simply rebelling against God. Rebellious tendencies are also manifested in the feminist advocacy of "unisex," in which an attempt is made to overcome God-ordained differences between the sexes.

3. *Feminism is often a form of Marxism.* The feminists see themselves as the oppressed and alienated sex, and their goal is to throw off the chains of oppression in order to liberate themselves. What they are seeking liberation from, of course, is the traditional family structure. They are also able to make the claims that Marxists do about the ideas of their opponents. Scholars who draw attention to the psychological and biological differences between men and women are dismissed because they are simply interested in maintaining the status quo. This tactic is often simply an attempt to dismiss evidence that is not consistent with the feminist outlook.

4. *These presuppositions of equality and liberation work out in a consistent social program.* As summarized by George Gilder, the ERA, if passed, would in all likelihood have had the following effects:

> 1) eliminated all rights of wives and mothers to be supported by their husbands, except to the extent husbands could claim an equal right; 2) eliminated all laws in any way restricting the rights of the gay liberation movement publicly to teach, proselytize, or practice their sexual ideology; 3) forced sexual integration of all schools, clubs, colleges, athletic teams, and facilities; 4) forced the drafting of women and the sexual integration of all military units; 5) threatened the tax exemption of most religious schools; and 6) compelled the use of government funds for abortions.[49]

Culture is also to be feminized. In fact, feminism has already made remarkable progress in transforming our culture into a feminist ideal. As one "biblical feminist" notes,

> Feminism since the early 1960s has begun to color interpersonal relations, the language we speak, family life, the educational sys-

tem, child-rearing practices, politics, business, the mass media, religion, law, the judicial system, the cultural values system, and intellectual life.[50]

The feminist goal is nothing short of social, political, and cultural revolution.

The New Humanism

In the modern world, classical "humanism" has been in decline. Humanism in this context may be defined as the belief that man is an inherently dignified being, and that education in literature and history can produce men and women who are characterized by an appreciation of beauty and reason. The rise of modern technology and science, however, led many to see man as nothing more than a machine, while Darwin claimed that man was little more than an advanced ape. In the wake of two world wars, philosophies of despair became widespread as men were reminded again of their potential for evil. Man was seen as nothing more than a pawn in a meaningless sea of meaningless forces. Freud argued that men are controlled by subconscious appetites and drives. In all of these, man's dignity as the master of the world and the ability of his reason to discover meaning was called into question.

Recently, however, there has been a revival of the ancient and Renaissance idea of man as the "measure of all things," and of the ideal of a classical liberal education that will produce cultured and reasonable men and women. Secretary of Education under Ronald Reagan, William Bennett, for example, has outlined a new curriculum for the public schools. He proposed that school children be given a good dose of foreign languages, history, grammar, and literature. Similar proposals have been made for the university. In his surprise best-seller, University of Chicago professor Allan Bloom called for a return to the classical curriculum based on the "great books," particularly on Plato and Rousseau.[51]

Some of these "new humanists" trace their lineage back to the critical and cultural theories of Matthew Arnold, a nineteenth-century critic and poet. Arnold's great enemy was not sin, but "philistinism," the term he used to characterize vulgar middle-class culture and tastes. Unlike some of his contemporaries, Arnold did not turn toward the Middle Ages for values. He believed that England could never return to the Christian culture of that period, and insisted instead that men could lead good lives without any appeal to God or to revelation. In the place of the

"Hebraism" of the Middle Ages, Arnold proposed a return to Hellenism, to Greek thought and culture.

In his essay "Sweetness and Light," Arnold argued that the only hope for the future was a cult of beauty (sweetness) and reason (light).

> He who works for sweetness and light, works to make reason and the will of God prevail. . . . Culture has one great passion, the passion for sweetness and light . . . It is not satisfied till we all come to a perfect man; it knows that the sweetness and light of the few must be imperfect until the raw and unkindled masses of humanity are touched with sweetness and light.[52]

Good taste and the cultivation of reason are the goals of education. What all these "new humanists" leave out is, of course, the Bible. Arnold self-consciously rejected a return to Christianity as a viable alternative for Victorian England. Allan Bloom likewise believes that the Bible, while a source of truth, is only one source among many. And he places himself squarely in the Enlightenment tradition in education, in which "all things must be investigated and understood by reason."[53] Man, in this view, remains the measure of all things, and is not bound to submit himself to the Word of God. Though far less radical than the previous two worldviews, the new humanism is no less rebellious in principle.

The "new humanism" is less a consistent worldview than a philosophy of education. But because it is a philosophy of education, you will encounter it on the college campus. The popularity of Bloom's book, and the efforts of Secretary Bennett make it likely that many colleges will begin to adopt this agenda. This is certainly preferable to the revolutionary scholarship of feminism and Marxism, but lacking a biblical foundation, this vision of education and society is ultimately doomed to failure.

Behaviorism

Behaviorism originated with the work of John B. Watson, an American psychologist. Watson claimed that psychology was not concerned with the mind or with human consciousness. Instead, psychology should be concerned only with behavior. In this way, men could be studied objectively, like rats and apes. Watson's work was based on the experiments of Ivan Pavlov, who had studied animals' responses to conditioning. In Pavlov's best-known experiment, he rang a bell as he fed some dogs several meals. Each time the dogs heard the bell they knew that a meal was coming, and they would begin to salivate. Pavlov then rang the bell without bringing food, but the dogs still salivated. They had been "conditioned" to salivate at the sound of a bell. Pavlov believed, as Watson was later to emphasize, that humans react to stimuli in the same way.

Behaviorism is associated today with the name of B. F. Skinner, who made his reputation by testing Watson's theories in the laboratory. Skinner's studies led him to reject Watson's almost exclusive emphasis on reflexes and conditioning. People respond to their environment, he argued, but they also operate on the environment to produce certain consequences. Skinner developed the theory of "operant conditioning," the idea that we behave the way we do because this kind of behavior has had certain consequences in the past. For example, if your girlfriend gives you a kiss when you give her flowers, you will be likely to give her flowers when you want a kiss. You will be acting in expectation of a certain reward. Like Watson, however, Skinner denied that the mind or feelings play any part in determining behavior. Instead, our experience of reinforcements determines our behavior.

Behaviorism originated in the field of psychology, but it has had a much wider influence. Its concepts and methods are used in education, and many education courses at college are based on the same assumptions about man as behaviorism. Behaviorism has infiltrated sociology, in the form of sociobiology, the belief that moral values are rooted in biology. What are the presuppositions of behaviorism?

1. *Behaviorism is naturalistic.* This means that the material world is the ultimate reality, and everything can be explained in terms of natural laws. Man has no soul and no mind, only a brain that responds to external stimuli.

2. *Behaviorism teaches that man is nothing more than a machine that responds to conditioning.* One writer has summarized behaviorism in this way:

> The central tenet of behaviorism is that thoughts, feelings, and intentions, mental processes all, do not determine what we do. Our behavior is the product of our conditioning. We are biological machines and do not consciously act; rather we *react* to stimuli.[54]

The idea that men are "biological machines" whose minds do not have any influence on their actions is contrary to the biblical view that man is the very image of God—the image of a creative, planning, thinking God. In fact, Skinner goes so far as to say that the mind and mental

99

processes are "metaphors and fictions" and that "behavior is simply part of the biology of the organism."[55] Skinner also recognizes that his view strips man of his "freedom and dignity," but insists that man as a spiritual being does not exist.

3. *Consistently, behaviorism teaches that we are not responsible for our actions.* If we are mere machines, without minds or souls, reacting to stimuli and operating on our environment to attain certain ends, then anything we do is inevitable. Sociobiology, a type of behaviorism, compares man to a computer: Garbage in, garbage out. This also conflicts with a Christian worldview. Our past experiences and our environment do affect the way we act, of course, but these factors cannot account for everything we do. The Bible teaches that we are basically *covenantal* creatures, not biological creatures. Our nearest environment is God Himself, and we respond most fundamentally to Him. We respond either in obedience to or rebellion against His Word.

4. *Behaviorism is manipulative.* It seeks not merely to understand human behavior, but to predict and control it. From his theories, Skinner developed the idea of "shaping." By controlling rewards and punishments, you can shape the behavior of another person. As a psychiatrist, one of Skinner's goals is to shape his patients' behavior so that he or she will react in more socially acceptable ways. Skinner is quite clear that his theories should be used to guide behavior:

> The experimental analysis of behavior has led to an effective technology, applicable to education, psychotherapy, and the design of cultural practices in general, which will be more effective when it is not competing with practices that have had the unwarranted support of mentalistic theories.[56]

In other words, Skinner wants behaviorism to be the basis for manipulating patients, students, and whole societies.

The obvious questions, of course, are: Who will use the tools? Who will pull the strings? Who will manipulate the technology? No doubt, Skinner would say that only someone trained in behavioral theory and practice would be qualified to "shape" the behavior of other persons. But this is contrary to the Biblical view, which commands us to *love* our neighbor, not to manipulate him.

In sum, the ethical consequences of behaviorism are great. Man is stripped of his responsibility, freedom, and dignity, and is reduced to a purely biological being, to be "shaped" by those who are able to use the tools of behaviorism effectively.

CONCLUSION

Naturalism was destined to fail. But it has left a number of disintegrating world views in its wake. These collapsing worldviews have sent thousands to look elsewhere for meaning. The lives of Charles Manson and his "Family" are tragic examples. But there are lessons in what happened. Manson appealed to the dregs of society, to those who were without hope. These "Family" members took a leap into the void of Manson's distorted world. What else could they do? Their spiritual craving had to be satisfied. In some twisted and perverted way, Charles Manson filled it.

> Most of the people at the ranch that you call the Family were just people that you did not want, people that were alongside the road, that their parents had kicked out, that did not want to go to Juvenile Hall. So I did the best I could and took them up on my garbage dump and I told them this: that in love there is no wrong.[57]

Manson's description of his worldview as a "garbage dump" is important. The naturalistic worldview led him and his followers into its logical consequence: If the world is all there is, then man must find meaning in himself. Manson "believe[ed] you could do no wrong, no bad. Everything was good. Whatever you do is what you are supposed to do; you are following your own karma."[58] Who can argue with such a premise? Only the Christian worldview has an answer.

6
SPIRITUAL COUNTERFEITS

> Every religious cult has two sets of differing creeds: the exoteric and the esoteric. The exoteric creed is the official, public doctrine, the creed which attracts the acolyte in the first place and brings him into the movement as a rank-and-file member. The esoteric creed is the unknown, hidden agenda, a creed which is only known to its full extent by the top leadership, the "high priests" of the cult. The latter are the keepers of the mysteries of the cult.[1]

FEW people find solace in the various worldview expressions of irrationalism. Many leave these bankrupt philosophies and return once again to Jesus Christ. But some turn to other forms of religions that often resemble Biblical Christianity. They are spiritual counterfeits, close to the originals but not close enough. The college campus is a haven for non-Christian cults. Be on the alert.

It's been said that "the cults are the unpaid bills of the church."[2] The vacuum caused by a retreating Christianity has made it possible for all types of spiritual counterfeits to invade our nation and capture the hearts and minds of the unsuspecting and vulnerable. The cults are one of the many options to which spiritual seekers turn when they are in need of spiritual vitality. But the surprising thing is that most cults cater to disenchanted church people. It seems that the cults offer what many churches have neglected. The spiritual vacuum must be filled. Unfortunately, many cult leaders are ready to seduce the broken hearted with a "different gospel" (Galatians 1:6).

What is a cult? Generally speaking, a cult is a religious movement that often claims support for its views by using the Bible but is fundamentally wrong on the basics of the Christian faith. To be more specific, a cult is any religious group which claims to be a more authentic expression of Christianity with its own distinctive interpretation on major doctrines. We know that not all Christians agree on every doctrine. But there are certain "core" doctrines that all Christians must believe in order to be called "Christian." Cults strike at the heart of these core doctrines.

WHAT TO LOOK FOR

Cults are not new to the Church, although most cults that we see today have not been around for more than a hundred years. While their contemporary expressions are new, their doctrinal distortions have been with us for centuries. Here's what to look for:

1. *There is more than one standard of authority.* Numerous cults have additional revelational books that are considered equal to the Bible in authority. Mormonism, for example, has the *Pearl of Great Price, Doctrine and Covenants, The Book of Mormon*, and continuing authoritative revelations by the "apostles" among the Mormon leadership. Other cults have an *interpreting* authority. While they might use the Bible and consider it to be authoritative, they believe that it takes a certain degree of spiritual discernment by a self-appointed or designated leader from the group to tell the members what the Bible *really* means. Sometimes books are designed by the hierarchy in the movement to be read along with the Bible. These books or "new revelations" become the interpreting code for the members to understand properly what God is saying. In time, the cult-produced books become the new authority.

Let's look at some of the cults and see how they misuse and reinterpret Biblical authority. The Jehovah's Witnesses have their own version of the Bible, *The New World Translation*, that obscures certain texts that are not compatible with their doctrines. This is most evident with those verses that teach the divinity of Christ. The Witnesses also determine doctrine by an unnamed hierarchy from the "Watchtower" organization. The Unification Church, whose members are often described as "Moonies" after its founder Sun Myung Moon, looks to Moon's *Divine Principle* to throw further light on the Bible: "It may be displeasing to religious believers, especially to Christians, to learn that a new expression of truth must appear. They believe in the Bible, which they now have, is perfect and absolute in itself." Christian Science has *Science and Health with Key to the Scriptures.* Mary Baker Eddy had this to say about the book's authority:

> I should blush to write of *Science and Health with Key to the Scriptures* as I have, were it of human origin and I apart from God its author, but as I was only a scribe echoing the harmonies of heaven in divine metaphysics, I can not be super-modest of the Christian Science Textbook.[3]

There are other groups that claim similar divine authority for their writings, prophecies, or doctrines: The Way International, The Children of God, Unity, Theosophy, Hare Krishna, and Scientology. You will probably encounter others. Your first question should be: "Is the Bible the only authority you have or must I look to some other book or a group of interpretations handed down from your leadership?" Of course, since cults are very deceptive, you may not get a straight answer.

2. *Jesus Christ is less than God, a great teacher, or a son of God just as we are all sons of God.* "Who do people say that the Son of Man is?" This was Jesus' question to His disciples. But Jesus went even further: "But who do *you* say I am?" This is the single most important question you can ask someone who seems a bit off concerning the basics of the Christian faith. The doctrine of the divinity of Christ, that Jesus is God in human flesh, is the single most important doctrine for the Christian Church. The divinity of Jesus separates Christianity from *all* other religions, philosophies, and cults.

Jesus is God in human flesh. He is not just *a* god or Michael the archangel (as the Jehovah's Witnesses teach), a pre-existent spirit, also the Father, one of many gods (as Mormons teach), a great moral teacher (as in most Eastern religions), a prophet (as in Islam), a reincarnated spiritual master (as in the New Age movement), or a son of God not much different from mankind in general (as probably most religious Americans who call themselves Christian believe). Some might go so far as saying that Jesus never existed. Or, if He did exist, then His life and deeds were manufactured by His disciples so they could start a new religious movement in His name. He is, therefore, the "ideal" for all of us to follow. This is the view of most theological liberals.

God became man in the person of Jesus Christ, the second Person of the Trinity (Godhead). This is why there are passages in the New Testament that refer to Jesus as a man. He was a man in the fullest sense of the word, except for one fallen human condition: sin. At the same time,

Jesus is God in the way the Father is God and the Spirit is God. "In the beginning was the Word [Jesus], and the Word was with God, and the Word was God. . . . And the Word became flesh, and dwelt among us, and we beheld His glory, glory as the only begotten from the Father, full of grace and truth" (John 1:1, 14). Here is a comparison chart to show how divine attributes are given to or claimed by Jesus:[4]

"THERE IS ONE GOD" (1 Corinthians 8:6)

GOD IS . . .	YAHWEH IS JESUS	. . . JESUS IS
Genesis 1:1 Job 33:4 Isaiah 40:28	CREATOR	John 1:1-3 Colossians 1:12-17 Hebrews 1:8-12
Isaiah 41:4 Isaiah 44:6 Isaiah 48:12	FIRST & LAST	Revelation 1:17 Revelation 2:8 Revelation 22:13
Exodus 3:13, 14 Deuteronomy 32:39 Isaiah 43:10	I AM (EGO EIMI)	John 8:24, 58 John 13:19 John 18:5
Genesis 18:25 Psalm 96:13 Joel 3:12	JUDGE	2 Timothy 4:1 2 Corinthians 5:10 Romans 14:10-12
Psalm 47 Isaiah 44:6-8 Jeremiah 10:10	KING	Matthew 2:1-6 John 19:21 1 Timothy 6:13-16
Psalm 27:1 Isaiah 60:20	LIGHT	John 1:9 John 8:12
Psalm 106:21 Isaiah 43:3, 11 Isaiah 45:21-23	SAVIOR	John 4:42 Acts 4:10-12 1 John 4:14
Psalm 23 Psalm 100:3 Isaiah 40:11	SHEPHERD	John 10:11 Hebrews 13:20 1 Peter 5:4

In Israel, the worship of any god other than Jehovah brought with it the death penalty. So then, for Jesus to accept worship if He were not indeed God would mean that He was either a lunatic or a deceiver. If Jesus believed Himself to be God and was mistaken, then He was insane. He certainly would not be worthy of our worship. If Jesus misled the people into believing that He was God, then He is no more than a con artist who deserves our scorn. But if He is what He said He was, then He deserves our worship.

Neither men nor angels are to be worshipped, and yet Jesus willingly accepted worship. In Revelation 19:10 an angel refuses worship from the Apostle John: "Do not do that; I am a fellow servant of yours and your brethren who hold the testimony of Jesus; worship God." A similar incident occurs in Revelation 22:9. In Acts 10:25-26, Peter refuses worship from Cornelius. In Acts 14:11-15, Paul and Barnabas refuse worship at Lystra.

But notice the difference when it comes to the worship of Jesus. First, the wise men came to worship Him: "Where is He who has been born King of the Jews? For we saw His star in the East, *and have come to worship Him*. . . . And they came into the house and saw the child with Mary His mother; *and they fell down and worshipped Him*" (Matthew 2:2, 11). At that point Mary could have said: "Wait! He is no more than a man."

Second, Jesus accepted worship from others and did not rebuke those who came to worship Him: "And behold, Jesus met them and greeted them. And they came up and took hold of His feet *and worshipped Him*" (Matthew 28:9).

Third, Jesus accepted the title of "Lord and God": "Thomas answered and said to [Jesus], 'My Lord and my God!'" (John 20:28). Jesus' response was far different from that of Peter, Barnabas, and the angel in the book of Revelation: "Because you have seen Me, have you believed? Blessed are they who did not see, and yet believed" (v. 29). There is no rebuke for Thomas. Jesus accepted the titles "Lord and God."

The Christian faith revolves around the doctrine of Jesus' divinity. All cults distort this fundamental doctrine and turn Jesus into something less than God in human flesh.

3. *There is the need for a new interpretation of what true Christianity is all about.* Cults usually begin through the leadership of an individual who has become disenchanted with some aspect of Biblical Christianity and now presents his system as the "true" interpretation of the faith. An example of this is found in the writings of Herbert W. Armstrong, founder of the Worldwide Church of God:

I found that the popular church teachings and practices were not based on the Bible. They had originated, as research in history had revealed, in paganism. Numerous Bible prophecies foretold it; the amazing unbelievable truth was, the SOURCE of these popular beliefs and practices of professing Christianity, was quite largely paganism, and human reasoning and custom, NOT the Bible![5]

What is Armstrong's "truth" as opposed to these "popular church teachings and practices"? First, the gospel message of Jesus' saving work has not been preached since A.D. 69. It has only been since Herbert W. Armstrong's resurrection of the gospel that we have had the truth. Second, there is more than one God. God is a "family" that is open to others to join. This teaching is similar to that of Mormonism and some branches of eastern mysticism and the New Age movement. Third, the destiny of man is to become God. Armstrong says, "You are setting out on a training to become creator—to become God!" Fourth, man is saved by his own "good works." According to Armstrongism, "People have been taught, falsely, that 'Christ completed the plan of salvation on the cross'—when actually it was only begun there." Of course, it's for us to finish by our own supposed good works. These are the doctrines that have been hidden for nearly two thousand years.

People who talk this way are usually pushing a cult, whether old or new. Here's a list of some cults and their leaders:

Christian Science—Mary Baker Eddy
Jehovah's Witnesses—Charles Taze Russell
Mormonism—Joseph Smith
The Way International—Victor Paul Wierwille
The Unification Church—Sun Myung Moon
The Children of God—David Brandt Berg
The Worldwide Church of God—Herbert W. Armstrong
Unity—Charles Sherlock Fillmore
Forum (formerly known as est)—Werner Erhard

People looking for answers are often convinced by these admittedly charismatic figures. They appeal to the dissatisfaction that some may feel about their waning spiritual vitality. Many people are seduced because their circumstances have made them vulnerable: loss of a loved one in death, divorce, dissatisfaction with their present church, loneliness, or the unfulfillment of any number of heart-felt needs. As a college student you are especially vulnerable to the appeals of the cults. You are in a new environment, far away from friends and family. Your college experience may not be what you had hoped. A relationship may have just soured, making you susceptible to the appeals of someone who assures you that when you join this new religious group everything will be all right. You're looking for answers and this leader seems to have them.

The best antidote to seduction is a thorough knowledge of Scripture, knowing what you believe and why, and a strong church where the Word of God is preached faithfully and your spiritual needs can be met. The best way to spot a counterfeit is to be familiar with the original.

4. *Salvation is gained by good works.* If there is a new or twisted authority and a different Jesus, then we should expect a different gospel.

> I am amazed that you are so quickly deserting Him who called you by the grace of Christ, for a different gospel; which is really not another; only there are some who are disturbing you, and want to distort the gospel of Christ. But even though we, or an angel from heaven, should preach to you a gospel contrary to that which we have preached to you, let him be accursed (Galatians 1:6-8).

There is no grace in the cults, only works. What Jesus did on the cross was not enough. We have to add our good works to His less than sufficient sacrifice. What question should you ask of a cult evangelist?: "What must I do to be saved?" If he tells you anything more than "Believe on the Lord Jesus Christ," then it's time to bring *him* the true meaning of redemption.

Salvation by works is the most common doctrine the cults use to deny the sufficiency of Christ's death. But there are variations:

• *Salvation by faith in the leader of the cult.* Jim Jones of the Guyana tragedy became the focus of salvation. He was called "Father." Jesus may be important to these cultists, but He is still not enough. Charles Manson, while he did not create a new cult that gained wide acceptance, did structure his "Family" along cultic lines. One Manson cult member said this about him: "He represented a God to me that was so beautiful that I'd do anything for him."[6]

• *Salvation through "god-consciousness."* This type of salvation is found in most cults with an Eastern flavor such as the Unification Church or "Moonies." But it is also found in Christian Science. For Christian Scientists, the world is an "illusion." (In Hinduism, a similar concept is described by the world *maya.*) "Hence, evil is but an illusion, and it has no real basis. Evil is a false belief."[7] The New Age movement stresses god-consciousness. For all these groups, god-consciousness is very subjective.

Some Additional Cult Characteristics

The four pillars discussed above are found in all cults to one degree or another. But there are additional peculiarities that show up in the more extreme cults. Keep in mind that not all cults will manifest these characteristics. Some of them will only be exhibited in lesser degrees and may not be immediately obvious to a prospective cult member:

• An elite membership: "God has chosen us by giving us the truth. All other groups are wrong. Only our way is right."

• Demand to break family relationships: "We are your true family. You must forsake your earthly father and mother. Our leader is your new father."

• Surrender of possessions: "If you are truly committed to God's plan for your life, you must be willing to turn your possessions over to God's chosen leader."

• A change in daily routine: "You must work on a daily basis to prove your faithfulness to your religious commitment. This will mean witnessing, raising money, and avoiding contacts with family and friends. You will have to stop eating meat since we believe all life is sacred."

• Threat of losing your "salvation" if you leave the group: "If you leave the true religion, there will be no hope for you either in life or death. You will lose your salvation."

• Doctrinal ambiguity: "Well, you are not ready to understand our doctrines. Don't question new concepts. You are just a beginner. You must trust our leader. Your thoughts don't count. Do not trust your mind, your thinking processes."

• Scripture twisting: "You were taught, 'Blessed are the pure in heart, for you shall see God.' While this is true, there is more: 'Yes, blessed are those who purify their consciousness, for they shall see themselves as God.'"

• A corrupt leadership: "You should not question the actions of our leader. He is far above us. He is much better than we."

• The destruction of individuality: "We must be like our leader so we must give up our individuality, our personal desires, even our possessions. Even our children must be like him."

• Control of incoming information: "We can't allow you to have contact with those outside. They might influence you with the things of the world."

PSYCHOLOGICAL SEDUCTION

Many cults take advantage of young people who seem to be confused about life. Some cults use psychological techniques to gain the confidence of skeptics. Instead of arguing with newcomers about doctrine, the cultists might turn to proven psychological techniques that work to fulfill a person's physical, psychological, social, or spiritual needs that are not being met anywhere else. This could include some of the following:

1. "Love Bombing": Many cults shower prospective members with an inordinate amount of attention and affection. From the moment a person enters a meeting, he will be assigned a "chaperon" to give him constant attention. This technique is designed to break down any barriers of resistance a person might have erected when he agreed to come to a meeting.

2. Information Overload: Cultists know that they must break down certain preconceived ideas that young people have about the world in general and religion in particular. They also know that most Christians do not know much about the "whys" of their faith. They prey on ignorance. In order to short-circuit a prospect's belief system, he may be subjected to confusing lectures filled with the cult's favorite doctrines, the failure of all Christian movements, and Scripture passages quoted out of context. In time, it all might "make sense."

3. Meaningless Activities: Cultists must keep prospective converts from thinking about the new information that they hear. Cult leaders know that much of what they will tell a prospective cult member is radically different from what he or she has been raised on. In order to keep the prospects from questioning the new information, they often will be kept busy by the leadership until the next overload session of information occurs.

4. Group Bonding: Some cults design techniques to "bond" potential members to the group and to the leader. A student may be asked (compelled) to join in a group game where she is at the center of attention and the group supports her psychologically, emotionally, and physically. This might mean trusting yourself to the group by falling back into the arms of a cult member. From an experience like this you will learn to depend on and trust the group more than your friends or family.

THE END OF THE WORLD LURE

Some cults entice prospective members by spinning a scenario that includes the near end of the world and the return of Christ in judgment. The Jehovah's Witnesses have made this a part of their "evangelistic" strategy since 1914. Converts are attracted to cults that maintain that Jesus is coming back on a certain day, and by joining with them, the bearers of the only true religion, they can avoid the impending judgment that will consume everyone else. Here's an extreme example:

> The group known as "The Lighthouse Gospel Tract Foundation," led by Bill Maupin, was located in Tucson. He originally calculated that the Rapture would take place on June 28, 1981. Some members of the group quit their jobs and/or sold their houses. When that date passed, Maupin said that he had miscalculated by forty days, and predicted that the Rapture would take place on August 7, 1981. The Return of Christ is to occur May 14, 1988. Maupin calculated his dates on the basis of Daniel's seventy "weeks," and the founding of the State of Israel on May 15, 1948.[8]

The important thing to pick up on in the above quotation is that they "quit their jobs and/or sold their houses." I've heard of students who joined similar cults and dropped out of school in anticipation of "the end." The Children of God began as a somewhat fundamentalist sect, but later turned into a doomsday cult. They believed that the end of the world was just around the corner. Their leader, David Berg, had had visions supporting the claim. Acting on their belief, the cult members embraced an itinerant lifestyle and lived in the shadow of Christ's soon coming.

New cults come on the scene without warning. Be very careful of the seemingly orthodox religious groups that tell you it knows when Jesus is going to return. Well-intentioned but mistaken prophetic speculators have been with us since the second century A.D., all of whom have been wrong in their predictions about when Jesus Christ will return.

CONCLUSION

The cults are Christian counterfeits. What is a counterfeit? A counterfeit is an illicit copy of an original designed to be passed off as the real thing. You're most familiar with the counterfeiting of United States currency. The important thing to remember about counterfeiting is that there is a genuine article that is being copied. If there is no genuine article, then there can be no counterfeit. If someone handed you a three dollar bill, you would know immediately that it wasn't real. You might, however, be hard pressed to spot a counterfeit ten dollar bill.

We do not often consider "theological counterfeiting" as a way the devil might hide the truth from Bible-believing Christians. Yet the Bible shows us that there are counterfeit Christs (Matthew 24:5; Acts 5:36, 37), counterfeit prophets (Matthew 7:15; 24:11), counterfeit miracles (Exodus 7:8-13), counterfeit angels (2 Corinthians 11:14), counterfeit gods (Galatians 4:8; Acts 12:20-23), counterfeit good works (Matthew 7:15-23), counterfeit converts and disciples (1 John 2:19), counterfeit spirits (1 John 4:1-3), counterfeit doctrines (1 Timothy 4:3), counterfeit kings (John 19:15), counterfeit names (Revelation 13:11-18; cf. 14:1), counterfeit gospels (Galatians 1:6-10), counterfeit kingdoms (Daniel 2; Matthew 4:8-11; Acts 17:1-9), and a counterfeit new age (Revelation 13:11-18). Cults are counterfeits. They want the *fruit* of Christianity without the *root*.

7
THE OCCULT EXPLOSION

> There are two equal and opposite
> errors into which our race can fall
> about the devils. One is to disbelieve
> in their existence. The other is to
> believe, and to feel an excessive and
> unhealthy interest in them. They
> themselves are equally pleased by both
> errors and hail a materialist or a
> magician with the same delight.[1]

WHO would have thought that the devil would still be popular as we near the end of the twentieth century, especially in the light of the reason-alone, rationalistic worldview that prevails in our nation, particularly on the college campus? Well, he is. "Theologian Protests 'Witchcraft at Indiana University'" is the title of a newspaper article that denounces the way college students are being duped by the supposed "reasonableness" of witchcraft. It seems that witchcraft is "better for women than Christi-anity." "Ms. Budapest," a self-proclaimed witch who claims to be descended from an eight hundred-year-old line of witches, presented a lecture on "Religion, Women, and Power." The professor who invited "Ms. Budapest" to speak is also a witch.[2]

Devil worship is showing up in criminal cases. Signs of it appeared in the serial killings committed in Los Angeles by the suspected "Night Stalker," Richard Ramirez. At one point during his trial, he left the court-room shouting "Hail Satan!" The death of a fifteen-year-old girl has been linked to the occult. A sheriff from Douglas County, Georgia, "said the suspects' motives in the killing involved sex, satanic devil worship and witchcraft. 'To a certain extent, I know they are involved in (devil worship). There's a good possibility that a portion of the motive has to do with sex, and additionally the motive has to do with devil-worshipping and witchcraft.' "[3]

Some cases of child abuse are being linked to "ritual abuse." Dr. Gregory Simpson, a Los Angeles pediatrician, began looking into the ritual abuse of children in 1985 as a result of seeing ritual scarring on patients. "One dead girl's chest was carved with a pentagram, he says. 'The conclusion I reached is that satanic abuse of small children does exist, and it's something that needs to be dealt with by the medical community.' "[4]

Investigative journalist and author Maury Terry believes the "Son of Sam" killings that terrorized New York City in 1977 involved Satanists. Similar suspicions arose during the trial of Charles Manson and his followers. The police no longer dismiss Satanism when they uncover what look like ritualistic murders like those in the "Night Stalker" case. Ramirez was fond of painting pentagrams, a favorite satanic symbol, in the homes of his victims.

Drugs, hypnosis, sexual abuse, brainwashing techniques, and intimidation are used to bring children and occult initiates under the control of the Satanists. Those who escape from satanic movements are often hunted down by members of the group. What "theology" do these members encounter that makes it so attractive? Patricia Pulling, founder of B.A.D.D. (Bothered About Dungeons and Dragons), an organization based in Richmond, Virginia, that seeks to educate young people about baneful influences, describes the perverted worldview of the occult:

> The satanists' theology derives in a perverted fashion from the Old Testament description of God as a jealous god—jealous, in particular, of Satan, says Pulling. If God and Satan are on equal planes and their battle is eternal, as satanists believe, why take the side of God, who places restrictions on what man may do? Why not take the side of Satan, who will help you satisfy your desires? Why try to deny the appetites that arise from the sin you are born into?[5]

The devil has become God's cosmic equal. Why believe in a God who restricts sinful desires when you can worship the devil and have all your desires met? This form of Satanism grows out of irrationalism, in which all things are possible, and monism, in which "all is god." There is also a sprinkling of Manichaeanism, an ancient philosophy in which the principles of Evil (Darkness and Matter) and Good (Spirit and Light) are deified. This view enabled Charles Manson to combine without conflict both Christ and Satan in himself.

THE TURNING POINT

There have always been movies with the devil as part of the plot. *Angel on My Shoulder* (1946) and *The Devil and Daniel Webster* (1941) are two of the best. *The Devil and Daniel Webster* is a sometimes comedic but always authentic portrayal of the devil and his schemes. It's reminiscent of C. S. Lewis' immortal *Screwtape Letters*. A simple, down-and-out farmer sells his soul to the devil in exchange for riches. In the end, the farmer changes his mind and turns to the great nineteenth-century orator and lawyer Daniel Webster to get him out of the contract. A jury of long-dead scoundrels, who had likewise sold their souls, is called up from the pit of hell to sit in judgment. After hearing the pleading by Webster, they allow the seemingly doomed farmer to break his former contract with "Scratch," the devil's apprentice who originally beguiled the farmer.

The devil had been trivialized in Walt Disney's 1937 first animated feature, *Snow White*, and the screen adaptation of Frank Baum's *Wizard of Oz* continued the trivialization process. "The influence of Walt Disney's witch in the animated movie, *Snow White*, while terrifying to young children, is amusing to adults. To a great extent, this is the traditional image of the witch: broomstick, black hat, black cat near at hand. It is as old as the medieval witchcraft trials."[6] The American public would soon be caught off guard by the new devil of special effects and a revived occultism.

Something happened at the movies beginning in the sixties. Prior to this time, the devil always knew his place. He was a defeated and doomed creature whose power was limited. He was real but under control. But today, the devil is no longer so accommodating. First, there was *Rosemary's Baby* (1968).[7] An overly ambitious actor "sells" his wife to a cult of devil-worshipers so he can gain fame and fortune. Why do these Satanists want her? You might have guessed: Mia Farrow, who plays the actor's wife, Rosemary, is raped by Satan in order to bring his child into the world. How does it end?: Rosemary grows to love her "demon seed." By the way, *Demon Seed* is the title of another occult "classic." A super-computer named "Proteus" (a god noted for his ability to assume different forms) mates with the wife of a computer scientist. The devil has entered the world of "high tech."

Then came *The Exorcist* in 1973. In this blockbuster movie the devil seems to get the upper hand again. The movie ends with the devil leaving the possessed girl, only to enter and destroy the exorcist. After seeing Father Karras hurl himself out the window in an act of desperation, the audience is left with the impression that the devil won the battle.

In the occult move *The Omen*, a 1976 box office hit, the devil is incarnated in the form of a five-year-old boy sired by the devil himself, and adopted by a wealthy American couple which was unaware of his origin. *The Omen* spawned two sequels, *Damien – The Omen II* (1978) and *The Final Conflict* (1981). In these movies Satan made a comeback – but as a different devil. No longer was he a submissive creature condemned to judgment. He was now an equal with God Himself. God seemed to be absent from the universe, or at least helpless to do anything.

Why the revival of the devil and the demonic at this point in history? And why his new status as God's equal? The devil has always had to be reckoned with. In the Christian worldview he was tempter, adversary, and accuser, but he always operated under the sovereignty of God (Job 1:6-22). He was always considered to be under God's control. Christians rarely believed that he had the upper hand. The Bible says that Satan is defeated, disarmed, and spoiled (Colossians 2:15; Revelation 12:7ff.; Mark 3:27), "fallen" (Luke 10:18), and "thrown down" (Revelation 12:9). He was "crushed" under the feet of the early Christians (Romans 16:20). He has lost "authority" over Christians (Colossians 1:13) and has been "judged" (John 16:11). He cannot "touch" a Christian (1 John 5:18). His works have been "destroyed" (1 John 3:8). He has "nothing" (John 14:30). He "flees" when "resisted" (James 4:7) and is "bound" (Mark 3:27; Luke 11:20).

Then something happened. The Christian message began to wane. The devil was seen as the one in control. Supposedly he rules the earth until Jesus returns to set up His earthly kingdom. Satan is considered to be "alive and well on planet earth" while God seems "to be holed up in his corner of the universe sulking,"[8] unable to lift a finger to stop the devil. Add to this the reduction of Christianity, the demise of rationalism, the rise of irrationalism, and the popularity of monism, and you have a volatile mix. There are those who will try anything to find fulfillment. Unfortunately, the occult is no longer off-limits.

Beyond Good and Evil

For the monist, good and evil are beyond this world. All is One. There are no ethical or moral distinctions in the One and no differentiation in being; that is, you are just as much a god as anyone else, and there is no god over you. The spiritual seeker must transcend the world of illusion and enter the world of unity with the One. "All actions are merely part of the whole world of illusion. The only 'real' reality is ultimate reality, and that is beyond differentiation, beyond good and evil. . . . So, like true and false, ultimately the category of good and evil fades away. Everything is good (which, of course, is identical to saying, 'Nothing is good' or 'Everything is evil')."[9] Tampering with evil in monism is no real problem since evil is no longer a category with ethical content.

So then, rationalism and monism are dangerous on two fronts. First, rationalism would have us dismiss the demonic, the world of spirits, and occult realities. Second, monism opens us to an unhealthy interest in the occult. In nearly all Eastern religions, there is open idolatry, superstition, animism (the belief that spirits inhabit objects), and spiritism.

OCCULTISM: PLAYING WITH FIRE

Occultism emerges in a society when the prevailing Christian worldview fails to impact people's lives by refusing to address the issues of life with concrete, life-transforming answers. When the Christian message becomes defeatist, retreatist, and otherworldly, the door is open wide to the occult. Occultism, then, prospers when Christianity is reduced. When the Church embraces a truncated Christian message and raises the white flag of cultural surrender, you can expect the devil to march in where he once feared to tread.[10] Os Guinness writes:

> Early hunters on safari in Africa used to build their fires high at night in order to keep away the animals in the bush. But when the fires burned low in the early hours of the morning, they would see all around them the approaching outlined shapes of animals and a ring of encircling eyes in the darkness. When the fire was high they were far off, but when the fire was low they approached again.[11]

We see that the encircling eyes of the occult are all around us because the Church has allowed the fires of a vibrant Christian faith to burn low. What were the steps of the ruin of Christianity and the rise of the occult?

First, a large segment of the Church "demythologized" the Bible. Anything that could not be explained rationally was discarded as myth.

Today, this view prevails in most colleges and many seminaries. The belief in the devil is counted as an old-world superstition that has no modern-day validity.

Second, the Bible itself is no longer considered authoritative. The Bible is presumed to be riddled with errors. Supposedly it is true only on matters dealing with "faith," that is, how to get to heaven and live a quiet life until Jesus returns. Many conservative Christians hold this view of the Bible. For them, Scripture does not address political, economic, educational, and legal issues, and is not considered reliable when it mentions a personal devil. For these anti-supernaturalists, there is no devil. The Bible used the devil only to enhance the story of Jesus' conflict between good and evil. While Jesus may have believed in the devil, He was just a man of the times. He was susceptible to all the then current superstitions. All this has had the effect of discrediting the Bible. Without an authoritative standard like the Bible to define truth and error, good and evil, and right and wrong, experience has became the norm, and the occult offers just one experience among many.

Third, the Christian message was diluted in its effect in and on this world. An otherworldly-only gospel was adopted: The Bible has answers in death but little to say in life. Those looking for answers to daily problems will try any option, including the occult. Many supposedly Bible-believing Christians refuse to turn to Scripture in any systematic and consistent way to deal with contemporary issues such as poverty, crime, education, and politics. For them, the Bible is a "spiritual," otherworldly book that should only be consulted for the latest in prophecy. What Jesus meant in John 18:36 when he told Pilate that His kingdom was not "of this world," was that His kingdom did not operate *in* and *over* this world.

Fourth, paganism, which supposedly has received a "bum rap" from Christianity and the scientific community (for different reasons), is now seen as a viable worldview option. Once the Bible is dismissed as authoritative on everything on which it speaks (and it speaks on everything),[12] we are left with a free-for-all when it comes to a choice of worldviews. The worldview of relativism makes all other worldviews possible and permissible. Witchcraft thrives in a relativistic world where Christianity is only one religious alternative among many, as the following quotation makes crystal clear:

> One need not be a witch—I am not—to understand witchcraft as a valid expression of the religious experience. The religion of witchcraft offers to restore a lost option, paganism, to our reli-

gious worldview. Both Christianity and scientism have taught us falsely that paganism is nonsense. We are taught that pagans worshiped idols, that they believed undignified things about a useless variety of silly gods, and that they invented interesting but irrelevant myths. . . . The religions of Egypt and Canaan, of the Celts and the Teutons, when properly understood, are rich, sophisticated, beautiful, and psychologically full of insight. The neopagan witches are attempting to recreate the positive values of pagan religion.[13]

The man-centered worldview of rationalism and the truncated worldview of Christianity produced a new worldview which is now being identified as the New Age movement, higher consciousness, holistic healing, psychic healing, astrology, eastern mysticism, life readings, and outright Satanism.

IRRATIONALISM'S OPEN DOOR TO THE OCCULT

But doesn't it seem rather strange that with the collapse of Christian belief that we should see a revival of the occult? Not too long ago Christians were ridiculed for believing in witchcraft. John Wesley wrote: "The giving up of witchcraft is in effect giving up of the Bible." The noted atheist Bertrand Russell nastily added, "I think he was right."[14] Ah, but the giving up of the Bible by Russell and others has turned the devil loose on the world. Today's devil is far more sinister. Rationalism declared that witchcraft, the devil, and a power-inducing occult were dead. But rationalism has been steadily losing its grip on certainty. The world is now up for grabs, and belief in the devil is just another brass ring. "The door to the non-rational, the irrational and super-rational is wide open. One of the many previous 'unthinkables' which has squeezed through the door is the occult."[15]

"POP" OCCULTISM

Many people are introduced to the occult through seemingly harmless practices, such as seances, Ouija boards, astrology, and *Dungeons & Dragons*. This is "pop occultism." At first, there is little that seems sinister. In fact, it seems like fun. It's a way "to escape from a drab and burdensome life."[16] Let's look at a few of the open doors that can lead to the acceptance of the occult as an acceptable worldview.

121

Astrology

Instead of seeking answers to life's problems in the Bible, millions of Americans turn to the stars each day to search for spiritual direction. There are over two thousand newspapers in the United States that carry a daily horoscope. Jeanne Dixon and other astrologers have a daily telephone horoscope. Just dial a number and get instant direction for your life. Astrology plays a major role in the lives of millions around the world. The Bible is no longer God's Word to man, and if it is, it's not enough. It's surprising how many Christians are horoscope readers. Millions of Americans (some estimate 32 million) are willing to trust their lives to the impersonal movements of the stars rather than a God who gives specific direction in the Bible.[17]

Astrology is also very irrational. You can't be born under a particular "sign." All the supposed "signs" are made out of non-patterned star points. It's like "connect the dots" with more dots than you need. You can then turn any group of stars into any sign you want. Find a book on constellations, choose the constellations Leo and Cancer, redraw the stars as points on a blank sheet of paper, and then hand the paper to a friend and have him connect the dots in the form of a lion (Leo) and crab (Cancer). Then ask someone else to connect the dots to look like two other animals. What's the point? The dots can be made to look like anything you want. The astrological signs are arbitrary renderings.

Then there is the problem of alignment. At your particular moment of birth, the sun, planets, and stars are in a particular alignment. But are they really? Light from the sun takes 8.3 light-*minutes*. This means that light from the sun, traveling one hundred eighty-six thousand miles per second takes more than eight minutes to reach Earth. Jupiter is nearly 51 light-minutes away from Earth, and Pluto 5.6 light-*hours*. This means that when you see the sun you are actually seeing what happened eight minutes before you actually see it. The closest stars are measured in light-*years*. None of these heavenly bodies are aligned in the way you see them. A planet has shifted position a number of times before you even see the light from a distant star.

The Ouija Board

The Ouija board is another pop occult "game." Thousands of children each year place their hands on a device that mysteriously travels across the face of the board, either spelling out words or simply answering yes or no to questions asked of it. But who or what is doing the answering? Is it possible to go further into the occult through this seemingly harmless game? Some people think so. The use of the Ouija board "suggests communication with a nonmaterial world, a world of ghosts and disembodied waves . . . a yearning toward contact with unknown powers, a seeking for what has been called the Unexplained."[18] Playing with the Ouija board can make the spiritual seeker a bit more inquisitive about the powers of the occult.

Dungeons & Dragons

Some enter the occult world through a seemingly harmless game called *Dungeons & Dragons*. The "game" is sold through toy stores as "fun and fantasy." Players compete to "summon demons to defeat opponents" and to "employ dark forces to win battles." Games are also used in classes for "gifted" children in some public schools. The games have been up-dated to include electronic versions to be used with computers.

> The motifs of FRPs [Fantasy Role Playing] are reinforced by other aspects of youth culture. Saturday morning cartoons feature the *Masters of the Universe*, muscle-bound barbarians living in a world of magicians, witches, and sorcerers. You can get *Masters of the Universe* dolls, balls, comic books, and videos. There's even a feminist version: *She-Ra, Princess of Power.*[19]

What harm can these games do? Well, they initially trivialize the occult by calling *Dungeons & Dragons* a "game." Remember the quotation that introduced this chapter? C. S. Lewis warned us about refusing to believe in the existence of devils or feeling "an excessive and unhealthy interest in them." *Dungeons & Dragons* moves a person from disbelief ("it's only a game") to an unhealthy interest ("an incredible sense of power"). A frustrated writer admitted that he had experienced "an incredible sense of power" as a Dungeon Master. "In some games," he acknowledged, "they don't call me Dungeon Master; they call me God."[20]

Now, not everyone who toys with astrology, the Ouija board, and *Dungeons & Dragons* becomes an occultist. My point is that they can open the door to an unhealthy interest in things that are not good to fool with.

THE BIBLE AND THE OCCULT

What is the "occult" and how can you spot occult practices? The word "occult" is derived from the Latin word *occultus*, and it conveys the idea of things hidden, secret, or mysterious. You should keep in mind that involvement in the occult is often very subtle. Many people may not know that they have been seduced by occult teachings. Of course, this is what seduction is all about. "Under the designation occult we could class at least the following items: witchcraft, magic, palm reading, fortune telling, ouija boards, tarot cards, satanism, spiritism, demons and the use of crystal balls."[21] To this list we could add astrology, Dungeons & Dragons, seances, preoccupation with UFOs, Masonry, astral projection, hypnotism, mind reading, ESP, life readings, psychic healing, the sorcery techniques and philosophy of Carlos Casteneda, and the New Age movement.

The purpose of the occult is to get around God's way of dealing with the world. In all occult techniques, the practitioner either wants something that God forbids or pursues a good thing contrary to God's expressed will. God wants things done His way. Man, as the perpetual rebel, believes that he can subvert God's moral order by going to a lesser self-appointed god, Satan. But even Satan exacts a price: Adam and Eve lost Paradise (Genesis 2:15-17; 3:5, 14-24), Saul lost his kingdom (1 Samuel 28:3-19), and Judas most certainly lost his soul (Luke 22:21-23). The following is a list of the Bible's prohibitions against dabbling in the black arts:

Witchcraft (sorcery)–Exodus 22:18
Necromancy-Spiritualism–Leviticus 19:31; 20:6; Deuteronomy
    18:11
Astrology–Isaiah 47:13
False prophecy
    inaccurate–Deuteronomy 18:20-22; cf. I John 4:1
    idolatrous–Deuteronomy 13:1-3
Divination–Deuteronomy 18:10
    arrows–Ezekiel 21:21
    livers–Ezekiel 21:21
    images–Ezekiel 21:21
Fire walking–Deuteronomy 18:10
Omens–Jeremiah 10:2
Wizardry (secret knowledge)–Deuteronomy 18:11
Charms (snakes)–Jeremiah 8:17

Enchantment (spells)—Isaiah 47:9-12

Times (lucky days)—Leviticus 19:26

The term translated "witch" by the King James Version is more
  accurately rendered "sorcerer."[22]

The Bible gives us the answers we need to live a full and abundant
life. Messing with hidden things is messing with trouble. "The secret
things belong to the LORD our God, but the things revealed belong to us
and to our sons forever, that we may observe all the words of this law"
(Deuteronomy 29:29).

To put yourself under the authority, and thus, the power, of another
being is an act of rebellion against God. It will lead to disastrous results.
But worst of all, submission to the occult is a way of despising God; it is
disobedience of the highest order. "For rebellion is as the sin of divination, and insubordination is as iniquity and idolatry" (1 Samuel 15:23). It
is no accident that divination and immorality are so often mentioned in
the same context (Acts 15:29; 1 Corinthians 10:6-9; Galatians 5:20; Revelation 2:14; 9:21). Those who choose the occult over Christ want power
and authority apart from Him. This is the worldview of the Satanist as
expressed by Anton Szandor La Vey, who founded the San Francisco–
based Church of Satan in 1969: "I wouldn't presume to improve on
Milton's quote, 'Better to reign in hell than serve in heaven.' "[23]

FLIM-FLAM

One last point needs to be made. While there are probably occult
phenomena that are truly linked to the demonic, most of what is passed
off as "supernatural" is nothing more than flim-flam. Some people are
ready to believe almost anything. Even in an era in which science is still
king, a good many suckers are still born. Some of the most rational people
become unbelievably irrational when it comes to psychic phenomena. You
might get sucked into groups that promote themselves through flim-
flam, believing that they "have the power." Flim-flam is the art of the
con. As George C. Scott said in the movie *The Flim-Flam Man*, "You
can't cheat an honest man." When it comes to psychic phenomena, you
can't fool a rational man who understands the limits of the devil, the in-
genuity of fakers, and the gullibility of the naive.

All of us want to believe in supernatural powers. This one fact is used
by some very talented but evil people to draw spiritual seekers into dangerous spiritual movements. The vulnerable and desperate are the most

susceptible. You may be shown what seems to be supernatural phenomena to attract you to a particular cult, pseudo-Christian religious group, or the occult. If you are particularly depressed, confused, or just desperate for answers, you might find yourself attracted to some of the most bizarre and sinister religious movements. Don't say "It can't happen to me." It happened to nine hundred desperate souls in Guyana, South America:

> "Reverend" Jim Jones was as charismatic a leader as any who ever swayed reason. Despite his farcical philosophy, he managed to convince a considerable number of California's populace that he had a direct pipeline to the gods and to salvation. With the kind of sleight of hand and sleight of mind that characterizes such charlatans, he "proved" that he could raise the dead—he performed the "miracle" forty-seven times in his church—and showed his followers that he was able to cure cancer and other afflictions by removing masses of organic junk from their bodies. After his death, cult members came forward to testify that, after threats from Jones, they had agreed to fake death and then stage instant resurrections. The surgery was even simpler than that still being performed by "psychic surgeons" of Brazil and the Philippines. Jones merely reached beneath the clothes of the intimidated faithful and pulled out chicken gizzards and other material, according to witnesses. Those who did not see through the tricks were convinced.[24]

Jones had his followers believing that he had supernatural powers. They would do anything for such a man. Over nine hundred of them followed him in death. Most of them went willingly.

Danny Korem, a world-famous magician, writes that it is possible "to convince almost anybody—under the right circumstances and through the use of trickery—that one may have supernatural powers." Korem argues "that unless one is schooled in how the mind can be deceived, one is at a potential disadvantage when trying to objectively report so-called manifestations of occult powers."[25]

Most of you probably know of Sherlock Holmes, the fictionalized English master detective. Holmes's creator was Sir Arthur Conan Doyle. Holmes the character is quite different from Doyle the author. As a detective, Holmes was scrupulously rational. He could deduce the most fantastic clues from only a few scraps of evidence. The angle of a stab wound would tell him the height of the assailant. A whiff of tobacco smoke left lingering at the scene of a crime would enable him to trace the thief through a local tobacco shop that blended the odd mixture. Everything was logical and reasonable. There had to be a rational explanation for even the most suspicious circumstances, even those in which the clues seemed to point to the paranormal. For Holmes, there was always a rational explanation.

But when it came to psychic phenomena, Sir Arthur Conan Doyle became especially irrational. On this issue, he did not personify Sherlock Holmes. He was willing to believe any fragment of evidence to support his unbending belief that mediums could penetrate the realm of the supernatural and communicate with departed spirits. Then he met up with Harry Houdini, the "Handcuff King."

Harry Houdini was the most famous magician who ever lived. His name is synonymous with magic. He could escape from any and all restraining devices: handcuffs, straight jackets, safes, locked boxes, and jails. He once escaped from Scotland Yard. He even escaped after being placed *inside* a locked safe.

Houdini was fascinated with life beyond the senses. He had a running battle with Sir Arthur Conan Doyle about the legitimacy of contacting the spirit world. Sir Arthur believed that certain people had the "gift" of being able to break through to the other side. Houdini wanted so much to believe, but could not. "I'm not denouncing spiritualism. I'm showing up frauds. If there is an honest medium, trot her out."[26]

Doyle was convinced that Houdini was himself a medium, capable of supernatural feats. He believed that Houdini could perform some of his tricks only by dematerializing himself and rematerializing himself later. Houdini objected.

> I do claim to free myself from the restraint of fetters and confinement, but positively state that I accomplish my purpose purely by physical, not psychical means. The force necessary to "shoot a bolt within a lock," is drawn from Houdini the living human being and not a medium. My methods are perfectly natural, resting on natural laws of physics. I do not *dematerialize* or *materialize* anything; I simply control and manipulate natural things in a manner perfectly well known to myself, and thoroughly accountable for and adequately understandable (if not duplicable) by any person to whom I may elect to divulge my secrets.[27]

In one sense Houdini should be an example to us all. Don't be afraid to question the supposed-supernatural, especially when it's linked to the occult. If you are ever tempted to believe, then investigate, question, and doubt. Don't be afraid to "test the spirits." This can also mean calling on an expert to help you out. On the other hand, we should never forget that occult phenomena can be real, although I suspect that the many reported occurrences are nothing more than wishful thinking, fakery, deception, and flim-flam. Again, if you believe it to be real, flee from evil.

> "See to it that no one takes you captive through philosophy and empty deception, according to the tradition of men, according to the elementary principles of the world, rather than according to Christ" (Colossians 2:8).

CONCLUSION

With the erosion and decline of a Christian culture, we have seen the vacuum filled by a revival of beliefs that would have been unthinkable when a vibrant Christian culture flourished. The occult is the last spiral down into the void. It's man's last desperate lunge for answers. If this is the best the non-Christian worldview can offer, then we can expect a resurgence of the Christian worldview. There is no hope in a worldview that can only offer sorrow and tragedy. But if we are to keep the "encircling eyes" at bay, we must once again build high the fire of a comprehensive Christian worldview.

8
KEEPING YOUR FAITH ALIVE

Kids have no—or little—hope for the
future. They live in the present because
the future is frightening to them. They're
frightened by the economy, international
tensions, and everything else, and they
feel inadequate, as if they're unable to
deal with the world. For many kids, life is
very existential, with no meaning except
what they create for themselves.[1]

YOU probably belong to a church. You might be active in a Christian
youth group. There's a good possibility that you have made some profession of faith in Jesus Christ as your Savior, perhaps when you were quite
young. You may have even "walked the aisle" and been baptized. Not
one of these things alone nor all of them together makes you a Christian.

In a way, this is the most important chapter in the book. If you are not
a Christian, no matter how successful you are in college, your life will ultimately be a failure. Jesus said that there is no profit even if you own the
whole world, if you lose your soul. So, there are several things to cover in
this chapter. First, make sure you know what it means to be a Christian.
Second, keep your faith alive during your college years. Third, learn how
to study the Bible. Fourth, pray. Fifth, fellowship with other believers.
Sixth, participate in corporate worship in a church where the Bible is believed and preached and where the Lord's Supper is regularly celebrated.

WHAT IS A CHRISTIAN?
We live in an era of "decision Christianity." If a person makes a "decision for Christ," he is considered to be a Christian. Obviously, God
wants you to make a choice for Him (see Deuteronomy 30:15-16; Joshua
24:15; 1 Kings 18:21). But it is an oversimplification of Christianity to
think that making a decision is all there is to it. You must have some

131

understanding of what you are deciding. And there has to be some evidence that Jesus Christ has made a difference in the way you live.

One of the most neglected Biblical doctrines is the holiness of God.[2] Because God is holy and men are sinners, we are, by nature, hostile to everything God is and everything He demands. Many people do not associate salvation with the holiness of God. They do not understand that the holiness of God is the *reason* Jesus came to earth to live a perfect life (the requirement God demands because He is holy) and then to die a horrible death on the cross (the penalty God demands for sin). Until we recognize that God demands that we renounce our sinful lifestyle and turn to Him in humble submission to His divine grace, we cannot call ourselves "Christian." In fact, until we "unconditionally surrender" to God, we are His "enemies" (Romans 5:10). The apostle Paul tells us in Romans, chapter 5 that before we surrender to Christ in repentance we are "helpless" (v. 6), "ungodly" (v. 6), and "sinners" (v. 8). In another place, the Apostle tells us that we are "dead in trespasses and sins" (Ephesians 2:1).

This does not mean that we work for our salvation. We can do absolutely nothing to gain enough favor to win our own salvation. *God* saves us. We surrender ourselves to Him, repenting of our sin and crying out for mercy. No amount of good works can merit God's favor. One sin is enough to cast us into hell, yet we commit dozens of sins daily. Jesus didn't commit one sin. It is His life that God accepts. We must find favor with God on Jesus' merits.

So then, first things first. Come to Christ! Repent of your sins and humbly rely upon Jesus' redeeming death and resurrection to make "peace with God" for you (Romans 5:1). If you choose not to come to Christ, the "wrath of God abides on" you (John 3:36). You cannot do it in your own strength or with your own supposed good works.[3] Call upon Him to redeem you from the wrath to come. If you think college is going to be rough, try life without Jesus Christ. More than this, think what death will be like without Jesus Christ.

How Strong is my Faith?

You may already be a Christian but still a mere "babe" in the faith. The "babe in Christ" is not ready for "solid food"; that is, he's not able to handle Biblical doctrines that take time and study to understand and apply: "But solid food is for the mature, who because of practice have their senses trained to discern good and evil" (Hebrews 5:14). An immature Christian can be easily bullied by a hostile professor and just as easily influenced by the lack of morality found on many college campuses.

To become mature, you must do the following:

1. Submit and surrender to God all personal rights and claims on your life. In our day there is the clamor for "human rights." Somehow we have gotten away from the belief that "rights" are related to "righteousness"; therefore, we cannot claim our "rights" before God. We must submit to His requirements for *right*eous living.

2. Pursue God and His righteousness and rest in His unfailing love for you. This means learning from the Bible what pleases and what displeases God. While it is true that the Christian is freed from the "curse of the law," he is not freed from the obligations of the law.

3. Look to God alone to satisfy you. Too often we are inclined to seek satisfaction in material things, relationships, good grades, prestige, athletic recognition, and honor by our peers. These certainly are not evil things. But there is no lasting satisfaction in them. God wants us to be fully satisfied in Him. This is the meaning of the verse which tells us to seek *first* the kingdom of God, *then* all these other things will be added (Matthew 6:33).

4. Forgive in your heart all those who have offended you and make peace with those who might hold grudges against you. Life is miserable if you are always holding a grudge.

5. Accept with thanksgiving all the circumstances and challenges that face you with the understanding that "God causes all things to work together for good to those who love God, to those who are called according to His purpose" (Romans 8:28).

6. Turn away from sin and every appearance of evil, repent of your sins, and ask God to forgive you and cleanse you from all unrighteousness (1 John 1:9).

7. Follow the law of God as the standard of righteousness for personal behavior, interpersonal relationships, economic and political policies, foreign affairs, science, and every endeavor under the sun.

There's no "crash course" you can take that will prepare you for the shaking your faith may undergo. But you should start right now by arming yourself with some ammunition. The book *Unconditional Surrender*, by Dr. Gary North,[4] is a good place to start. It will introduce you to the basics of Christianity. It is comprehensive, yet brief. You will find information on God, man, law, family, church, civil government, and economics, as well as an explanation of the kingdom of God and its implications for worldwide dominion by Christians.

Keeping Your Faith Alive

The faith of the typical Christian will be rattled in college. Many students return home as skeptics. Their faith is destroyed by atheistic professors who long ago sold their souls for a mess of intellectual pottage.

But you say that you're going to a "Christian" college. Well, there are still come good ones, but some colleges that pass themselves off as "Christian" are no more Christian than the State university. In fact, your faith may be most vulnerable in the wolf-in-sheep's-clothing "Christian" college. Your guard is down. You're expecting a solid "Christian" education. But you may be getting baptized humanism. You will tend to trust a professor who teaches at a Christian college. But you should remember that most Christian colleges have received accreditation from statist accrediting agencies. The professors of these colleges probably received their advanced degrees from humanistic State universities.

How can you avoid being seduced by humanistic rhetoric that could destroy your faith? You have to keep growing in the Lord, in the knowledge of the Bible, and in the knowledge of Jesus Christ.

BIBLE READING AND STUDY

It's easy to let your spiritual life go down the tubes when you are preoccupied with the new obligations of college life. In order to keep things in perspective, you must *read and study the Bible daily.* The Bible is a blueprint for life.[5] It will define what your obligations are to both God and man. It will nourish you, for "man does not live on bread alone, but on every word that proceeds out of the mouth of God" (Matthew 4:4; see Deuteronomy 8:3). "But I've never learned how to study the Bible." You are not alone. Making up lost ground is difficult. It will take time to get to know your Bible. But you need to get started. There are a number of books on the market that will help you.[6]

To get a daily diet of the Bible, I recommend a systematic reading program. A very good chronological guide that will take you through the Bible every year is a monthly publication from Walk Thru the Bible Ministries, 61 Perimeter Park N.E., Atlanta, Georgia. But reading is not enough. You need to *study* the Bible, and not just for your own spiritual health. You need to study the Bible in conjunction with your school work. If you're assigned a reading on inflation or debt or family relations or political theory or whatever, you need to study Scripture to discover what God's Word has to say.

In addition to the books mentioned earlier, there are many tools available to help you study the Bible. You will be able to find most of these at any Christian bookstore. First, you need a good Bible. There are many study Bibles on the market in many different translations. Different translations are useful for different purposes. I use the New American Standard Bible for study. Whatever translation you get, make sure that it has good cross references. Cross references direct you to passages where the same topics are being discussed. This is an invaluable help, because the first principle of Bible interpretation is that the Bible interprets itself.

Second, you need a topical Bible. A topical Bible arranges Bible passages according to subject. You can look up, say, "land," and it will list passages that tell about land. You could do the same thing using good cross references, but a topical Bible saves a lot of digging. The best topical Bible is *The New Nave's Topical Bible*.[7]

Third, you need a good Bible dictionary. A Bible dictionary gives you background information about places, people, and events in the Bible. Often, knowing about the place where a Bible story happened helps to illumine the meaning of the story. There are many on the market, of varying sizes. A good one-volume Bible dictionary is the *New Bible Dictionary*.[8]

Fourth, you need a concordance. Concordances list every word in the Bible in alphabetical order, and the passages where those words are found. This can be a helpful tool, but you should realize that there are limits and dangers with "word studies." Still, a concordance is an indispensable aid, particularly if you are looking for a specific passage. Of course, you will have to get a concordance that uses the same translation that you are using, but they are not difficult to find. There are concordances available for the New American Standard Version, the New International Version, and the King James Version.

Fifth, take a look at commentaries. You don't need to buy a big set of commentaries, but sometimes a commentary will help you understand a passage. Your pastor probably has commentaries that you can borrow.

Buying a good Bible, topical Bible, concordance, and Bible dictionary probably sounds like a lot. It will cost you over one hundred dollars to get started. But that's cheaper than buying a set of commentaries, and if you are diligent, you will be able very quickly to study passages in more depth than most commentaries, even if you don't know Hebrew or Greek. And, it's a priceless investment, because understanding the Word of the Lord is more precious that gold and jewels.

Of course, all of these extra books are tools, and, in fact, there are many more tools available. All these tools aid your reading. But in the end, there is absolutely no short cut to learn about the Bible. The only way to develop a solid Biblical worldview is to keep reading the Bible, carefully, over and over and over again. Read it prayerfully. Use whatever tools you find helpful. But above all, read God's Word, and pay attention to what you read.

Now that you have all these tools, how do you go about studying the Bible? Let's assume that you have a particular issue in mind, and you want to find out what the Bible has to say about it. For example, you want to discover what the Bible teaches about gold. Very briefly, let me outline several steps that will help you study this topic.

1. Look up the word gold in a concordance. This will give you all the passages that use the word.

2. Read the passages that you have found from the concordance. What you're looking for, after all, is not simply the word gold, but the Bible's teaching about gold. This means you have to read and meditate on sentences and paragraphs that deal with gold.

3. Look up any cross references.

4. Look up gold in the topical Bible. This may give you some passages that don't use the word gold, but are still relevant to your study.

5. Expand the focus of your study: look up silver and jewels and treasure and wealth in your concordance and topical Bible. Look up the cross references.

6. Take notes as you read. For example, on Genesis 2:12, you might make a note that gold is "good," and that it was near the Garden of Eden.

7. When you have assembled as much information about gold as you can find, try to put it all together. Try to find connections between different passages, looking for similarities and differences, and try to get a full picture of the Biblical view of gold.

8. The Bible is our guide for all of life, but its main focus is on the life, death, resurrection, and ascension of Jesus Christ. Whatever you study in the Bible, ask what it teaches about Jesus.

These steps are very brief, but they will get you started. The most important point, to reiterate, is that you need to keep reading and studying. Don't get discouraged. The more you study the Bible, the more wonderful it becomes, and the more wisdom you will be able to glean from its pages.

Looking for Patterns

When you read any book, you need to look for recurring patterns and references from one part of a book to another. In *The Plague* by Albert Camus, for example, the author tells us in one place that the sea is a symbol of the constant flux and clamor of human life. Later, Camus writes that the plague-ridden town of Oran has its back to the sea. The point is that the people of Oran have forgotten their place in the cosmos, have become "humanists" who think they can control plagues and wars in their own strength. A careful reader of Camus will pick up the symbolism, but only if he is looking for patterns and repetitions.

One example of a recurring pattern is the following four-point pattern, which is often used in the historical books of the Bible:

1. God speaks (command or promise).
2. Man responds (faithfulness or unfaithfulness).
3. God evaluates (cursing or blessing).
4. God redeems (salvation).

We find hints of points 1 and 3 in operation even before man was created. God speaks, and then something comes into existence (Genesis 1:3, 6, 9, 11, 14, 20, 24, 26, 29). At the conclusion of God's command He makes an evaluation: "And God saw all that He had made, and behold, it was very good" (v. 31). There is even a hint of point 2 in this sequence of events: "Then God said, 'Let there be light'; *and there was light*" (1:3). (Of course, we do not find point 4 mentioned prior to the Fall. There was no need to redeem a creation that did not need redemption.) God's evaluation of His handiwork in Genesis 1:31 was ethical and not just aesthetic. Five times previously God declared after various creative acts "that it was good" (verses 10, 12, 18, 21, 25).[9]

If God evaluates His work in this way, how does God evaluate our work? In the same way. Later in Genesis, we find the following: (1) God *commands* Adam to "cultivate" and "keep" the garden and not to eat "from the tree of the knowledge of good and evil" (Genesis 2:15, 16); (2) Adam and Eve *respond*: "She took from its fruit and ate; and she gave also to her husband with her, and he ate" (3:6); (3) God *evaluates*: First, He asks for Adam's evaluation: "Where are you?" (3:9). Second, He gives His evaluation: Genesis 3:14-24. (4) God *redeems*: "And I will put enmity between you and the woman, and between your seed and her seed; He shall bruise you on the head, and you shall bruise him on the heel" (3:15) and "the LORD God made garments of skin for Adam and his wife, and clothed them" (3:21).

Often, God's command will not be stated explicitly in the passage. For example, 1 Kings 10:26-29 tells us about Solomon's numerous chariots and horsemen. It sounds like a commendation. What a great king! If, however, we find a cross reference to Deuteronomy, chapter 17, we discover that God specifically commanded the kings *not* to multiply horses and chariots. In other words, even when a particular passage does not mention God's command, some command is assumed. We need to use the tools mentioned above to find out what commandments or promises are in the background of the events that are recorded. Whenever we read one of the historical books of the Bible, we need to keep referring back to the laws in Exodus, Leviticus, Numbers, and Deuteronomy. Otherwise, we will misunderstand what's happening in the historical sections.

Sometimes, God's evaluation is implicit. God commanded Abram to leave his home in Ur, and to go to a new land to live. God also promised that Abram would be blessed. Abram obeyed, and as soon as he got to the land of Canaan, God added the promise of the land (Genesis 12:1-9). By adding a further promise, God was showing his approval of Abram's obedience.

There are other patterns in the Bible as well. The death (or suffering) and resurrection (or exaltation) pattern can be found in the lives of Joseph, Daniel, and above all Jesus Christ. There is the pattern of warfare, victory, and exaltation in the book of Joshua, the career of David, and the life of Jesus Christ. The entire book of Judges follows a cycle of deliverance, sin, enslavement, and deliverance, over and over again. The "exodus pattern" is found not only in the book of Exodus, but also in the later chapters of Isaiah. You should also look for recurring symbols, such as the garden, the wilderness, the mountain, etc.[10] And, the overall structure of the Bible should be kept in mind: The Old Testament points forward to the coming of Christ, and the New Testament tells of the fulfillment of the Old Testament promises. Other books that we have mentioned will suggest other patterns. The important thing is to read carefully and to look for places where one part of the Bible refers back to another.

CHRISTIAN FELLOWSHIP

"There is strength in numbers." Take a stick and break it in half. Even a child could do it. Take eight sticks of the same size and bundle them together. Now try to break them. You might be able to do it, but it will be very difficult. A larger bundle of sticks makes the task nearly impossible. This illustrates something that is true about the Christian life. As a Christian, you cannot make it alone. You will get eaten alive by temptation and the assault on your faith. Even the Lone Ranger had Tonto.

Jesus sent out His disciples "two and two ahead of Him" (Luke 10:1). The listing of spiritual gifts and the role they play in making up the functioning body of Christ is indicative of the corporate nature of the Christian's experience (1 Corinthians 12-14). You cannot go it alone. Your best bet is to make contact with someone who will be going to the same college. Since you've spent a good deal of time selecting a college, you should know someone who could introduce you to other Christians. The classroom will be a good place to spot Christians, especially if you have an antagonistic prof who ridicules religion in general and Christianity in particular.

There are also campus ministries at most colleges. They provide Bible studies and often sponsor campus evangelism drives. The most important consideration in evaluating these ministries is the quality of the leadership. It is hard to make specific recommendations since the leadership varies from campus to campus. It would be best for you, your parents, and your pastor to contact and meet personally with the campus leader.

ASSEMBLING TOGETHER

As helpful as campus ministries can be, they are limited. Campus ministries are simply not capable of doing what God intended the church to do. So, it is extremely important that you get involved in a local congregation. You should join a church basically for two reasons: worship and accountability.

Worship is the most important thing we do. Our whole life is to be a living sacrifice to God (Romans 12:1-2), and we are to seek the glory of God even in the most mundane details of our daily lives (1 Corinthians 10:31). In a sense, then, everything we do is to be worship, because it is done for the glory of God through Jesus Christ. But the Bible also lays upon us a special duty of worshiping with His people in public assembly. The writer of Hebrews warns his readers not to forsake the assembly (Hebrews 10:25). In worship, we enter into the very throne room of God, the true heavenly sanctuary to present ourselves before the Lord with praise and thanksgiving. We hear the Word preached, the Word that sanctifies and nourishes us. We receive the bread and wine of the Lord's Supper, and are refreshed for another week of battle. If you are not regularly and whole-heartedly participating in the public worship of a church, you will not be able to withstand the pressures of college life.

This also means that you need to leave the Lord's Day to the Lord. It may sound strange in a book on surviving college, but the Bible is clear: Do not work on the Lord's Day. This may even sound absurd. But it works. When I was in graduate school, where the academic pressures are much greater than they are at college, resting on the Lord's Day never harmed my school performance, and in fact was a great help. Even looking at it pragmatically, you need a rest from reading and studying one day a week. That's the way God has made you. That's what you need to do.

The church is a place of worship, but it is also a government. The leaders in the church are responsible for your welfare, and you are obligated to submit to their jurisdiction and counsel: "Obey your leaders, and submit to them; for they keep watch over your souls, as those who will give an account. Let them do this with joy and not with grief, for this would be unprofitable for you" (Hebrews 13:17). You need to find a church in your college town. Before you leave home, go to your pastor and have him locate a church for you near the college. You must remain accountable to some leadership. A local church, which has a relationship with your home church, will serve that purpose.

You need to be under the authority of some church leadership because God commands you to be. But it also has many other advantages. Invariably, church families will invite you to dinner, and provide a more home-like environment. You may be a long way from home, and, whether you believe it now or not, you will miss the home cooking and the atmosphere of normal life. It is also important that you get to know some people who are not in college. College tends to isolate you from the rest of the world. Colleges operate on schedules different from the working world. College students and faculty are preoccupied with different issues. It will be helpful to have friends outside the campus community to give you a more realistic perspective on things. You might also want to seek career advice from someone in the church. In many ways, joining a church and becoming an active participant will be of great help to you.

FELLOWSHIP WITH GOD IN PRAYER

Let's face it: Prayer is one of the most important things Christians are supposed to do. Every Christian knows he is supposed to pray, but many do not know how. Many have difficulty maintaining a consistent prayer life. If this has been your experience, you can at least take some comfort in the fact that you are not alone. But this is no excuse for not getting better. While there are no shortcuts to a good prayer life, the following suggestions may help you get started.

First, it might help to recall something about the importance of prayer. According to the Reformer John Calvin, prayer is like a great conduit, a pipe, that brings us all that God promises. God has promised to do "immeasurably more than all we can ask or imagine" (Ephesians 3:20-21). How do we get a hold of that abundant store of blessing? By asking. "Ask and you shall receive," Jesus told His disciples. James tells us that wisdom will be granted to those who ask. Over and over again, God encourages us to pray by promising that He will answer (Luke 18:1-8; Matthew 7:9-11). Whatever you lack, prayer is the key to receiving the benefits that God has promised.

Prayer is also one of the greatest weapons we have in fighting for the Lord on the college campus. Look at the great things that God has accomplished through the prayers of His people: battles have been won

(Exodus 17:8-13), rain has been withheld (James 5:17-18), fire has been cast down to the earth (Revelation 8:1-5). The prayers of God's people change the world!

We should always remember, of course, that God is God and we are but dust and ashes. God can rightfully answer "no" to our prayers. But God doesn't answer "no" without a good reason. He may delay answering our prayers to strengthen our faith, to make us pray more fervently. He may answer "no" because He knows that what we ask is not really good for us. But God has promised to answer prayers that are in accord with His will. And we can boldly and confidently present our petitions before Him (Genesis 18:22-33; Hebrews 10:19-25).

Second, your prayers need not be long and involved. They can be short and offered throughout the day. Your goal should be to make prayer so much a habit that you naturally respond to crisis situations with prayer. Prayer should be your first response to all situations. Read the book of Nehemiah, and notice how often he prayed short, spontaneous prayers. These are every bit as pleasing to God as long, eloquent prayers.

Third, we should also set aside some time every day specifically for prayer. If you read Nehemiah carefully, you will discover that he had fasted and prayed for months before he offered his spontaneous prayers. We need to have both: spontaneous prayers throughout the day, and specific prayer time. Unfortunately, modern Christians have been silenced partly because they believe that their prayers *must* be spontaneous. They needn't be! God is not displeased with prayers just because they are not spontaneous, nor is He necessarily pleased with spontaneous prayers. God is pleased with Godly prayers. Of course, our prayers must be heartfelt; it is the *fervent* prayer of the righteous man that accomplishes much (James 5:16). But prayers can be fervent without being spontaneous.

My point is simply this: Throughout the history of the Church, many excellent prayers have been written, and we should use them. The prayers of the Anglican Book of Common Prayer are tremendous. Many editions also contain all of the Psalms, divided up as morning and evening prayers on a thirty-day cycle. That means you can pray through the Psalms, the Bible's own prayer book, every month. This is often a helpful way to get started with your prayer time: read through the Psalms for the day, and make the Psalms your own prayers. The Lord's Prayer is also a model prayer that can be used as a "springboard" for our own thanks and petitions. There is no better training in prayer than God's own Word.

Fourth, you need to schedule time for prayer. If you don't schedule something, you won't do it. This is true in every area of life: study, marriage, raising children, work, church. If you don't make time for prayer, you will never pray. It's that simple. Observe your own rhythms. Some people function better in the morning, some in the evening. Get up an hour early if that's what you need to do. The great leader of the Reformation, Martin Luther, in the midst of writing hundreds of tracts and leading the fledgling Reformation movement, prayed up to three hours a day. The Bible indicates that prayers should be offered in the morning, at noon, and in the evening. This kind of pattern breaks up the day, and keeps your focus on the Lord throughout the day. But some people simply cannot follow that kind of pattern. Schedule your prayers whenever you can, but *do schedule your prayers*. Make prayer a daily habit. Don't worry too much about how much time you spend. As you become more accustomed to prayer, you will discover more and more how much you have to pray about.

Fifth, keep a prayer notebook. That probably sounds silly. But how else are you going to remember what to pray about? How else are you going to keep track of your own requests and the requests of your friends? Your requests can be very general, but don't be afraid of specific requests. A prayer notebook will also help you keep track of answers to prayer, and will strengthen your faith in the Lord's goodness.

Sixth, remember that there are many different kinds of prayer. One helpful way of remembering these is the acronym, ACTS: Adoration, Confession, Thanksgiving, and Supplication (Requests). This pattern shouldn't become a straightjacket, but your prayers should include all these elements. Prayer is not just a matter of asking for things, but includes praise, thanks, and confession of sin.

There are many books on prayer available, as well as many prayer books. They will motivate you, give you some pointers, and provide patterns for your prayers. Work out a prayer schedule and find aids that help you. But whatever you do, PRAY!

CONCLUSION

To be really successful in anything, we must be pleasing to God. But we can't be pleasing to God without being Christians, or without growing as Christians. To be a truly successful college student, get right with God, study your Bible, worship and fellowship with God's people, and pray. Any other approach to college success is prideful, humanistic, and ultimately doomed to failure.

PART TWO

LEARNING HOW
TO ACHIEVE

9
GETTING READY FOR COLLEGE

George Villegas squeaked through high
school with a 1.7 grade point average, and
now he's paying the piper.

Last fall he enrolled in a community
college and joined the burgeoning ranks
of college freshmen who are so poorly
prepared for college-level work that they
must take remedial courses in math,
reading or writing in order to have a
chance at completing a college program.

I had too much fun, he says with a grin.
"Once in a while I studied, but not every
night."[1]

GEORGE is not alone. Some estimate that one in four to as many as
three out of five freshmen require remedial work. They just didn't prepare themselves while they were in high school. Study patterns were
never established. With each passing year these students fell further and
further behind. Many of them are probably C students, even C+ students. But the foundation for learning needed at the college level was
never laid. Wayne H. Slater, a professor who teaches remedial English at
the University of Maryland's College Park campus, says: "The majority
want a college education without studying. They honestly don't know
what studying is. They don't know that in reading a textbook they must
go slowly and concentrate and take notes. They read for a physics test
the way they'd read *Reader's Digest*. They aren't non-readers. They are
superficial readers."[2]

You might be saying at this point: "I've graduated from high school. My grades are pretty good. I was accepted to a number of good colleges. Why should I be concerned about how well I'll do in college?" Many students will not need much preparation beyond what they received in high school. But for others, college is going to be a shock. For some, the realization that they could be in academic trouble will not hit them until they hear their first college lecture. This chapter is designed to help you avoid a lot of surprises, surprises that could give you an immediate anxiety attack.

Grades are not always indicators of how much you know or what you can really do. Generally they only reflect how well you did in relation to how everyone else did in your graduating class. What if the education you all received was mediocre? You need something more than good grades and good test scores. These will certainly help you get into college, but they will not keep you there. The best protection is adequate preparation.

While it's not too late to strengthen the areas in which you might be academically weak, new knowledge is hard to retain, bad study habits are hard to break, and good study habits are even more difficult to cultivate. But we are capable of change. We grow up and understand that new responsibilities mean new resolutions and new opportunities. Sure, you may not have done your best in high school, but you understand what you need to do to make it in this world. While a college education doesn't mean what it once did, according to all the available statistics, you'll need it in most professions. In financial terms alone "the latest Census Bureau figures show that the average graduate earns one and one half times as much as the average high school graduate."[3] Many companies are not as concerned with what you learned at college as they are with your ability to follow through on a commitment and finish a difficult task with little supervision.

I'm firmly convinced that what you did in high school does not necessarily represent what you will do in college or in your chosen profession. So you want to be prepared to confront every obstacle. This chapter will get you started.

THE COST FACTOR

For which one of you, when he wants to build a tower, does not first sit down and calculate the cost, to see if he has enough to complete it? Otherwise, when he has laid a foundation, and is not able to finish, all who observe it begin to ridicule him, saying, "This man began to build and was not able to finish" (Luke 14:28-30).

Most of our daily life is occupied with financial decision-making. There isn't a day that goes by without at least one financial transaction taking place. As you face additional responsibilities, you will encounter more financial transactions. College becomes the first major outlay of cash you and/or your family will make for at least four years. The following illustrates the point:

Recently in Harvard Yard, a student was spotted wearing a T-shirt with a message meant to terrify parents with large ambitions for their young: THIS SHIRT COST MY FAMILY $50,000 . . . HARVARD 1985. If you think that's a shocking sum to pay for a Harvard B.A., wait fifteen years. By 2000 the figure on the shirt could be $154,000.[4]

Why be concerned about preparing for college? For one thing, the cost. Of course, there is always the need for a college education just to make it in this world. No matter how you look at it, it all boils down to finances. Most parents and students, while they might not admit it publicly, look at college as a way of getting ahead. There is certainly the desire to increase one's knowledge, but basically, a prestigious job that pays well is the real goal. Now, there isn't anything wrong with this if getting a good education is part of the plan. But let's be realistic. Financial considerations are high, maybe the highest, on the list of priorities for choosing college.

College costs are astronomical. Some of the "bargain" colleges will still set you back nearly five thousand dollars per year in tuition and fees and room and board. This doesn't include transportation costs, books, and miscellaneous expenses, such as entertainment, clothing, eating out, and dating. At prestigious institutions like Harvard in Massachusetts, Dartmouth in New Hampshire, Yale in Connecticut, University of Chicago in Illinois, and Brown in Rhode Island, you can expect to pay nearly eighteen thousand dollars per year. This would be like purchasing a new medium-priced automobile every year for four years with no trade-in allowance.

If you are going to spend this kind of money, you had better be prepared to get your money's worth. There are no refunds. Flunking out after one year still sets you back at least five thousand dollars. Those who flunk out do so because they do not study, never learned to study, or just goof off. All these handicaps can be corrected if you decide to apply yourself.

THE DOMINION FACTOR

But what should be the ultimate reason for pursuing a college education? A good job and lots of money never saved anyone. There are many men and women with great educations who are sending this nation into the very pits of hell. For the Christian, education is a tool and an expression of our commitment to our Lord. Getting a good education makes us better servants for our Master. Someone who understands how the world works is best able to have dominion over it. All our efforts should be directed to bring glory to God. What is man's chief end? In the words of the Shorter Catechism, "Man's chief end is to glorify God and to enjoy Him forever." Education then is simply a means to an end. The end is service to our great God and King. If Christians fail to see education in these terms, we can expect others to pick up the concept of dominion and run with it in service to a different god and king. This is why Christian students should be the best students, motivated by the greatest purpose.

Those who teach set the agenda for the nation. Whatever worldview prevails in our universities will filter through the entire nation. Today's students are tomorrow's doctors, lawyers, judges, engineers, teachers, politicians, and economists. America's earliest colleges were established to set the agenda for all of life. Harvard was our nation's first college in the colonies. It's reason for existence was clearly spelled out.

The University in Colonial America

Harvard College was founded in 1636, only six years after the settlement of the Massachusetts Bay Colony. Its purpose was clearly Christian:

> Let every student be plainly instructed, and earnestly pressed to consider well, the main end of his life and studies is, to know God and Jesus Christ which is eternal life (John 17:3), and therefore to lay Christ in the bottom, as the only foundation of all sound knowledge and Learning.[5]

The same theme was echoed over one hundred years later at the founding of King's College, the predecessor of Columbia University. In 1745, the president of the school wrote:

The chief thing that is aimed at in this college is to teach and engage the Children to know God in Jesus Christ, and to love and serve Him, in all sobriety, godliness, and righteousness of life, with a perfect heart, and a willing mind.[6]

Yale in the early 1700s stated its primary goal: "[E]very student shall consider the main end of his study [to be] to know God in Jesus Christ and answerably to lead a Godly, sober life."[7]

The Puritan educational system trained church and civil leaders. The emphasis, however, was to train men so that future generations would not be left with "an illiterate ministry." The curriculum of Harvard, for example, emphasized the study of Biblical languages, logic, divinity (theology), and skills in communication (public speaking and rhetoric). Churches expected their ministers to read the Bible in the original languages. Remember, ministers were the primary educators and sources of information in the colonies. This was especially true in the New England colonies.[8] At Princeton, even those who did not enter the gospel ministry were expected to know their "Bible from cover to cover."

Since civil government was a major concern in the colonies, courses in ethics, political science, and history were also required. Many of the eighteenth-century framers of the Constitution had been steeped in basic Bible doctrines. These Biblical concepts were incorporated into our Constitutional political system (e.g., decentralized political power; checks and balances; a republican form of government; abhorrence of democracy; jurisdictional separation of family, church, and State; a design for stability in the rule of law; private property; the gold standard; the keeping of the Lord's Day; and the protection of Christian worship).

Courses in law and medicine were offered, along with astronomy, physics, botany, science, and mathematics. During the colonial period, from 1636 when Harvard was established to 1769 when Dartmouth was founded, nearly all the colleges were established as Christian institutions for the purpose of establishing a Christian civilization.

These early collegians were thoroughly versed in all branches of knowledge, including Greek and Roman writers and philosophers. Students had to be "able extempore to read, construe, and parse Tully, Virgil, and the Greek Testament; and to write true Latin in prose."[9]

The Christian's goal, therefore, is to bring every thought captive to the Lord Jesus Christ. Every branch of knowledge should be studied so it can be used for the extension of His kingdom. Anything less is less than true Christianity. I believe that it's a fair conclusion that without these early Christian colleges our nation would never have been born. **149**

GETTING A HEAD START

The purpose of the following sections is to evaluate where you are academically, to locate weak points, and to see how they can be strengthened. There is very little you can do to make up all the ground you may have lost. But it's not hopeless. If you're a high school sophomore or junior, you can put much of this material to work for you NOW! Seniors do not have the luxury of time on their side. For them, time is the great enemy. But there is always time for some improvement.

TAKING A PERSONAL INVENTORY

Socrates (469-399 B.C.) wrote: "The unexamined life is not worth living." There is truth in this. Examining ourselves for our strengths and weaknesses is not a pleasant task. We don't like to learn that something might be wrong with us. In fact, this is one of the reasons some people avoid going to the doctor for a checkup! They might find that something is wrong. But the point is to identify what's wrong and then correct it. Correction can never take place if you don't know what's wrong.

Academic Ability

First, evaluate yourself as a student. This might require having honest discussions with your teachers concerning your abilities. Their views are important. Teachers have been students, have graduated from college, and probably have done some graduate work. They know what it's like to go through the grind. (They may not have seemed so wise while they were teaching you, but their wisdom increases as you get closer to graduation. This goes double for parents.)

Don't be discouraged if the evaluation comes out negative. Many high school students with poor grades make it in college. They grow up. There's more at stake.

Don't dismiss your teachers' criticisms and suggestions. And don't be devastated if they tell you that you're not "college material." Negative comments should make you all the more prepared for what might be coming. It's better to be over-prepared than to be deceived about your abilities: "Pride goes before destruction, and a haughty spirit before stumbling" (Proverbs 16:18; cf. 11:2; 18:12). I mentioned in the Introduction that one of my high school counselors told my parents that I was not "college material." Based on the work I did in school, they were probably right. But I went to college with greater resolve to prove them wrong. If you are anything like me, your work in high school is not indicative of how well you can do in college. I do wish, however, that I had those years back to be a better student.

Make sure you talk to *all* your teachers. Your parents should be a part of this. *Do not exclude them from your affairs.* Take some notes. This will get you into practice for the rigors of college life. The common evaluations will be most helpful. If all your teachers give similar criticisms about the same areas, whether academic or attitude, then you know that this is something you'll have to work on. If you can, get a copy of your transcript. Teachers are often required to make year-end comments. They are usually brutally honest. This is where I learned that "Gary is not working up to his abilities."

Here are some additional ways to evaluate yourself:

1. *How well did I do on the SAT (Scholastic Aptitude Test) and/or the ACT (American College Testing Program)?* The SAT tests English and Math skills. The English section is much more important than the Math, unless Math will occupy a major portion of your course work. The ACT tests a broader range of knowledge. Your scores will give you *some* idea of your abilities. I'm not convinced that these tests rightly measure a student's abilities to do college work. There's much more to academic life than standardized tests. While you should not minimize the importance of these tests, don't get too bent out of shape if you don't score above nine hundred on the SAT. Of course, don't forget that colleges look at, in addition to standardized tests, your grade point average (GPA) and class rank in determining if you are fit for college. They will even glance at how active you were with clubs and general school activities.

2. *Do I read well?* Getting through college is going to be a problem (but not an insurmountable one) if you have difficulty reading. Nearly every course is loaded with reading material. You won't have the luxury of reading just one book a month. Each course you take may require that you read three to four books per semester. This is in addition to your textbooks. Speed is not the essential element, however. Understanding, remembering, and having the ability to present the author's thesis and his display of facts are most important. Much of what you'll be reading will be boring and seemingly irrelevant (more often than not it will be irrelevant). But, the practice of reading will make you a better reader. You will be surprised how well you understand and remember if you read on a regular basis. Reading is like any activity; the more you practice the easier it gets.

3. *Do I write well?* Reading, spending time in class, and writing papers will occupy most of your time. Nearly every professor will require papers. Many tests are made up of essay questions. Writing skills are mandatory. I'm going to assume that you have done very little writing in high school. While you may have written book reports and a few essays, your ability to research a topic thoroughly and write a lengthy paper is probably minimal. Most high school English departments will have you do one long paper your senior year. What you really need is at least two research papers each year of high school. What if you feel inadequate in this area? Take a course during the summer at a local college or junior college. Do some writing on your own and do a lot of reading.

4. *Are my poor grades the result of a lack of intelligence or a lack of hard work?* If you expended little effort in high school (and made it) and are willing to put forth a lot of effort in college, you'll probably make it there as well. Remember, it's hard to break bad habits. Most students see their grade point average drop one point when they enter college. If you're getting B's now, expect C's for a while. If C's fill your report card, then you had better be on your guard. You must get to work the first day of class and keep it up. Don't relax until you feel you have a handle on what's going on. All is not hopeless. Good grades have more to do with self-discipline and strong motivation than with a high IQ.

5. *Am I a good thinker?* Can you follow a discussion, analyze its main points, find the presuppositions the speaker is using to support his thesis, and determine if the facts support the presuppositions? Can you then marshal an adequate defense? You may not be able to give an answer on the spot, but you should be able to formulate the parameters for an answer. Reread the first seven chapters in this book. High school rarely teaches you to think. Some colleges expect it. You might want to study a few books on how to think. I've found the following ones to be helpful:[10]

- S. Morris Engel, *With Good Reason: An Introduction to Informal Fallacies* (3rd ed.; New York: St. Martin's Press, 1986).
- James Greene and David Lewis, *Know Your Own Mind: Nine Tests That Tell You What You Do Best* (New York: Rawson Associates, 1983).
- Allen F. Harrison and Robert M. Bramson, *Styles of Thinking: Strategies for Asking Questions, Making Decisions, and Solving Problems* (Garden City, New York: Anchor Press/Doubleday, 1982).
- A. J. Hoover, *Don't You Believe It!: Poking Holes in Faulty Logic* (Chicago, IL: Moody Press, 1982).

- David Lewis and James Greene, *Thinking Better* (New York: Wason, Wade Publishers, 1982).

- Linda Perigo Moore, *You're Smarter Than You Think* (New York: Holt, Rinehart and Winston, 1985).

- Alex C. Michalos, *Improving Your Reasoning* (Englewood Cliffs, NJ: Prentice-Hall, 1970).

- Robert A. Morey, *The New Atheism and the Erosion of Freedom* (Minneapolis, MN: Bethany House, 1986).

Most bookstores will carry books on how to think, but reading them will be of little value unless you implement their suggestions on a daily basis. Practice these new skills by evaluating what you read in the newspapers and what you hear and see on radio and television newscasts. Radio talk-shows are great for putting thinking courses to work.

6. *Do I enjoy learning?* The answer to this question might not seem very important, but it may detect an attitude problem that is hindering some very important intellectual gifts. While it helps to be academically oriented, it's not necessary. Many students see college only as a stepping stone to a job. This is fine if you understand that you're going to have to put up with academics for at least four years. But there is much more to life than getting a degree. Learning is part of the Christian life. The Bible tells us that we are to worship God with all our "mind." We are not being a complete Christian if we put our mind on a shelf and only pull it down on those rare occasions when we think it will come in handy. Learning is "thinking God's thoughts after Him." Johannes Kepler (1571-1630), an eminent Christian scientist, wrote: "O God, I am thinking thy thoughts after thee." The idea that all knowledge must originate with God led Kepler to learn more about the Creator in His creation. He discovered the laws of planetary motion and established the discipline of celestial mechanics. Kepler wrote: "We astronomers are priests of the highest God in regard to the book of nature, not of the glory of our minds, but rather, above all else, of the glory of God."[11]

7. *How "culturally literate" am I?* Recent studies by the Department of Education and the National Endowment for the Humanities were critical of the level of education that high school seniors generally receive. Keep in mind that there's no way to tell how well you're doing if your classmates are receiving the same inadequate education. When you get to college, you will be competing with the best from all over the world. The level of excellence increases at the college level. So it's important

that you know how good of an education you received. If it was a good one, then you shouldn't have any problems. A poor or even a fair education, however, could bring unwanted and unnecessary anxieties. But even here, things are not hopeless.

A good place to begin is with "cultural literacy." "To be culturally literate is to possess the basic information needed to thrive in the modern world. The breadth of that information is great, extending over the major domains of human activity from sports to science."[12] Consider the following results of a survey of college freshmen in the state of Georgia:

> While nearly half of today's Georgia college freshmen can name the four ex-Beatles, only two in one hundred can list four current members of the U.S. Supreme Court. Thirty percent can't name either of Georgia's two U.S. senators. One-quarter of them think that the population of the United States exceeds 1 billion.[13]

How well did you do? Can you name the two Senators from your own state? Do you even know that there are only two senators? A study sponsored by the National Endowment for the Humanities found similar deficiencies across the country. A generally accepted theory has been adopted that says concepts are more important than facts. The adage goes something like this: "Teach them *how* to think not *what* to think." The truth is, facts *and* thinking are important. An individual may be taught how to think but have very little to think about. If a student is unaware of how problems were solved in previous generations or even of the issues that arose over two hundred years ago, what good are his "thinking skills"? The past teaches us valuable lessons. Why repeat past mistakes and pay the same or even a greater price? What would you think of a doctor who had the skills necessary to be a doctor but knew very little about how the human body works, where your organs are located, how to identify diseases, and what treatment to prescribe for a cure? You wouldn't want him operating on you.

How does cultural or "world knowledge" help you in your pursuit of a college education? What you know about the world acts as background information to help you network ideas, words, figures of speech, and literary concepts. It is this background information that allows you to pick up anything and read without always asking this question: What does he mean by this? If an author writes, for example, that "the many dialects of China have turned this once great nation into a babel of confusion," you will understand his meaning. Your knowledge of the confusion of tongues in Genesis, chapter 11 helps you understand the author's meaning without his having to elaborate. His reference to "babel" tells a large story with just one word. But the important thing is that he assumes you know the meaning of the word. Most writers assume that their readers have a reservoir of background knowledge, that they've read Shakespeare, John Bunyan's *Pilgrim's Progress*, Milton's *Paradise Lost*, and a whole host of other famous writers and their works. How many times have you heard "It was the best of times, it was the worst of times" without ever understanding the depth of meaning attached to the words because you have never read Charles Dickens' *A Tale of Two Cities*? These immortal words open the book's entry into one of the darkest periods of human history, the French Revolution. Most have heard the book's closing lines as well without fully grasping their rare and heart-rending meaning: "It is a far, far better thing that I do, than I have ever done; it is a far, far better rest that I go to than I have ever known." It also takes a Bible to understand Dickens. Can Melville's *Moby Dick* be neglected if we truly want to be culturally literate? Without a broad spectrum of knowledge, reading becomes extremely difficult and frustrating. Too much is missed.

Cultural literacy tests do not measure a person's intelligence. You could be a genius and still not be culturally literate. But there is a correlation between cultural literacy and college performance.

8. *What's my IQ?* Most high schools make it a policy not to tell a student his or her IQ. For obvious reasons. A low IQ can be a self-fulfilling prophecy, and a high IQ can make a potentially good student lethargic. But too much has been made of the results of IQ tests. Who knows how many people have stayed out of college because of low IQ's. These tests are far too limited in measuring the intelligence of young people. They test only a small segment of human ability. Intelligence can be measured in a number of ways. The standard IQ test is not designed to measure all facets of intelligence. Consider the following list of "Seven Ways to be Bright":

Linguistic: Language skills include a sensitivity to the subtle shades of the meanings of words.

Logical-Mathematical: Both critics and supporters acknowledge that IQ tests measure this ability well.

Musical: Like language, music is an expressive medium—and this talent flourishes in prodigies.

Spatial: Sculptors and painters are able accurately to perceive, manipulate and re-create forms.

Bodily-Kinesthetic: At the core of this kind of intelligence are body control and skilled handling of objects.

Interpersonal: Skill in reading the moods and intentions of others is displayed by politicians, among others.

Intrapersonal: The key is understanding one's own feelings–and using that insight to guide behavior.[14]

I would hazard a guess and say that there are probably more than seven ways to be bright. You've probably known some really "IQ smart" people who just can't get it together. At the same time, someone who did not do well in school can turn out to be a "genius."

Thomas Edison, for example, overheard a teacher say that he was "addled."[15] Telling a kid he's stupid and confused is the same as telling him that he has a low IQ and will not amount to much. Edison also had a profound "distaste for mathematics" after a long study of Isaac Newton's *Principles*.[16] Edison ridiculed the "academical philosophers," believing that they were "engrossed with barren syllogisms, or equational theorems . . . and disdained to soil their hands with those handicraft operations at which all improvements in the arts must necessarily begin."[17]

The "addled" Thomas Edison is a rare genius with 1093 patents issued in his name, the most famous being for the light bulb and phonograph. As one critic of IQ tests says: "You can be smart in one thing and stupid in something else."[18] One long-range study found that a third of all the professionals it tracked had below-average childhood IQ's.

Here's "An IQ Test for the Real World":[19]

Insight questions

1. Fifteen percent of the people in a certain town have unlisted telephone numbers. You select two hundred names at random from the local phone book. How many of these people can be expected to have unlisted telephone numbers?

2. A man who lived in a small town married twenty different women in that same town. All of them are still living, and he never divorced any of them. Yet he broke no laws. How could he do this?

3. According to the United States Constitution, if the Vice President of the United States should die, who would be the President?

Novel thinking questions

Assume that the statement given before the analogy is true, and use that statement to solve the analogy.

4. VILLAINS are lovable. HERO is to ADMIRATION as VILLAIN is to: CONTEMPT / AFFECTION / CRUEL / KIND.

5. LEMONS are animals. LIME is to GREEN as LEMON is to: YELLOW / ORANGE / GROW / PICK.

6. NEEDLES are dull. THIMBLE is to BLUNT as NEEDLE is to: SHARP / SMOOTH / STAB / BRUISE.

7. SPARROWS play hopscotch. TROUT is to SCALY as SPARROW is to: FEATHERY / BUMPY / EAGLE / CANARY.

8. COBRAS drink lemonade. ROBIN is to BIRD as COBRA is to: DESERT / LIZARD / SNAKE / JUNGLE.

Inference questions

How would you classify the relationships between these words?

9. COVER : BOOK

10. EMPTY SET : NULL SET

11. EARLY : LATE

12. CLUE : HINT

13. NEW : ORLEANS

14. X OR Y : NOT X AND NOT Y

15. HEAVENLY : HELLISH

How well did you do? The answers are found in Endnote 19. Don't ever allow a low IQ to discourage you, not even one designed for the "real world." Much of what passes as "intelligence" and "genius" is simply hard work, which is, by the way, a mark of intelligence. Too often we evaluate the finished project of a supposed genius and don't realize how much work he actually put into the enterprise.

Ludwig van Beethoven was a genius. But when his music is heard few people really consider how much time he actually put into a finished symphony. "Yet, upon inspection of his sketchbooks, over five thousand pages of preliminary musical themes, phrases, and revisions make it clear that Beethoven worked hard to perfect his genius."[20] Don't be dismayed if things don't come easily the first time. Intelligence should be measured by willingness to take on, persist in, and complete a task, and learning what works and doesn't work in the process.

STUDY HABITS

Disciplined study habits can turn an average student into an academic marvel. Most "smart" students just work hard. There aren't that many geniuses out there. Perseverance is what you're after. By staying with a task long enough you'll gain proficiency. Here are a few questions to help you evaluate your study habits:

		Preferred answer
1.	Do I schedule my study time?	*Yes*
2.	Do I stick to my schedule?	*Yes*
3.	Do I have trouble settling down to begin my studying?	*No*
4.	Am I easily distracted when I study?	*No*
5.	Do I find any possible excuse to delay my studying?	*No*
6.	Do I work without my parents always prodding me?	*Yes*
7.	Do I work hard and not just enough to get by?	*Yes*
8.	Do I get my work in on time?	*Yes*
9.	Do I participate in class discussions?	*Yes*
10.	Do I sit in the back of the class?	*No*
11.	When I have trouble with my work, do I talk over any difficulties with my teacher?	*Yes*
12.	Do I take good lecture notes?	*Yes*
13.	Do I read over my lecture notes the day I take them?	*Yes*
14.	Do I wait to the last minute to get assignments in?	*No*
15.	Do I panic when exam time comes?	*No*
16.	Do I stay up late to study for exams?	*No*
17.	Do I quit in frustration when I encounter a difficult problem?	*No*
18.	Do I turn in clean and neat papers?	*Yes*
19.	Do I put extra effort in my assignments?	*Yes*
20.	Do I often fail surprise exams?	*No*
21.	Do I maximize my time?	*Yes*
22.	Do I prepare adequately for class?	*Yes*
23.	Do I begin my day in Bible study and prayer?	*Yes*

Disciplined study habits take time to develop. Make every effort to change any and all bad habits you have. The poor student can pull his grades up a point or two by following the *mechanics* of study. More often than not, poor grades are the result of not knowing how to study. Taking this short inventory will give you some idea of how well you perform. Let me give you an example. When a master carpenter wants to build, say, a cabinet, the first thing he does is make a drawing. This is his plan. He will then choose the materials he needs. But one of the most important aspects of carpentry is having the appropriate tools. Many do-it-yourselfers leave a partially constructed project in frustration because, halfway through, they learn that the tools needed to do a very simple task are nowhere to be found. These amateurs may never attempt another project because they think they lack the necessary skills. They fail to see the importance of having perseverance and the right tools. Persevere in the tasks you need to perform and find out what tools you need. Finally, use those tools for all they're worth, and your skills will develop.

AVOIDING ACADEMIC ATROPHY

A fitness craze has been sweeping the country for some time. The young and the old and the fat and the flabby want sleek, revitalized bodies. But most people who enter the exercise grind find out that getting a lethargic and lifeless body into shape is not an easy task. Firming up a walking corpse takes a lot of time and work.

The first day is the toughest. After a minute of vigorous activity, you begin to realize how out of shape you really are. You can't keep up with that energetic instructor who looks like she could go all day. And she's not even sweating! Your shortness of breath turns into gasping. The legs that get you from the dorm to the classroom now feel as heavy as logs. Your arms have turned to lead. All you can think about is rest. Being out of shape isn't really so bad compared to the self-induced agony of the exercise room.

A day after lifting weights, doing aerobics, and peddling on a Life-Cycle, your body goes into a stage-two reaction. You're sore and stiff. The slightest movement brings on a rush of pain from muscles you never realized you had. Why? An unused muscle gets soft. It's still there, but it's not used often enough during your daily routine to stretch its fibers. On your first day in the gym you forced these dormant muscle groups to "get physical." Oh, they responded, but they didn't like it. The following day tells you why. It hurts!

In time, however, your muscles adjust to the rigors of exercise. Like Milo of Crotona,[21] you find yourself getting stronger with each day's routine. What was once a sorry excuse for a body gradually becomes toned and physically fit.

The mind is like the body. When it isn't pushed into service, it does as little as possible. But when concentrated critical thinking is demanded, an untrained, atrophied mind behaves like an undisciplined body—it falters under the demands of rigorous mental activity. Getting the mind into mental shape is no less difficult than getting the body into top physical condition. Progress is slow and often imperceptible. Incremental change is not very rewarding, but it's the only way to achieve long-term success.

Don't take an academic vacation during the summer months. As any athlete knows, it's harder getting in shape than staying in shape. Your mind has been exercised during your senior year of high school, especially during final exam week. Take a *brief* rest, continue your academic pursuits, and work on any academic deficiencies you have. Here are some suggestions:

Maintain Heavy Academic Training

1. *Read at least one non-fiction book a week.* Diversify your reading to include philosophy, theology, history, American and English literature, fiction, economics, ethics, politics, law, art, music, etc. This is to bolster your "cultural literacy." Focus on reading where you are the weakest, where you have little knowledge. Practice your note-taking and reading techniques.

2. *Write to the college you're planning to attend and find out if there is a freshman reading list.* Many schools have a general English course that all freshmen are required to take. Get a jump on your classmates and relieve some first semester tension by sending a self-addressed stamped envelope to the appropriate department. You can save some money by checking the books out at your neighborhood library.

3. *Develop and maintain a daily schedule of study, work, reading, and recreation.* This will prepare you for freshman shock. Get up early. (Plan on having an eight-o'clock class. Freshmen get the leftovers when it comes to scheduling. Freshmen who have eight-o'clock classes also get the newest teachers. Teachers with tenure get to pick their hours.)

4. *Get a job during the summer months and save as much as you can.* You'll need it. Maintaining good grades while working at a job is an arduous task. This will give you some idea of what to expect if you decide to work while going to college. Some colleges, however, prohibit freshmen from working.

5. *You might want to take a course or two at a local college or junior college to keep you in academic shape.* Choose your weakest subject. Summer classes are often easier and less expensive. There's a relaxed atmosphere during the summer. Make sure your summer courses will transfer to the college you have decided to attend. Get their assurances in writing.

Working on the Finer Points

Vocabulary: One of the ways to give flair to your writing is to color it with a rich vocabulary. There are a number of ways to build your vocabulary in such a way that the use of new words does not become stilted. You can memorize lists of words and their various meanings. The Visual Education Association (Vis-Ed) has a set of one thousand cards (English Vocabulary Cards). A word is printed on the front, and spelled phonetically for proper pronunciation. Each word is used in a sentence and is printed on the back of the card along with a definition. These cards can be ordered from any bookstore, but your nearest local college bookstore should have a good supply. Obviously, this is not the best way to learn new vocabulary. But it can help you with your reading.

The *Reader's Digest* has a section called "Building Your Word Power." There are numerous books that promise to help you build a better vocabulary. *Thirty Days to a More Powerful Vocabulary* by Dr. Wilfred Funk and Norman Lewis is just one. But the best way to build your vocabulary is to *read, read,* and *read.* Underline the words you do not know or are unsure of. Look them up in a dictionary as you go and place brief definitions in the margins of the book. When you finish a chapter look back over it and review your list. A rich vocabulary is not designed to impress your classmates or your professors. I'm thinking more about building a vocabulary to help you with finding just the right word when writing those many college research papers. One of the most frustrating things about writing is trying to come up with the right word without using the same words over and over again. *Roget's Thesaurus* (many editions) is quite good as is *The Synonym Finder* by J. I. Rodale.[22] These are all helpful vocabulary builders.

Another good reason for building a rich vocabulary is to understand the technical jargon of your chosen field of study. Also, professors like to use their own specialized lingo. In order to cope, you'll have to know some of what they're talking about.

Learning prefixes, suffixes, and commonly used roots can be a great help in building your vocabulary. Many English words are made up of

Greek and Latin prefixes and suffixes. For example, atheism is made up of two words, *a* which means not and *theos* which means god. An atheist believes there is no God. Agnostic is a combination of two words: *a* meaning not and *gnosis* meaning knowledge. An agnostic does not know if God exists. A table of prefixes, roots, and suffixes is included in the back of the book.

Foreign language: Check your college catalog to see if you will have to take a foreign language. Keep your high school language skills alive by reviewing vocabulary, verb forms, syntax, and case endings. There are a number of audio cassette courses available. The Visual Education Association has vocabulary cards for nearly every language, even Biblical Hebrew and Greek. The best way to learn a foreign language is the way you learned English: hearing it and using what you've heard. There are numerous audio and video language courses on the market today. If you are really interested in learning a foreign language, then I would suggest getting Mary Pride's *The Big Book of Home Learning* (1986) and *The Next Book of Home Learning* (1987). These books contain a wealth of information on foreign languages as well as many other subjects. They are published by Crossway Books, Westchester, Illinois.

General knowledge: Writing papers is rough on the uninitiated. Successful writing depends on a number of factors. One flaw in otherwise good writing manuals is the lack of emphasis on collateral support material from seemingly unrelated subject matter. You will impress your prof if you can show, for example, how epistemology (get that dictionary) is broader than philosophy. Epistemology is the foundation of every discipline. You should be able to show that before an adequate economic, political, and legal social policy can be formulated, the epistemological foundation must first be established. Quoting appropriate sources in each of these fields will enhance your writing by leaps and bounds. Read everything you can get your hands on. Play "Trivial Pursuit" or "College Pursuit" every night during the summer. Keep some note cards with you to jot down ideas or bits of information from casual reading in magazines, novels, and newsletters. Get *Cultural Literacy* by Hirsch and *What Do Our Seventeen-Year-Olds Know?* by Diane Ravitch and Chester E. Finn, published by Harper & Row.

Spelling: Poor spelling can ruin even a great paper. Some instructors will deduct points for even one misspelled word. Get a book on improving your spelling. Pick up an English Grammar book and review some of the rules (i before e except after c and in words like neighbor and weigh). It wouldn't hurt to review basic phonetic rules.

Speaking: There are some courses that require oral exams. This can be quite a shock if you're not used to speaking in public. A high school course in public speaking can be of great value. If you have a real fear in this area, avoid any classes that require an oral exam. There will be times, however, when you will have to make an oral presentation to your class. Speaking is like writing. Practice makes perfect.[23]

The Library: Visit a local college library and familiarize yourself with the reference section. Determine what reference materials will be of great value in writing essays, book reviews, and research papers. Learn how to use the *Guide to Periodical Literature*. Make sure you know how to use the card catalogue (author, title, subject). Learn the basics of the Dewey Decimal System and/or the Library of Congress System before you get to college. Your college catalog should indicate which system the library follows.

Typing: Sign up for the basic typing course that your school offers, if you're still in high school. Finding a good available typist in college may be difficult. Paying for one may be impossible. You might pay two dollars per page. If there are footnotes as opposed to endnotes, the cost might be higher. You can teach yourself to type well enough to get you through. Taking a class during the summer would probably be a better idea. The course will force you to do the repetitious exercises necessary to become a proficient typist. A shorthand course might not be a bad idea if you want some real help with your note-taking.

Going the Junior or Community College Route

One way to save money and, at the same time, get many of your difficult courses out of the way is to enroll in a junior college. If you're looking for academic prestige, don't worry. In most cases your future employer will only be concerned about where you earned your degree. He'll know that you can cut it. Four-year institutions will know that you can make the grade if you were an average student in high school but picked up your grades during your junior college stay.

The junior or community college route may be the way to go if high school was a disaster, but you've now come to your senses and want to improve your academic standing. It may be that you're not ready to move away from home. You got yourself a good job during the summer, and you've found you can work and go to college and stay at home. This way you can finance your first two years with no debt.

Whatever you do, make sure that the courses you take will transfer to a four-year institution. Don't be satisfied with general answers like,

"Most colleges accept our graduates," or "Our courses transfer easily." Get it all in writing. You should spend some time with your junior college counselor to find out what four-year institutions accept the credits of the junior college you're considering attending. If you have a four-year college picked out, coordinate your courses at the junior college with those required by the transfer school.

Gaining College Credits Without Taking a Course

Many educational institutions have developed policies and procedures for granting academic credit for college equivalent skills and competencies. There are a number of ways to receive this credit. If you know a subject well enough, you can receive college credit by passing a test. One of the most well known tests is the College Level Examination Program (CLEP). The College Board and Educational Testing Service offer free information on the CLEP as an option for credit. Write to: CLEP, P.O. Box 1822, Princeton, New Jersey 08541. The test covers five general areas (English composition, mathematics, humanities, natural sciences, and social studies/history) and a number of specific subject areas. Sometimes a school department (e.g., the history department) will construct an exam similar to the CLEP. (You'll probably have to pay the same tuition fees.) You can find the CLEP study manuals at most bookstores. These manuals will give you some idea of your readiness for taking the test. For departmental tests, you'll have to contact your college.

You will receive either a grade for your score or a pass/fail. (You can get credit for the course but no grade. When figuring your GPA, a pass/fail course will not be included in the computation.) Check out the policy before you test. A good grade will help your GPA; a pass mark won't hurt it.

CONCLUSION

Preparing for college is a full-time job. It includes more than just taking a few tests. The heart, mind, and body must be ready to do the job. In order to be equipped for the academic contest that awaits you, you must begin now to develop the proper skills.

10
HOW TO STUDY

Most of us have gone through the rather painful experience of cramming for an exam. The "magic-marker syndrome" is a well-established academic phenomenon. That's when, the night before a test, the student takes out a yellow magic marker and proceeds to underline large sections of the textbook in hopes of memorizing and retaining giant chunks of data just long enough to regurgitate them back onto the test page in the classroom the following morning. Within twenty-four hours of the test, chances are good that little or none of the data has been retained. What has been retained, however, is a massive hangover which often lingers on for several days. Students get "up" for the exam and afterwards they "crash." This is the typical pattern set in the American education system.[1]

WE would all like to learn through osmosis. Unfortunately, it just doesn't happen that way. Putting a book under your pillow at night won't cut it. Studying takes time and persistent effort. In this sense, studying is really no different from any other discipline you've mastered. You have "studied" and learned a whole variety of complicated subjects. The same procedure should be followed for classroom subjects. If there is a difference between life courses and school courses it's in the area of immediate relevance or (let's be honest) interest. But if college is required for your career choices, then you are stuck with the system. So make the best of it by understanding the best methods for study.

Learning to do the things you did well as you were growing up was not as difficult as studying for a Western Civilization exam. You didn't "study" the rules for baseball, football, or basketball. By the time you were old enough to drive you knew most of the traffic laws and the general procedures for operating an automobile. What about cooking, writing, reading, and swimming? There are numerous things that you do well that took very little effort to master. At least now it doesn't seem like it was that difficult. You have been following the elements of a study methodology all your life. Now it's time to transfer those naturally developed techniques to new learning situations.

DEVELOPING A METHODOLOGY

Henry Wadsworth Longfellow (1807-1882) wrote: "If you would hit the mark, you must aim a little above it; every arrow that flies feels the attraction of earth." He also penned this bit of verse: "I shot an arrow into the air, it fell to earth, I knew not where." Putting a modern twist to Longfellow's words, we get: If you aim at nothing, you're bound to hit it.

Studying requires planning, a method for reaching a set of goals. The reasons for this are obvious. First, all types of activities compete for your time. We want to aim "high" to avoid the "attraction" of these outside interests. A workable methodology for study will keep you on track when you are tempted to follow short cuts to learning. Second, a method of study establishes goals. You "aim" at something and work to achieve it. You know you've been successful when you "hit" it. A study methodology is a tool to help you accomplish what needs to be done. If there's nothing to aim at, then there's nothing to hit.

Learning by Bits and Pieces

When I was in high school, I was really *interested* in track and field. I participated in a number of events, all *field* events. Very rarely did I ever run in a *track* event like the 100 meters. I never ran a *distance* event. There was a time when I could recite the world record in every event and the athlete who held it. After looking at the results of a track meet in the Sunday paper, I could tell you the time, heights, and distances of all the winners after only one reading. What makes a task like this easy? I believe there are four facets of developing a good study methodology:

interest, familiarity, categorization, and *discipline.* Let's go back to the track and field example.

First, there is an obvious *interest* in the subject. The most interesting subjects are the easiest to learn. But if we were interested in everything then there would be no need for this chapter. Learning would be easy. Sometimes it's just not possible to summon interest when we need it most.

There are times when you can create interest in a subject that seems to hold no interest for you. Let's say you are studying the philosophy of science, but your real area of interest is political science. Are there points of contact between these two seemingly diverse subjects? Can the information you gather in the philosophy of science help you in political science? There are probably many points of contact, but let's take just one. Does science have anything to do with politics at any level? I believe it has. If the scientific community creates ethical dilemmas with their theories, how should legislation be drafted to accommodate or overrule them? When science makes the determination, for example, that human embryos are nothing more than tissue, can a legislature draft a bill to allow laboratories to harvest developing embryos for potential organ transplantation? These courses and the questions they raise can be coordinated with courses in ethics, philosophy, and history. "Noted Berkeley biologist Thomas H. Jukes has declared that in a few years we will hear of 'the rights of bacteria,' since all that differentiates bacteria from humanity is a 'disparity in the length and sequence of DNA molecules.'"[2] What does the political scientist do with this?

Second, familiarity with a subject is a great help in learning. The more you work with a subject the more familiar you become with it. Unfortunately, most learning is one-time learning. The immediate goal is to learn it for a test. After the test there is no more need for the material. You then move on to other unfamiliar material. The best way to familiarize yourself with this new material is to associate it with things you already know. Again, look for contact points in fields that have familiar subject matter. This takes some practice. The chapter on memory will outline this technique in more detail.

Third, the sport of track and field is broken down into categories: *track* and *field* events. Track events are broken down further: sprints, hurdles, distance events, and relays. Field events are the weight or throwing events and jumping events. The categories look like this (all distances are in meters except where noted):

TRACK EVENTS

Sprints: 100, 200, 400, 800 (sometimes considered a distance event).

Hurdles: 110, 400.

Distance: 1500 (also called the "metric mile"), mile, 3000-meter steeple-chase (with stationary hurdles and water jumps), 5000, 10,000, marathon (26 miles, 385 yards).

RELAYS

4 × 100, 4 × 400

FIELD EVENTS

Throwing: shot-put, discus, javelin, hammer.

Jumping: long jump, triple jump, high jump, pole vault.

The Decathlon is the Olympic event that seems to get the most attention. It is made up of ten (from the Greek *deka*) events taken from each of the track and field categories except the relays. The women compete in the Heptathlon which consists of seven events (from the Greek *hepta*). The women do not have the triple jump, hammer throw, steeplechase, or pole vault. Team events consist of sprint and distance relays. Spectators are more familiar with the outdoor events, but there are also a number of indoor events, such as the 50-and 60-meter dashes, 600 meters, 60-meter hurdles, and the thirty-five pound-weight throw.

What can this categorization teach us? If you were asked to learn this scheme for a physical education class, how would you go about it? You probably have little interest, but you have to pass the test. A physical education course is needed to round out your liberal arts requirements. Do you have a *system* for studying? Do you just dive in or do you work out a *methodology* that acts as a track to take you through each bit of new information?

Without a study methodology, most students get overwhelmed with the enormous amount of new information they must learn. Many give up in frustration or do just enough studying to get by. Add the simple physical education learning task to all the other things to be learned, not only in the physical education class but also in the more difficult subjects, and you begin to see the formidable task that's before you. The key is found in the track and field example. By breaking down your study assignments into bite-sized pieces, the difficulty factor is minimized.

Science has categories of study that include the following: *biology* (the study of living things); *physics* (the study of the properties of and interactions between matter and energy); *astronomy* (the study of celestial bodies, including galaxies, stars, planets, moons, etc.); *geology* (the study of the earth and its physical history); *anthropology* (the study of man and his origins). Each of these areas can be broken down into even smaller categories.

History has its broad sweeps of historical demarcations that go back as far as "pre-historical." (Of course, this is a deceptive way of denying the Biblical revelation which maintains that the opening words of Genesis begin history: "In the beginning, God created the heavens and the earth.")

This technique of categorizing new material is crucial to student study success. It works equally well in scheduling time.

Fourth, without discipline, the best intentions and the best techniques are useless. You must commit to follow through with putting these techniques to work. This will mean changing the way you think and work. Changing old habits is a three-step process: (1) stop doing what's wrong; (2) substitute a new good habit for the bad habit; (3) change bad habits in degrees. The third point is important. A person who is overweight got that way over time. If that person wants to lose excess weight, he or she will have to lose it over time. Frustration and defeat set in when unrealistic goals are set and never met. Set realistic goals and work to meet those goals one at a time.

THE TYRANNY OF TIME

You will find that generally your classmates have the same number of hours to study as you have. Fifteen hours of class time (the average on a semester system) means that you will have to spend nearly thirty hours in study time each week. Two hours should be devoted to study in one form or another for each hour in class. Of course, this will vary with each class. But you should *plan* for this schedule at the beginning of your course work. You can always adjust your schedule accordingly after the second and third weeks.

I can remember taking an English class that met only once. In that meeting, the class was divided up into two groups. I never did know what happened to the other group. In fact, I don't know what happened to the people in *my* group. To show the absurdity of the entire course, *I never sat through one lecture!* Every week we were to turn in an essay of our choosing, slip it under the professor's door, and return to his office the next week for a critique. That was it. This was a three-credit-hour course (three class periods each week, fifty minutes each). Ideally, I should have allocated six hours of study time. There was no need. My study schedule went through an immediate revision.

If you do not schedule your time, time will schedule you. If you want to get your papers in on time, have time to study for tests, play a few games of racquetball or tennis, date on the weekends, and take part in college life in general, a *detailed* schedule (subject to modification for sanity's sake) is a must. There's probably not one student in a hundred who will develop a schedule, and there's not one student in a thousand who will follow it. Success comes to those who plan for it. Ask any successful businessman.

Before I could get into graduate school I had to take two required courses that were not part of my undergraduate course work. The two courses were a year's course work jammed into ten weeks. I was scared to death. Fear is a good motivator. It works well with me. In fact, the Bible tells us: "The fear of the LORD is the beginning of knowledge; fools despise wisdom and instruction" (Proverbs 1:7). When you have to get something done, you sit down and do it because you fear the consequences of not doing it.

Here's what I did: I got up at 4:00 A.M. I showered, ate breakfast, and began to study until 7:15. Class began at 7:30 and concluded at 9:30. There was a half hour break before the next class at 10:00. The second class was also two hours. I ate lunch at 12:30 and took a one hour nap from 1:00 to 2:00 P.M. The rest of the day and evening was taken up with studying. I went to bed at 10:00 p.m. sharp. I didn't watch TV for ten weeks. Cold turkey. I followed this regiment for ten weeks. I succeeded in getting A's in both courses, courses that I had never taken before in any form. My secret? I scheduled my time down to the half hour until I felt I was able to handle the work.

When the regular school year started, I was able to revise my schedule. You probably will not have five extremely hard courses. But you don't know that going into your first week of classes. It's best to schedule the study time and then revise your schedule as you get a better idea of the course load.

Long-Term Scheduling

The first thing you want to do is set up your *long-term* schedule. You'll need a monthly calendar with spaces to fill in exam dates and due dates for special projects and papers. Researching and writing a paper takes quite a bit of time. You won't be able to crank one out the night before it's due and expect to get a good grade (B or better). Remember, as hard as it is to believe right now, you may want to go to graduate school. You'll need good grades in all your courses.

Set yourself deadlines for completing your project work, such as papers, essays, observation notebooks, lab notebooks, and anything that can get away from you if you don't write it down and plan for it. You won't be able to remember all the things you'll have to do, especially when you may have as many as five papers to write over the course of a semester. This doesn't even count your scheduled tests. By scheduling all your known assignments, you will be able to tackle each task one day at a time. Your cumulative course work will not seem so awesome if you spread it out and tackle it in bits and pieces.

A planned schedule saves time and effort and helps you work more efficiently. Without a schedule you will find yourself locked in indecision: "What do I study first? How much time should I spend on this? Will I have enough time to complete this?" You want to make studying *habitual* and *automatic* like every other thing you do well. Scheduling also helps keep you from letting time get away: "I'll get to that after I watch the evening news. Sure, I'll go to the store with you. I'll look at my history notes when I get back. There's plenty of time." Does any of this sound familiar?

The biggest advantage of scheduling is relieving yourself of the frustration and guilt of not doing an adequate job on your assignments. You want to be sure that you are giving each assignment the best possible attention. Planning is the only way this can be accomplished.

You will also want to schedule campus activities. Get a list of what's happening on campus: concerts, guest lecturers, movies, sporting and social events, etc. Also, don't forget to schedule trips home.

But before we go on, observe and record the way you spend your time now, from the time you get up in the morning until you go to bed. How much of that time is wasted? Where could you save time? What are some of your bad time-wasting habits? How long after you wake up does it take you to do the first constructive thing of the day?

Weekly Scheduling

Weekly scheduling is also imperative. For the first two weeks you'll need to write in your class times. Once your schedule is finalized, you can write it in on a master form and have it copied. Don't let your schedule master you, however. Give your schedule two weeks or more of tinkering. Make the necessary adjustments as you go. You may find that you do not need two hours each evening for an education course, a very real possibility. Math, science, and language courses require study *every evening*. Transfer the extra study time to your more difficult courses. Schedule the following:

- Morning Bible study, Scripture memorization, and prayer.
- Class times
- Labs
- Meals (Breakfast, Lunch, and Dinner): There are scheduled hours for meals if you eat in the dorm.
- Laundry day: This one can really get away from you. My suggestion is that you schedule the time weekly. Pick a time that's inconvenient for others. Take along a reading assignment.
- Recreation
- Social and sports events
- Job hours
- Study time
- Library time: Two hours each week should be scheduled for going through periodicals, journals, and newspapers. This is best done between classes.
- Sunday worship and ministering to others
- Group Bible study
- Free time

Class assignments should be written in daily. You should take either your schedule or an assignment notebook to class. Transfer the information to your weekly schedule when you get back to your room. A sample weekly schedule form is found in the back of this book.

You can make your own schedule form, copy the one supplied in this book, or purchase one ready-made in the form of a weekly plan book. Visit your local school supply store or business store. Be sure the plan book covers the hours from 6:00 A.M. to 11:00 P.M. There should be sufficient space to make notes for class assignments, long-term projects, tests, etc. Make enough copies for the term and some extra ones in case you drop a class or two (ten copies for a quarter or sixteen for a semester), one copy for each week. Have it enlarged to increase the size of the boxes. A commercial copy center normally can do this. Punch holes in the pages and put it into a three-ring binder. Your own procedure is the best. Be creative.

Scheduling your time will give you more free time than you could ever have dreamed of. Don't forget that Saturday is a workday. We are to labor six days. Study or get a job. Sunday is a day for worship, rest, and fellowship; it's not a time for booking it. The temptation will be to use this day for work. Avoid the temptation. Giving your mind and body a rest one day a week will do wonders for you.

Don't expect miracles from your schedule; procrastination, resistance to change, and laziness will not disappear just because you've mapped out a workable schedule. Your first six weeks of college are going to be rough, especially if you're a poor or even fair student. Your biggest obstacles will be your peers and the lure of campus activities. Do your work first. While you're getting on a solid footing, your classmates are digging their own graves. Your time will come to relax. With a properly laid out schedule, you should have time for these activities.

Fine Tuning

Here are some things to keep in mind:

1. Put your semester schedule in a definite place. If your dorm room has a study desk, put the schedule on the wall in front of you. You should check your weekly schedule periodically throughout the day. You don't want any surprises.

2. Study the same thing at the same time each day. This will help you avoid procrastination. You will also establish regular habits this way.

3. Fit your schedule to your needs and your gifts. There is a delicate balance here. There will be some assignments on your schedule that you will dread, but you still *need* to accomplish them. On the other hand, some things will come easy, and you will want to do them first. You may find that you never get around to the tough stuff. Let your schedule be the balance. I recommend that you study the more difficult and less interesting (for you) courses first.

4. Build some flexibility into your schedule. Don't make it a grind. As time goes on, you will find that you can cut back on some things. If you anticipate through planning, you will rarely be caught by surprise.

5. If a worthwhile unscheduled event comes up, don't automatically say, "I can't make it because I have something scheduled for that time." The beauty of a schedule is that you can adjust it. You can find a way to move something around. But don't rationalize. And don't let it become a habit.

6. Find the best spot in your room to study. The bed is out. A well-lighted desk is the best place. All your basic study materials should be at

175

your finger tips: pens, pencils, paper, assignment book, file folders, index cards, etc.

7. A small library of reference materials, especially a dictionary, should be at your desk or at least on a nearby shelf.

8. Avoid all distractions. Don't study while watching television. You may have to retreat to the library to avoid dormitory life for a while.

STUDY TECHNIQUES

I've taught enough students to know that the biggest problem poor students have is that they never learned how to study. Many very bright students never reach their full potential because they never learned a proper method of study. Of course, no single method will work for everyone. As a matter of fact, there is no single study methodology. There are basic study methods that can be employed for the type of student you are. For example, you may learn best by hearing something while your roommate may retain more by reading the same material.

Keep in mind that if you have not been a good student in high school, there are some skills you'll have to learn, skills that should have been second nature to you by now. Moreover, your storehouse of knowledge is limited, and your mental fitness is at a low ebb. The more difficult college curriculum, in most cases, takes a certain amount of knowledge for granted. Your professors will expect to build on what they think you learned in high school. They won't wait for you to catch up.

I remember sitting in a world history class where the professor was asking some basic questions: "When was the fall of the Roman Empire? To what did Gibbon attribute Rome's fall? When were the Dark Ages? The Reformation?" Many of the students stared in disbelief. They probably thought they had entered the Twilight Zone. It was the professor's way of weeding out the class. Right after the class was dismissed, I saw a number of students head for the registrar's office to drop the class. These freshmen probably did not belong in the class. They probably didn't belong in college.

It may be that you'll have to lighten your course load the first semester. As your study skills improve, you can resume a normal load your sophomore year. So what if you graduate in five years. If you are determined to graduate in four, you can always take summer courses. There is much more time to study since there are fewer activities during the summer months.

How much time should I spend studying?

A forty-hour work week is a good model to follow. This is the minimum. For example, if you just got a new job, you would probably put in some overtime because you would not be familiar with company procedures. If you have fifteen credit hours (fifteen class hours), figure on spending *at least* one and one half to two hours of study time for each hour in class. Fifteen class hours plus twenty-two and one half study hours = thirty-seven and one half hours total (fifteen class hours plus thirty hours of study hours = forty-five hours total). Again, some courses may be under the norm and some may be over. This is an average. Depending on your major, you may need to spend as many as fifty combined hours (class plus study time). If you're like most, plan on spending sixty hours in combined class and study time your first year, but work hard enough to bring it down to forty-five.

There will be times when you will have to boost the number of study hours for special projects and final exams. Remember, you've already planned for them. Your daily studying will give you more flexibility when test time rolls around. If you follow the study procedures listed below, you should be well prepared for any test. If you follow your paper-writing schedule, you will not need to pull an all-nighter.

When should I study?

Whenever you can. The eight-hour work day is our example. Of course, meals will consume some of the traditional nine to five work day. Once you go to class, *don't go back to your room until your last class is finished.* "What if I have an eight o'clock class, but don't have another class until eleven? Couldn't I go back to my room and pick up a few hours of sleep? Eight o'clock classes are rough." Yes, they're rough, but no rougher than getting up for work every morning, something you'll have to do when you graduate and get a job. Welcome to the real world. Instead of going back to your room, go to the library or some other quiet place, and either look over your notes from the previous class, or read the material for the eleven o'clock class. Since you have your papers scheduled, this might be the best time to do some research. Studying during this limbo time will save you from staying up all night (and going to bed at a reasonable hour will help you get up for that dreaded eight o'clock class).

The worst time to study is late afternoon, especially in the spring. This might be the best time to do that needed lab work. Hit the gym just before the evening meal. Of course, you might have a class during the fateful two to five time slot—the luck of freshman scheduling; you get the course leftovers. Friday afternoons are often wasted. Again, resist the temptation to relax. You may be able to complete all your work for the week and have the weekend free.

Should I ever skip a class?

No. Nothing else really needs to be said, but I'll say it anyway. Your parents are spending a lot of money to see that you get an education. There's always something you will learn, even in the most boring classes. Copying a classmate's notes is not the same as being there. When you hear the lecture and take notes, you are reinforcing your memory patterns.

Most professors do not follow the textbook material. You are expected to pick up the pertinent data on your own. Lectures are meant to supplement the textbook if there is one. Oftentimes the textbook material is not clear. Moreover, the emphasis the professor gives in his lecture material will give you the needed clues for his tests. In order to get the needed material from a skipped lecture, you're going to have to trust a classmate. He may be a worse student than you. Of course, you might have a professor who takes attendance.

Should I study alone?

In most cases, yes. Group study can be profitable for difficult courses with which you are having some problems. You might find, however, that a lot of time is wasted and not much studying is accomplished. Pick your group-study times carefully. As you get into your major course work, you will come into contact with the same people course after course. You'll learn who is a good student and who is not. If you're not a good student, you may not be asked to join a study group. You may be perceived as a study leech.

The greatest asset of group study is that it can be a real test of your understanding. You may go over your notes and really think you know the material. In group study you will be pressured into formulating an answer. There may even be gaps in your notes. Everybody misses some material. You will also get immediate feedback on your answers. You will hear the answers given by other members of the group. This will reinforce the memory patterns.

I do recommend a note-taking pool for some classes. "[Y]ou can work out a rotation system in which each of you attends one-fifth or one-eighth or one-tenth of the lectures."[3] When I was in graduate school, four of us had a note-taking pool. On my assigned day I would tape the lecture, and in the evening I would play back the lecture and fill in the notes I had missed. *But I still went to the lectures when it was not my turn.* I would make a complete set of notes for my assigned day and make copies for the others in the group.

What should I study?

You will have lecture notes, a textbook, outside assigned reading, and weekly homework (usually described as "course work") assignments. The homework will vary with each course. *Keep up with your homework assignments. Get them in on time, without fail.* Review your lecture notes daily. Do it immediately after each class if you have the time. Some of what you write will be hard to read. When you go through a comprehensive review of your notes for a test, that scribble will be incomprehensible. This is the time to clean up your notes. This daily review will reinforce the lecture material. You may be able to make some notations in the margins from your collateral reading.

Many courses have a class text. The reading is usually assigned on a daily (class time) or weekly basis. Some professors give you a course outline that shows you when the material is expected to be read. Read the material as assigned. Read in an active way.

• Before you begin to work on an assignment, get an overview of what you want to do.

• Follow the pertinent suggestions laid out in the chapter on "How to Read a Book."

• Go directly to the end of the chapter and read the questions if there are any. The author of the textbook obviously believes these are the key ideas that should be gleaned from the material. This will guide your reading. One of the best ways to study is to ask questions about the material before you begin your reading. The supplied questions will help. You can develop your own questions as you go along.

• Mark your textbook. Draw lines down the margin marking important paragraphs. Difficult sections merit a double line. These sections need to be gone over again for better understanding and contemplation. Put a question mark on material that you do not understand. Go to your professor for clarification or do your own independent research. Often a

179

professor has a teaching assistant (TA) who is a graduate student assigned to help the prof. He or she could be of some help.

• Underline important phrases and words. Put a check mark (in pencil) for anything that probably should go into your notes. Don't stop now to take down the information. When you finish with your reading you may find that it's no longer important.

• If the book doesn't have subheads, put your own in the margins. Keep them to the point.

• What are the key ideas? Distinguish key ideas from secondary ideas and supporting materials. Normally, a key idea is the topic sentence. Turn the topic sentence into a question. Your instructor's lecture will give you some idea of what he considers key ideas.

• Use the margins to outline the material. This will serve as a quick review. It will also help you "activate" your study time. By briefly summarizing the material in writing, deeper memory patterns are developed.

• Summarize the chapter in writing when you finish. Include your own thoughts, conclusions, disagreements, and questions. It's possible that this material will be used as an essay question. By briefly summarizing the material in writing, you will have some idea of where the gaps are in your understanding and of how well you have remembered the facts.

• Some items may have to be memorized. Pay attention in class to what your professor emphasizes. Determine whether he or she prefers that you memorize or summarize ideas. Some classes are filled with memory work. This is especially true in the sciences. If you take an anatomy course, expect to memorize.

• Charts and graphs are also important. Don't neglect them. If you are a visual learner, these will prove to be especially helpful. The graphs and charts can trigger your memory as you try to learn abstract concepts that don't seem to relate to reality. Try to hang some concepts on the chart as you study. Many of us are visual learners. We tend to remember when we can see it. As you call the chart to mind, you will find that it will bring other concepts forward.

• Make a list of formulas, specialized vocabulary, and any other important data that will be useful for a test.

• Go to your notes and place page numbers from the textbook that correspond to the lecture material. Be selective in your markings. It won't do you much good if everything is underlined. You want to be able to go back to your textbook and find the "meat" for a test.

• Write the questions you feel are the most important on index cards (the questions that will probably be asked on a test). These can be used for a quick review for tests. Make sure you note where the answer can be found (either in your notes or textbook). You may even want to put the answers on the back of the cards. In all of this you should realize a very important point. Your textbook may have cost you nearly thirty dollars, but the time you will put into reading that textbook will cost you a small fortune. Time is money. If you spend two hours each day studying your textbook, three days per week, at five dollars per hour, the cost of reading is thirty dollars per week. In ten weeks you've spent three hundred dollars in time. A purposely-marked textbook will save you a tremendous amount of time when review time rolls around.

How should I arrange my study time each evening?

You want to use your study time in the most effective way. One of the first things you must find out is the extent of your attention span. Do you drift after fifteen, thirty, or forty-five minutes? Be honest with yourself. If you're just developing your study habits, your attention span may be in the fifteen to thirty minute range. Give yourself the needed breaks. Five minutes at the most. Get up. Stretch. Walk around a bit. *Get right back to your desk.* Schedule the breaks and take them, even if you feel like going on. Take a longer break between subjects.

Divide up your daily study time over a variety of subjects. Don't spend three hours on English literature on Monday and three hours on biology on Tuesday. Study at least two subjects each evening. The ideal is three. This will mean that every two days you will have studied all your material. Another advantage to this approach is that dissimilar material will help you remember what you study. If you study similar material, one subject after another, you will not remember it as well. The facts in literature, for example, will become confused if you move on to history. Switch subjects every hour or so, and always try to make your new subject as different as possible from what you have just finished. A technical course, such as science or math, should be placed next to a social science course, such as psychology or sociology.

PROCRASTINATION

"Don't put off for tomorrow what you can do today" is an old proverb filled with wisdom. How many times have you postponed tackling an unpleasant task? "Well, I'll just watch this TV show before I work on my book report." What begins as a single show turns out to be a whole evening wasted. You might hurriedly copy something from the book's dust jacket to get the assignment in on time. It may be that you fail to do it at all.

Few people like to study. If you're a typical student, studying will not be one of your favorite activities. The key then is to minimize the displeasure. Let's face it, if you know that you will have to spend the time studying, then why not get it out of the way early. You know what it feels like when you finish a task. Relief! Procrastination is a mind-set that needs to be reversed. It takes will power to break this bad habit.

Procrastination is probably the most vexing problem that faces students when they enter college. College is less regimented. You don't have parents and teachers looking over your shoulder prodding you to get your work done. There is very little peer pressure in college. Not many people care if you make it. If it's a large school, few people even know you're there.

What can you do to break the procrastination cycle?

1. Don't try to be a super student overnight. Set a goal to accomplish small tasks at first. Success with these will make more difficult tasks seem less ominous.

2. Reward yourself when you accomplish a goal.

3. Give yourself enough time to accomplish your tasks. You may think that it will take you three evenings to read a book for English class but, in fact, it might take you a week. It's better to give yourself more time so that you can avoid the frustration and feel good about finishing early.

4. Utilize short segments of time. When you have an extra five or ten minutes, pull out that book you have to read for English class. You should always carry some assignment material with you. Reading material is the easiest.

5. Expect to fail sometimes and don't give up when you do. It's possible that one of the reasons you are a procrastinator is that you dislike failing. "It's better not to try than to try and fail." Break this habit now! Failure is complete when we don't try to correct our mistakes. The successful person learns from his mistakes and is not demoralized by them.

6. Don't wait until you feel like doing your work. If you wait that long, nothing will get down. Establish the time when you are going to perform your task and then do it until it's finished or until the time you alloted to complete the task is ended.

CONCLUSION

Studying is not much fun, but you know that it's necessary if you're going to make it through college. Instead of trying to avoid studying, learn the best ways to make your task easier. You will save yourself a lot of aggravation, stress, and frustration if you learn to study intelligently. Don't be fooled by those who say you either have it or you do not. You have a tremendous amount of potential that has never been tapped. Trust that God will bring it to the surface. This will mean doing what He requires of you. At first it will not come easily. Give it some time. Work at it. You will be amazed at your success.

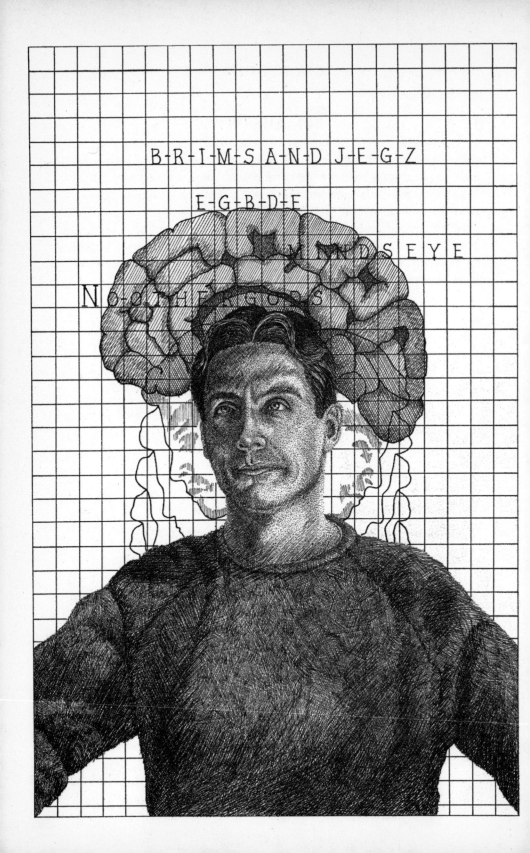

11
MEMORY MECHANICS

"I forgot!"

You have said it thousands of times with embarrassment, vexation, and self-reproach. In attempting to remember speeches, price lists, studies, statistics, names, and faces you have depended on the old, tiresome method of repetition to stamp them on your memory—and it went back on you at the critical moment.

This is all unnecessary. You have the proper mental equipment, but neglect and wrong methods have caused it to deteriorate.

Your memory is actually the most wonderful instrument in the world. You need only to know how to use it to do things that appear marvelous. The purpose of these lessons is to afford you a real opportunity for improvement.[1]

OUR brain is a magnificent creation. A typical adult's brain contains fifteen billion to one hundred billion neurons. If we accept the lower estimate, this means that you and I can remember two-to-the-ten-billionth-power bits of information. How big is this number? Well, it would take you ninety years to write it out if you wrote a zero per second. If we take the larger number of neurons, this would be equivalent to ten billion encyclopedia pages of information. The brain is a very big place in a very small space.[2]

Some see the brain as a highly evolved machine. It's not. There is something unique about the human brain and its relationship with the mind. While a computer searches all the possibilities before it can come up with a correct answer, the brain evaluates, sorts, compares, discards, and formulates. There is an evaluation process going on that no computer can match.

> The key word here is *evaluating*. By placing a value on a bit of information we let it advance to the forefront or recede to form a part of a larger picture. We can do this temporarily or permanently, and we can convert the images later if we want to. No tape recorder, camera, or even a computer can do all of this. Computers, in fact, are just very fast, efficient morons, with neither imagination nor common sense. It takes a computer four minutes to work out the right combination for a Rubik's Cube, considering every possible turn until all the correct ones have been made. An efficient teenager can do it in two minutes and the sixteen-year-old 1982 World Champion did it in 22.95 seconds![3]

But as scientists learn more about memory they are beginning to realize that there is no single entity called "memory." Consider an amnesiac. Clive Wearing once was an expert on Renaissance music and a producer for the British Broadcasting Corporation (BBC). Not long ago he came down with a rare form of encephalitis, an inflammation of the brain, which left him with a memory span of only a few seconds. He cannot recall a single event in the past. He couldn't tell you what he just had for lunch, even if he had eaten the meal ten minutes before. But not all his memory patterns have been wiped out. He can sing and conduct a choir. His musical ability is still intact. Wearing's wife, Deborah, says, he "is trapped forever in the groove of a scratched record."[4] Memory, then, is multi-faceted and much more difficult to describe and define than was once thought. "It seems, then, that some sections of the mind's archives store facts (names, images, events), while others store procedures (recollections of how to do things)."[5]

While it's important to understand what memory is, it's more important for a student to understand how it works and how to improve it. Students want a more efficient memory so that studying will be easier. This chapter will introduce you to methods that will expand your ability to remember.

MEMORY TECHNIQUES

The ability to have a good memory is present with each of us. And while superior intelligence might be an asset in developing a good memory, it's not a prerequisite. Memory is more a technique than a gift.

Memory is the ability to attach unknown ideas or facts to known ideas or facts. Parents transfer basic sounds to an infant and the infant mimics the parents. This continues with words, phrases, and sentences. Learning the alphabet leads to learning words, words are worked into sentences, and sentences are turned into complete and workable ideas. Not much thought is given to all this. It just seems so "natural." But listen to any two-year-old struggle with simple words and phrases. In time, he learns to put all those new sounds into coherent thoughts. What began as babbling turns into beautiful speech. One word turns into thousands.

There are times when a single event that happens in a split second is recorded in your mind for a lifetime. It can be recalled at any time with no trouble. On November 22, 1963, President John F. Kennedy was assassinated in Dallas, Texas. I can remember where I was and what I was doing. But there is little else I remember of that day. In fact, there's not much in that year that I remember. You probably have similar memory patterns. What makes these events "stick," while others seem to be as slippery as teflon? The key to a good memory is association: linking something you know with something you want to know.

Mnemonics

Your ability to memorize can improve by using devices and methods called mnemonics [pronounced nee-MON-iks or na-MON-iks]. The word comes from the same Greek root as that of *Mnemosyne*, the goddess of memory who was the mother of the nine sister muses who presided over the arts and sciences. (Did she have difficulty remembering all their names?) Our English word *mnemonic* means "helpful to memory."

Basically, all you must do is force yourself in unnatural and infrequent areas of learning to do what has been natural for years. Most learning comes by way of *associations*. You connect, associate, what you do know with what you do not know. You look for some relationship between the *new material* and the *familiar material*. While there may not be a subject connection (e.g., room and house), there may be an auditory connection ("In fourteen hundred and ninety-*two* Columbus sailed the ocean *blue*"). *Two* and *blue* have no subject connection, but they do sound alike. This is a forced memory connection.

187

If I were to ask you to name the Great Lakes, you might be able to remember two or three of them. But if I associate the five Great Lakes with something you already know, like HOMES, you will never forget them again: *H*uron, *O*ntario, *M*ichigan, *E*rie, and *S*uperior.

Many young children learned the word "arithmetic" as their first big word this way: *A* *r*at *i*n *T*om's *h*ouse *m*ay *e*at *T*om's *i*ce *c*ream.

The colors of the light spectrum, *r*ed, *o*range, *y*ellow, *g*reen, *b*lue, *i*ndigo, *v*iolet, can make up a fictitious man's name, Roy G. Biv.

The cranial nerves always present a problem for first-year medical students. The following memory device is a standard to remember *o*lfactory, *o*ptic, *o*culomotor, *t*rochlear, *t*rigeminal, *a*bducens, *f*acial, *a*uditory, glossopharyngeal, *v*agus, *s*pinal accessory, and *h*ypoglossal: "*O*n *O*ld *O*lympus' *T*owering *T*op, *A* *F*riar *A*nd Greek *V*iewed *S*ome *H*ops."[6]

The tribes of Israel: *J*udah, *I*ssachar, *M*anasseh, *B*enjamin, *R*euben, *A*sher, *N*aphtali, *D*an, *S*imeon, *E*phraim, *G*ad, and *Z*ebulun. If the tribal names are unfamiliar, look for a way of associating the *unfamiliar* tribal names with something *familiar*. You might try making up a little song, visualizing them on a map of Israel, or memorizing them in groups of three or four. (This is why your phone number and Social Security number have dashes between groups of numbers. It's much easier to remember a long number if it is broken down in smaller groups.)

Suppose that instead of following one of these devices (all good ones), you try taking the first letters of each tribal name to see if you can make something familiar with them. First you try B-R-I-M-S A-N-D J-E-G-Z. While it might be helpful, in time you would have difficulty remembering it because it isn't familiar enough. You try again and come up with J-I-M B-R-A-N-D-S E-G-Z. A name is easy to remember, and you can visualize twelve eggs with farmer Jim Brand picking them up. The only variation you have to make is to change the plural for eggs (the z sound) to EGZ (z substituting for the plural of egg).

It's easy to move from the tribes of Israel to the sons of Israel (Jacob). Two of the sons of Israel are not listed among the tribal allotments by name: Joseph and Levi. But we still have twelve tribes. Ephraim and Manasseh, we learn, are not the sons of Israel, but his grandsons. They are Joseph's sons, the same Joseph who is not listed among the twelve tribes. Levi is given cities throughout the tribal allotments. Ephraim and Manasseh are added to the other ten tribes and make up Joseph's inheritance.

Acronyms

An *acronym* is a word made up of the first letters of a list of names, items, places, etc. HOMES is a good example. You're probably familiar with FACE, an acronym used to help children remember the notes between the lines on the treble clef. In order to make an acronym work, you may have to reorder the list several times. While VIBGYOR might do for the light spectrum—it sounds more like some extraterrestrial being thrashing about with a laser weapon that emits the light spectrum— Roy G. Biv is probably better. If an acronym just doesn't work, you'll need to go on to some other technique.

Acrostics

An *acrostic* is very similar to an acronym. In an acronym the initials are pronounced to form a new word, either real or something pro-nounceable (e.g., NATO, NASA, HUD, etc.). An acrostic uses initials that are not pronounced but are used to form new words that make a sentence. For example, *E*very *G*ood *B*oy *D*oes *F*ine teaches a beginning music student the notes of the treble clef that appear on the lines: E-G-B-D-F. A student of biology devised the following: *K*ings *P*lay *C*ards *O*n *F*airly *G*ood *S*oft *V*elvet, for kingdom, phylum, class, order, family, genus, species, variety. You can remember the planets with this mnemonic device: *M*y *V*ery *E*xcellent *M*other *J*ust *S*ells *N*uts *U*ntil *P*assover, for Mercury, Venus, Earth, Mars, Jupiter, Saturn, Neptune, Uranus, and Pluto.

Visualization[7]

"A picture is worth a thousand words." If that's true, then the mind can save you a lot of words. You can picture almost anything. Picture what you read. Turn abstractions into visual ideas that have a close association, either in content or sound.

> *Eye-pictures are the most accurate of mental impressions.* And because the mind has this wonderful ability to see pictures long after the disappearance of the original pictures that the real eye made on the mind, we speak of the *mind's eye*, and of seeing in our *mind's eye*. The scientific name for the *mind's eye* is visualization, and the ability to use this wonderful faculty is invaluable to you.[8]

189

In time, the more you use the material, the artificial visual association will fade. Your mind will move directly to the idea. Visualize the three branches of government as a triangle with each side representing one branch. Then visualize that triangle perched on a *branch* of a cherry tree in Washington, D.C. Sure, it's not always this easy. But this method will take you pretty far.[9]

One adaptation of the visualization technique is the "Location System." Roman orators commonly used the *loci* system to remember the components of a speech. They didn't have the advantage of a Teleprompter or note cards. In this system, major parts of the speech were associated with a certain route from the speaker's home to the Forum where he was to give his address. Along the way, he would associate a familiar landmark with the points of his address. One landmark with one point in the speech. As he delivered his speech, he would recall the landmarks in order of their place along the route and each speech component would be recalled as well. The following story is told of a Russian's ability to recall items that were memorized years before.

> A Russian renowned for his memory could hear a list of fifty words and recite them back without error fifteen years later. As he heard each item he mentally placed it along Moscow's Gorky Street, outside a shop he knew well. To remember the items, he took a mental walk down Gorky and picked them up one at a time.[10]

If you have a group of similar concepts to learn, try to place them in a house with various rooms. For example, if you have to learn the names of the Popes from the sixteenth-century to the present, you can choose one room for each century. Then place the Popes for a particular century in different locations in a room (e.g., the living room), sitting on chairs, sitting at the piano, standing by the window, sitting on the sofa, etc. By visualizing the room and the furniture, you can easily recall the names by their location. Your own home or a very familiar building would be the best *loci* to choose. You could associate each Pope's name with an article of furniture that can easily be recalled for the test.

Vocalization, Rhymes, and Jingles

Some people are better auditory learners. Reading something aloud and emphasizing the main points with greater inflection may help. Most of us learned the alphabet this way. One way to remember names, for example, is to repeat the name of the individual you were just introduced to. Hearing it again helps the memory process.

Most of us can remember TV commercials because they have catchy tunes or clever associations: "Coke, it's the real thing." Or Eastern Airlines, "We have to earn our wings every day." How did you learn when to set your clocks ahead and back every year? "Spring ahead, fall back." In April (Spring) we move our clocks ahead one hour (spring forward). In October (Fall) we turn our clocks back one hour (fall backward).

Abbreviation

Sometimes it helps if you abbreviate a long section of material into its essential parts. For example:

THE TEN COMMANDMENTS

1. No other gods	6. No murder
2. No graven images	7. No Adultery
3. Name of Lord	8. No Stealing
4. Sabbath rest	9. No False witness
5. Honor mom and dad	10. No coveting

Instead of ten commandments to learn you now have two groups of five commandments. You can shorten this even further by leaving off the negatives, for abbreviation purposes only. Be forewarned, however; there was a Bible published that left the "not" out of the seventh commandment. It was called the "Adulterer's Bible."

Our nation's Constitution had attached to it ten brief amendments. Here's a handy way to learn the basics of each one:

THE "BILL OF RIGHTS"
(The first Ten Amendments to the Constitution).

1. Freedom of religion, speech, press, assembly, petition
2. Right to bear arms
3. Quartering of soldiers
4. Search and seizure
5. a. Indictment
   b. Double jeopardy
   c. Self-incrimination
   d. Legal trial
   e. Private property

6. Speedy and public trial
7. Suits at common law
8. Bail, fines, punishment
9. Rights not mentioned
10. State's rights

You can add your visualization techniques to many of these. Freedom of religion could be represented by a cross or Bible, speech by a podium or megaphone, press by a newspaper or book, assembly by a crowd or a group of picketers holding signs, and petition by a scroll with names written on it. Arms could be represented by a rifle or a revolver. Quartering soldiers could be remembered by visualizing troops coming to a home and hoping to gain entrance by paying a quarter. You can finish the visualization with your own associations.

Memory Connections

How can you remember a sequence of events? All those bits of meandering memory mechanics might make me mad miming mindless muddle. Good point. How can you best remember a list of events that have to be in order?: two facts at a time. By associating the first fact with the second fact, the second fact with the third fact, the third fact with the fourth fact, etc., you can learn a whole string of events, two facts at a time. Here's how the "Link Method" works:

THE MINOR PROPHETS

1. Hosea = *Hose* spraying out *jewels* instead of water.
2. Joel = *Jewels* falling on *a moss*-covered arrow.
3. Amos = *A moss*-covered arrow aimed at an *oboe* player.
4. Obadiah = The *oboe* player meets *Jonah* in a whale.
5. Jonah = *Jonah* goes to a *mic*rophone to sing.
6. Micah = The *mic*rophone sends out a *hum*.
7. Nahum = The *hum* makes the *haberdasher*'s hat vibrate.
8. Habakkuk = The *haberdasher*'s hat is blown off by a *zephyr*.
9. Zephaniah = The *zephyr* blows it to an old *hag*.
10. Haggai = The *hag* scares old *Zack*.
11. Zechariah = *Zack* runs to *Malachi* the *mail*man for help.
12. Malachi = *Malachi* the *mail*man delivers a closed Bible.

Associate each unfamiliar minor prophet with a visual sound-alike word. Visualize a *hose* (Hosea) spewing out *jewels* (Joel). The *jewels* come out and smash into a man aiming *a moss* (Amos)-covered arrow at a man playing an *Oboe* (Obadiah). His playing is so bad that he is swallowed by a whale where he happens to meet *Jonah*. Jonah tells his story using a *mic*rophone (Micah), but the only sound that anyone hears is a gentle *hum* (Nahum), etc.

Once you recall the hose, the visualization process takes over. The memory sequence starts with only two minor prophets in view at any one time. Once the memory link is made, the first minor prophet fades away and the new association takes over. This technique can be used with any sequence of events.

From the Abstract to the Concrete

Abstract ideas are some of the most difficult concepts to remember. There are few memory "handles" for your mind to hold on to. An abstract idea has to be turned into something concrete. For example, how can you make existentialism concrete? For a philosophy test you have to remember that Heidegger, Sartre, and Kierkegaard are existentialists. You know that existentialists believe that "existence precedes essence." Exist sounds like "exit." When you come into the world (a type of existence) you "exit" your mother's body.[11] And guess who's greeting you when you enter the world? *Heidi*, Captain James T. *Kirk* of the Starship Enterprise, and *Ser*geant (pronounced *sar*jent) York, the decorated World War I army hero. You can visualize a delivery room at a hospital with Heidi dressed up in her mountain-climbing clothes, Captain Kirk in his ship's captain attire, and Alvin York in his sergeant's uniform.

Here's a list of some abstract concepts and a list of concrete equivalents:

ABSTRACT CONCEPT	CONCRETE SYMBOL
1. Intelligence or mind	1. Brain
2. Grief	2. Someone in tears
3. Peace	3. Dove or olive branch
4. Ignorance	4. Dunce cap
5. Security	5. Padlock or vault
6. Hope	6. Anchor
7. Speed	7. Sprinter or race car
8. Language	8. Dictionary
9. Happiness	9. Mask with a smile
10. Death	10. Coffin

Pegging and Linking

Have you ever had trouble remembering numbers, dates, or a long list of related facts or dates? Well, do I have a system for you. Numbers and dates are abstract by themselves. You can have twelve eggs to make a dozen, twelve inches to make a foot, twelve tribes to make up the nation Israel, and twelve apostles to make up the number of men Jesus chose to be His closest disciples. It's difficult to make a number stand out as something more than a number. What if you have to remember various dates for the many battles that occurred during World War II? Did it happen on May 12, 1943 or May 13, 1945? Consider sixty events strung out over a period of five years. But what if each date could be turned into a picture? The month of May could be represented by a flower ("April Showers bring May *Flowers*"), twenty-three becomes gnome, and 1945 becomes tub and rail. A battle on this day would be associated with a flower shading a sleeping gnome who has just finished collecting a tub full of rails. How did I come up with this? Let me show you.

The pegging system is a comprehensive memory device that uses a number system that corresponds to the letters of the alphabet and their *sounds*. Keep in mind that the *sounds* are what's important, not the letter. For example,

t and d represent the number 1 (one down stroke of letters, and both sound alike)

n represents the number 2 (2 down strokes of letter)

m represents the number 3 (3 down strokes of letter)

r represents the number 4 (fou*r*)

l represents the number 5 (L is the Roman numeral for 50)

j, soft g, ch, and sh represent the number 6 (j [a backward 6], g [an upside down 6], ch and sh all sound alike)

k and hard g represent the number 7 (k has a backward leaning 7)

f and v represent the number 8 (a script f makes an 8)

p and b represent the number 9 (p is a backward 9, b is a backward and upside down 9)

s, soft c, and z represent 0

Other letters that *sound like* the above letters represent the same numerical value. For example, a word with a hard c and hard g sound would be a 7 along with k. A soft c sound (when it sounds like an s) would be a o as in daises, which would mean 100. A v could substitute for an f (have or half), a p for a b (pat or bat). This really is not very complicated, but it does take a little time to learn.

The following letters have *no numerical value* (all vowels and the letters that make up the word why):

A E I O U and *W H Y*

I'll take you through the first ten words/numbers to show you how it works.

1. hat (h and a have no numerical value, t is 1)
2. hen (h and e have no numerical value, n is 2)
3. ham (h and a have no numerical value, m is 3)
4. hare (h, a, and e have no numerical value, r is 4)
5. hill (h and i have no numerical value, the sound l is 5)
6. jaw (j is a backward 6, a and w have no numerical value)
7. cow (c is a hard k sound, o and w have no numerical value)
8. hive (h, i, and e have no numerical value, v sounds like f which in script looks like an 8)
9. ape (a and e have no value, p is a backward 9)
10. toes (t is 1, o and e have no numerical value, the *sound* of z in the s is 0)

You associate the first word, hat, with the second word hen. Then associate hen with ham. You want to make up some wild associations so you will never forget them. Continue until you learn all ten this way (there are one hundred words to learn). Once you have the ten associated, you can put ten unfamiliar words with the ten now familiar words—by associating hat with the first new word, hen with the second, ham with the third, and so forth. Since you know the ten linking words, it's just a matter of recalling one word at a time until you get all ten. Theoretically, you could learn a list of one hundred items in order in less than thirty minutes and recall it the next day for a test (I've done it).

What about the numbers? Notice that h-a-t has an h and an a, two letters that have no numerical value. The t represents 1. So it is with all the words. Numbers can be translated into words, and words can be *visualized* and *associated*. So, an

195

abstract number like 1903 (the year of the first flight by the Wright Brothers) becomes two words: Tub (T is 1, u has no numerical value, and b is 9) and Ham (H has no numerical value, a has no numerical value, and m is 3). From this you get the Wright Brothers delivering a new *tub* filled with a huge smoked *ham* to celebrate their first flight.

There's much more to this system. Even if you never use it, it's a lot of fun. Here are a few books that go into great detail with all the specifics and applications:

1. David M. Roth, *The Famous Roth Memory Course* (New York: Sun Dial Press, Inc., 1918, 1934). This book is no longer in print. You may be able to find it in a used bookstore. It is very rare. All the modern memory books use Roth's system, but few give him the credit he deserves.

2. Harry Lorayne and Jerry Lucas, *The Memory Book* (New York: Ballantine Books, 1974). This book was a number one coast-to-coast bestseller. In their chapter on "Some History of the Art," they state that it is their "pleasure to bring the art of trained memory back into the foreground." Unfortunately, not once do they mention David M. Roth. You can find this book in most used bookstores. It may still be in print.

3. James D. Weinland, *How to Improve Your Memory* (New York: Barnes & Noble, 1957). A very helpful book. He mentions Roth (p. 108).

The Six Serving Men

One of the best ways to remember is to ask questions. When you want to get the basic information out of a lesson, follow the prescription of Rudyard Kipling:

I keep six honest serving men
(They taught me all I knew);
Their names are *What* and *Why* and *When*
and *How* and *Where* and *Who*.

These indicators will help you retrieve key information. Since you now know the serving men, recalling the needed information comes more easily. Also, it's a great way of organizing information that you read. Put the six serving men across a sheet of paper and fill in the questions as you read.

Flash Cards

In order to work for the Post Office, you must take zip code tests on a frequent basis. Sometimes mail comes in without a zip code. You do not have time to look up the street number and name. You must know it *immediately*. Time is money. There are thousands of streets in our large cities. You are required to know the zip code of nearly every street in the city if you work as a letter sorter. The only way to do it is with flash cards. The name of the street on one side, the zip code on the other.

This technique can be used for learning vocabulary words for foreign language study. All the memory techniques discussed thus far can be applied to the flash card approach. Be sure to mix the order periodically so you will not memorize them based on familiarity with the previous card.

SQ3R

For broad review learning you will not be able to use mnemonic devices. Another method is needed. Mnemonic devices, however, will come in handy within the broad concepts. In 1946 Dr. Francis P. Robinson wrote *Effective Study*, in which he explained a study method that contained five simple steps: *S*urvey, *Q*uestion, *R*ead, *R*ecite, *R*eview: *SQ3R*. I've added another: *P*review.

The following is a brief explanation of this very popular and effective system.

PREVIEW

Look at any introductory material that is supplied with the material that you are about to survey. Is there an introduction, preface, or foreword? Check out the table of contents.

SURVEY

Reading boldfaced type, topic sentences, summary paragraphs, and review questions will give you an idea of the contents of the assignment.

QUESTION

After you have completed the survey, ask yourself what will be the important information contained in the assignment. Questioning will also help you to link the information in the assignment to what you already know. An easy way to create the questions is to turn the boldfaced type or the topic sentences into questions. Some texts supply questions at the end of each chapter.

READ

Read for ideas—especially to answer the questions you have created or read. Read one section at a time, and then go to the next step.

RECITE

Answer the questions you have asked, without looking at your notes or at the notebook. After you have finished answering the questions, go on to the next section of the assignment. Read it, and answer the questions you have asked. Continue reading and reciting until you have finished the assignment.

REVIEW

After you have finished the assignment, look away from the book, go over your notes, and get a comprehensive grasp of the complete assignment.[12]

The *SQ3R* formula will go a long way in helping you formulate the context of what you need to know. You may not pick up some of the *particulars*, but you can always go back and spend specialized time on the rote memorization sections.

Pulling it All Together

All of the above techniques can be used to memorize large sections of poetry and prose. Why not try your hand at Abraham Lincoln's *Gettysburg Address*. But before you make the attempt, consider these suggestions.

First, understand the setting for the *Gettysburg Address*. Why did President Lincoln give it? Where did he give it? What are the circumstances surrounding the event? This will help you understand the terms being used and give you a feel for the time: civil war, battlefield, final resting place, brave men living and dead, etc. The more familiar you are with something, the easier it will be for you to memorize it.

Second, familiarize yourself with the entire address before you begin to memorize it. Understand the flow of thought. Anticipate what will come next.

Third, divide up the address into smaller sections. Find its natural rhythm: Fourscore and seven years ago/our fathers brought forth on this continent/a new nation/conceived in liberty/and dedicated to the proposition that all men are created equal.

Fourth, apply some of the memory techniques, especially visualization and linking. You might even want to try locating the address on a battlefield while you walk through it, associating portions of the address with items you might find there. Creating a sing-song effect might be of some help. Combining these techniques could also prove helpful.

Fifth, when all else fails, repetition or vocal emphasis can get you over a sticking point.

> Four score and seven years ago our fathers brought forth on this continent a new nation, conceived in liberty, and dedicated to the proposition that all men are created equal.

> Now we are engaged in a great civil war, testing whether that nation, or any nation so conceived and so dedicated, can long endure. We are met on a great battlefield of that war. We have come to dedicate a portion of that field as a final resting place for those who here gave their lives that that nation might live. It is altogether fitting and proper that we should do this.

> But in a larger sense we cannot dedicate, we cannot consecrate, we cannot hallow this ground. The brave men, living and dead, who struggled here, have consecrated it far above our poor power to add or detract. The world will little note, nor long remember, what we say here; but it can never forget what they did here. It is for us, the living, rather to be dedicated here to the unfinished work which they who fought here have thus far so nobly advanced. It is rather for us to be here dedicated to the great task remaining before us, that from these honored dead we take increased devotion to that cause for which they gave the last full measure of devotion; that we here highly resolve that these dead shall not have died in vain; that this nation, under God, shall have a new birth of freedom, and that government of the people, by the people, and for the people, shall not perish from the earth.

Lincoln was wrong on at least one point. The world has noted what was said commemorating those who died on that Gettysburg, Pennsylvania battlefield.

CONCLUSION

Memory, like all mental activity, takes practice. When we were very young, memorizing was easy; it was natural. As we grew older, the memorizing process was dulled because we no longer learned at the rate we did when we were infants. What we had to learn became less and less, and the process we used to remember changed. Our initial experience with memory was not in the classroom or over books. Memory work seemed so natural that it wasn't work at all.

Times have changed and so has our ability to memorize. But maybe we can capture some of that youthful technique. The process has not really changed. In fact, we still use it; we're just not aware of it. This chapter has given you some tools to help you revitalize your memory processes.

12
HOW TO READ

Some great men—Gibbon was one and
Daniel Webster was another and the great
Lord Strafford was a third—always, before
reading a book, made a short, rough analysis
of the questions which they expected to be
answered in it, the additions to be made to
their knowledge, and whither it would take
them. I have sometimes tried that way of
studying, and guiding attention; I have never
done so without advantage, and I commend
it to you.[1]

IN this country, at any given time, there are about seven hundred fifty
thousand books in print. At the same time, there are more than 100 million out-of-print books that continue to circulate! This doesn't count
magazines, daily newspapers, newsletters, professional journals, and the
flood of material that comes into our mailboxes every day. You can't read
everything, especially when you have to turn in nine papers in one
semester, all supported by collateral reading and footnoted. Your reading
will have to be very selective. The clock is always ticking and there's
always something else to do, whether scheduled or not. The development of good reading skills depends, once again, on a well-thought-out
methodology.

Reading has fallen into disfavor today. "Twenty-seven million adult
Americans are unable to read. At least 30 million more are functionally
illiterate—they read and write so poorly that they cope only marginally.
In just fifteen years the functionally illiterate population could be as
much as seventy percent of adults. Every year 2.3 million functionally illiterate people are added to the ranks; some are immigrants who may or

may not be literate in languages other than English, and, incredibly, 1 million come out of our public schools."[2] A generation that cannot read is open to the most subtle forms of propaganda. Non-readers are then dependent upon other sources for their information, namely television and radio. Those who do not read are just as dependent. The college classroom becomes another vehicle for information. You should keep in mind that instructors are the ones who choose the reading material.

THE DEMISE OF READING

There are a number of reasons for the sad state of reading in our nation today. The preference of the "look-say" method of teaching reading has much to do with it.[3] Many who are taught to read with this system often find it frustrating. They rarely get to a point where they can analyze what they read. For them, reading is drudgery. To even consider critical thinking as part of reading is out of the question. These readers at least have some excuse.

Then there is television. Watching Ronald Colman play the lead in the movie version of Charles Dickens' *A Tale of Two Cities* is certainly easier than taking the time to read the full-length literary treatment of it. Many poor readers find their "reading enjoyment" in front of the tube because they were never taught to read properly and thus to enjoy it. Few movies ever do full justice to a book. But for many, this is all they have. Rudolf Flesch writes in *Why Johnny Still Can't Read*:

> During the writing of this book, I've talked to many of my friends and acquaintances about the reading problem. Invariably the first reaction is an accusation of TV. "They don't read any good books any more because they spend all their time watching TV" is the standard view. In truth, it's just the other way around. The kids haven't been taught to read fluently and so they use their leisure hours to watch TV. Reading for them is a painful chore. How can anyone expect them to turn to leisure reading voluntarily? They're astronomically far away from the stage of reading a book because its *enjoyable*.[4]

Television viewing feeds the poor reader. He goes to television to look for entertainment when he is bored. Before the time of radio, which at least forced the listener to picture what he heard, and television, boredom was often overcome by picking up a good book. With more entertainment options competing for our attention, the poor reader gravitates to television because it is non-threatening. He doesn't have to worry about his reading ability. Television viewing is effortless and enjoyable for the poor reader. In fact, it's relaxing. Television is not evil. Like any entertainment medium, it can be abused. Its convenience and availability make it an easy entertainment option.

Television viewing seems to turn off the desire to analyze, a very important skill in good reading, and especially needed in college level work. "Fred Allen, the comic genius of early radio, once called television 'chewing gum for the eyes.'"[5]

A final point needs to be made about the demise of reading. Reading skills must be coupled with thinking skills. Thinking skills are useless unless there is a foundation of values to give the reader something to compare what he reads with what is real and right. But how can you develop thinking skills when the prevailing philosophy of our day, as the opening song in *Indiana Jones and the Temple of Doom* tells us, is "Anything Goes"?

ANYTHING GOES

Many young people and adults alike have surrendered themselves to philosophical and ethical pluralism; every view of reality has an equal chance in the free market of ideas, except a system of values that says there are absolutes. How can you analyze what you read if there are no absolutes? On what do you "bounce off" your concerns, evaluations, and analysis? It seems that for today's reader there are no evaluating standards except those you create for yourself. Critical thinking has degenerated into openness. The following exchange might not be an uncommon theme on our nation's campuses:

Cornell University President Frank H. T. Rhodes suggested it was time for universities to pay "real and sustained attention to students' intellectual and moral well-being."

This elicited gasps and even catcalls from the audience of professors and students. One indignant student arose to challenge Rhodes. "Who is going to do the moral instructing?" he demanded. "Whose morality are we going to follow?" The audience applauded thunderously, believing that the student had settled the issue and shut Rhodes up simply by posing these unanswerable questions.[6]

So, when a book is read, there is really no right way or wrong way to evaluate what the author has written. Non-Christian educators and many Christian educators believe that facts are neutral. For them, the task of the reader is to glean and absorb the facts and shape them independent of any fixed standard. In time, it is thought, the facts will come together in some coherent whole. But while students are being told to be open, to accept every and all options, their teachers and the books they assign are pushing a different agenda. There is no openness in the views of the authors or the professors. They want you to adopt their worldview while you open your head to all sorts of non-Christian options.

The Neutrality Myth

This openness can have a devastating effect on reading, not only because it makes you a poor reader, but also because it makes you a susceptible reader. Your unformed worldview will begin to take shape in terms of the material you read, in most cases unknowingly, if you do not recognize that all facts are interpreted facts, by you and the author.

Mortimer Adler, in his classic *How to Read a Book*, falls into the isolated-fact trap when he states that "reasonable men can agree" when they agree on the facts. He writes:

> I think that knowledge can be communicated and that dis-
> cussion can result in learning. If knowledge, not opinion, is at
> stake, then either disagreements are apparent only–to be
> removed by coming to terms and a meeting of the minds; or, if
> they are real, then the genuine issues can always be resolved–in
> the long run, of course–*by appeals to facts and reason.*[7]

He never considers that all men, writers and readers, interpret the facts from a certain presuppositional grid. All men choose, write about, align, and interpret the facts according to a set of preconceived ideas about the nature of God, man, and reality in general. Even Christians have been trapped. Too many believe that if only the facts are presented in a logical and systematic way, unbelievers will be convinced and come to Christ. This is nonsense. A quick survey of the Bible tells us that this is not even near the truth. There was certainly ample evidence that Jesus rose from the dead. But did the facts convince the presuppositional skeptics? Hardly. The facts did not fit their worldview. It's no different today:

This is true of even the most "convincing" Christian argument—a cogent case for the historicity of the resurrection. Upon hearing such an argument, one listener may reply, "Aha, this *is* ultimately a chance universe in which even the most unexpected of things can happen once. A man rising from the dead, can you imagine that?" Or another may say, "Erik Von Daniken must be right. Jesus must have been one of those men from outer space, evidently from a planet where men are so constituted that they come back to life after dying." In neither case has the data been seen to confirm that claim which it was intended to confirm—that Jesus is divine, the Son of God.[8]

Are the facts acknowledged? Yes. Do the interpreters of the facts associate them with Jesus as the Son of God? No. Why? Their worldview won't allow it.

Reading is not an easy skill to master. But it is obtainable. It will pay off. Reading is an expensive enterprise, not just in the price of the book but in the time spent in reading. If there is no informational pay back, then why continue to read? So most college graduates either stop reading or turn to passive reading materials like magazines and newsletters. Stick with it. While the average college graduate will quit reading when he lands his first job, you can continue your education and become a source of information for the Church of Jesus Christ and the advancement of His kingdom.

READING WITH A WORLDVIEW IN MIND

Philosophy is usually relegated to a semi-impractical field of study where jobs are hard to come by. But philosophy is broader than the discipline itself. All actions are tied to a philosophy. Our actions are motivated by our philosophy of life, our worldview. An author's worldview is simply the way he looks at things.[9] His worldview is his perspective of reality, his means of interpreting the facts, experiences, and circumstances around him. Everyone has a worldview. According to Alvin Toffler in his scenario of the future, *Future Shock*, "Every person carries in his head a mental model of the world, a subjective representation of external reality."[10] This philosophical model is, he says, like a huge filing cabinet that contains a file for every item of information we encounter. This giant filing system organizes the bits and pieces of information and serves as a grid from which to formulate our thinking.[11]

The author's mind is not blank, *tabula rasa* (a blank tablet), and his perspective is not open and objective. When he puts his thoughts to paper, he can only do so because his mind is already filled with all sorts of ideas with which to think. These more or less fixed ideas with which he thinks make up his philosophical model of the world, his frame of reference for marshalling the facts to support his thesis. His worldview comes to expression in everything he writes.

Reading, as in everything we do, must begin with worldview thinking. An effective reader must understand the style of the book, but more importantly, he must find the author's intent (his worldview or philosophy). In most cases, there will be a clash of worldviews with the author and the reader. There can be no critical reading if the author's worldview is not known. Moreover, there can be no critical analysis and interaction with the material if your own worldview is not formulated. More importantly, if you do not have a Biblical worldview formulated *before* you read, it's likely that you will be persuaded by his "reasonable" argumentation in an area where you have little knowledge.

Developing A Grid

What things should you be looking for to identify the author's worldview? There are at least four basics: What is the author's view about God, man, ultimate reality, and authority? There is no way that you or your professors can read, write, or lecture without considering these four first principles. Of course, there are certainly additional points that come into play, but these are the essential ones. You will see each of them emerge as your instructor handles questions from you and your fellow classmates. He will not be able to hide them.

Why is finding the author's presuppositional grid (philosophy of life) so important for the college student? Speaking practically, there is really only one reason. When you take a test, usually an essay test, forty-five minutes is all you have. If you've read the textbook (if any) and five books for the course, and have studied your lecture notes, you will have more material than you can ever put down in the time limit. If you know an author's thesis then you know the book. The many facts just support the thesis. Your professor wants to know if you *understand* the material and are able to interact with it.

Bits and Pieces

When most students tackle a book, they have no plan, no interpreting grid for absorbing, assimilating, and finally interpreting the facts.
When the reading task is completed, the student walks away from a
book and finds that he can't remember what he read. There are bits and
pieces of information, some disjointed facts here and there, but no
coherent whole. The opening words of Francis Schaeffer's classic, *A
Christian Manifesto*, while not related to reading directly, are important
here: "The basic problem of the Christians in this country in the last
eighty years or so . . . is that they have seen things in bits and pieces instead of totals."[12]

Reading and the Trinity

The Trinity seems like such an abstract piece of theology. For many,
the doctrine of the Trinity is useful only when determining whether a
particular campus religious group is a cult. It's unfortunate that the Trinity is rarely discussed outside academic theological circles. There are
some tremendous applications of the Trinity in the areas of science, politics, economics, and, yes, reading. All of life is a reflection of the character of God, with the exception of sin.

Reading reflects a trinitarian view of reality. God is both One and
Many[13]: One God and Three Persons each of Whom is God. Men and
women, created in the image of God, reflect God's trinitarian character.
Man's "creations" reflect the same trinitarian image. The structure of the
book, the author's worldview, is the integrator of the facts. The facts will
get lost if you do not first determine where the author is coming from.
This can best be remembered by keeping in mind that a book is both *one*
and *many* – a reflection of God's image in every author, whether acknowledged or not: *One* overall theme, structure, or grid and *many* supporting
facts, anecdotes, examples, personal experiences to support the thesis of
the book. It is your job to find out what the book is about *before* you do
any extensive reading.

Men and women, whether they are Christian or not, reflect the Trinity in their writings. Some may do a better job of expressing the Trinity
than others, but the pattern is there.

WHERE TO BEGIN:
DEVELOPING A READING METHODOLOGY

Few of us would attempt to travel across the country without a road map and some preliminary preparations, and yet many of us just dive into a new book with little or no preparation. Remember, you are reading to gain something—knowledge. You won't just stumble across it. You need to know what you're looking for, and you need to have the necessary tools to dig out the information. Once you get it, storing it and remembering it at the appropriate time (for an exam or a paper) are the most essential elements. Here are some simple steps to follow:

1. Title and Subtitle

Read and understand the title and subtitle of the book. They can reveal a lot about the book and will give the first clues you'll need to gather additional information. Let's look at a few examples:

• Herbert Schlossberg, *Idols for Destruction: Christian Faith and its Confrontation with American Society* (Nashville, TN: Thomas Nelson Publishing Co., 1983). The title does not give us much information, but the subtitle tells all, especially when it's tied to the dust jacket and introduction. The idols must be part of or make up American society in some way. Christianity is going to be the standard used to evaluate these idols.

• Harold J. Berman, *Law and Revolution: The Formation of the Western Legal Tradition* (Cambridge, MA: Harvard University Press, 1983). The book is obviously about law and revolution. The subtitle gives us information about the legal aspect of the book, but nothing is said about how it relates to revolution or the type of revolution discussed. The Preface, Introduction (forty-five pages), and the back cover give the reader all he or she will need to determine the author's thesis and definition of the nature of law and revolution.

• Konstantin M. Simis, *USSR: The Corrupt Society: The Secret World of Soviet Capitalism* (New York: Simon and Schuster, 1982). The Soviet Union despises capitalism. This book exposes the underground capitalistic system that operates within the Soviet Union. But there seems to be a sinister twist to this Soviet "capitalism"; it is actually corrupt. While the subtitle does not give us any more information than this, a brief reading of the dust jacket supports our initial conclusions about the book's contents:

When a squad of KGB men confiscated the manuscript in Simis' apartment, they discovered a triple threat—the exposure of the bribery, blackmail and corruption that are rampant in the Soviet Union today. . . . We learn of officials who are secretly paid hundreds of thousands of dollars; provincial bosses who systematically extort goods and services; the sale of almost everything from government posts to high school diplomas for the right price [inside flap of dust jacket].

Konstantin Simis has written an utterly fascinating book about a side of Soviet Life that we have never had a glimpse of before. He has given us an irresistible gallery of Russian rogues and scoundrels, and a vivid portrait of the Soviet bureaucracy at work. I recommend this book without reservation [back of dust jacket].

At this point I would recommend that you write down your initial thoughts on a three by five or five by eight card and use it as a book mark. You can fill the card with introductory data as you read the dust jacket, preface, foreword, and introduction. This summary information will keep you on track as you read. It will also serve as an integrator for the explanatory features of the book.

2. Dust Jacket

Read the dust jacket. Here you *should* find the essence of the book reinforcing the title and subtitle information. We have seen that this is the case in *USSR: The Corrupt Society*. Of course, if it's a paperback, you will not get all the valuable information. Paperbacks do not have inside dust jacket flaps. Moreover, if it's a library book, you will often find that the dust jacket has been taken off the book. In some cases, however, libraries keep the dust jackets by enveloping them in a protective see-through cover or gluing them to the inside hard cover. Sometimes you might find a review glued there as well. Let's look at Herbert Schlossberg's *Idols for Destruction* again:

"Our culture is dying," say modern social critics. Herbert Schlossberg, however, argues that the biblical concepts of idolatry and judgment provide better models for understanding our society than ones that focus on inevitable change and disintegration.

While this might not make a whole lot of sense by itself, it will be reinforced as you read the book, especially in the introduction. This, along with the subtitle information, will become your *interpreting grid*. Without it you will be reading a series of disjointed facts. By understanding the author's basic presuppositions up front you will be better able to follow the track he is laying down for you. Store any additional dust jacket information on your three by five card. It will come in handy.

A very straightforward *interpreting grid* is found on the dust jacket's inside flap of Rousas John Rushdoony's *By What Standard?*:

> Basic to this study is the belief that the presuppositions of human thought in every field must be basically one in order to arrive at any concept which both validates biblical faith and human knowledge. The sovereignty of the self-contained God is the key to every field, in that only the God of Scripture makes all things possible and explicable and is thus the basic premise not only of theology, but of philosophy, science and indeed all knowledge.

Someone always claims to be sovereign. When God is denied as the only independent Sovereign, sovereignty itself is not denied; it is only transferred from God to man, from man to the State.

3. Endorsements

Get some information about the book from those who endorse or reject the author's thesis. Let's take another look at *Idols for Destruction*. The back jacket gives us three brief reviews—all favorable, of course. It matters to us who these people are. Carl F. H. Henry is a well-respected writer. His six volume series, *God, Revelation, and Authority*, is a massive work that has gotten rave reviews. He was the founding editor of *Christianity Today*, a magazine that has seen better days. James Hitchcock has written an excellent exposé of secular humanism entitled, *What is Secular Humanism?* He also has an article, along with the late Francis Schaeffer, in *Who is For Peace?* His article asserts that the United States Catholic bishops' unrealistic view of the Soviet Union, as revealed in their pastoral letter, threatens the cause of world peace. Franky Schaeffer also quotes Schlossberg favorably in his *Bad News for Modern Man. Eternity Magazine, The Presbyterian Journal*, and *The New York Times* all had favorable reviews. By reading these reviews you will learn something valuable about the book that will help in your reading comprehension. I realize that you are not privy to all this information. But it is available. Of course, many good books never get reviewed.[14]

4. Reviews

Certainly every college student should go to great lengths to search out the reviews of those books that are required reading, especially in the area of their major. By going to the scholarly journals in the field of study in which the book falls, you will find a number of reviews by those who either teach or write in that field. A book that has just been published will probably not have been out long enough to be reviewed.

One place to find reviews is in the *Book Review Digest*. It's set up by years. Brief reviews are included that summarize more substantial reviews found in numerous periodicals. If you like what a review says, you can look up the periodical and read the more complete review. Make a Xerox copy of these reviews, either the ones in the *Book Review Digest* or the more substantial reviews in the periodicals cited, and mark the pertinent data. This will help you interact with the book in oral discussions, papers, and essay tests. Your professor will be quite impressed if you can interact with experts in the field.

The author's name is listed along with the name of the book and a number of magazines where additional reviews can be found but which are not summarized in the *Digest*.

The *Book Review Index* is also very helpful. Instead of giving brief reviews, it lists the periodicals where the reviews can be found. You might find a periodical not listed in the *Book Review Digest* that would better suit your purposes.

5. Author's Background

Learn something about the author and how he came to write the book. Check *Contemporary Authors* for the educational background, publishing history, and work history of the author. This will give life to what you read. Not all publishers supply you with this information, however. Again, when test time rolls around, this type of information makes interesting reading if it relates well to some question on an essay test. For example, Thomas Sowell and Walter E. Williams are economists who happen to be black. Sowell is a former Marxist. Their assessment of present-day welfare programs is contrary to that of most economists, white or black. They believe that welfare programs actually hurt the poor and that race has very little to do with economic mobility. It helps to know that these men are black and came from what we would call "underprivileged conditions."

One of the interesting aspects of *Contemporary Authors* is that it sometimes contains "Sidelights." Here the philosophy of the author is spelled out in great detail.

6. Table of Contents

It always helps to know where the author is taking you. The best way to learn his "route" is to read the table of contents. When you find a good table of contents, photocopy it and have it before you when you read through the book. The really important chapters can be checked and the most important pages you have read can be written down in the margin of your copy. When you finish your reading for the day, transfer your notations to the table of contents in the book you are reading. When test time comes, you will have already keyed yourself to the most important chapters. After listening to your professor's lectures you will learn that in *his* mind some chapters are more important than others. After your initial reading, and after listening to your professor, you may find that an adjustment is needed on your evaluation of the important chapters. When it's time to review for a test, you might be able to skip the unimportant chapters and save some time. Also, you should make a mental note of those chapters he did not discuss. By making reference to them in an essay test, you'll show him that you've read the material.

7. Preface

The preface is the author's statement of why he wrote the book. "Material normally included in an author's preface consists of reasons for undertaking the work, [and] method of research (only if this has some bearing on the reader's understanding of the text) . . ."[15] Greg Bahnsen writes in his preface to the first edition of *Theonomy in Christian Ethics*:

> Central to the theory and practice of Christian ethics, whether personal or social, is every jot and tittle of God's law is laid down in the revelation of the Older and New Testaments. The Christian is obligated to keep the whole law of God as a pattern of sanctification, and in the realm of human society the civil magis-

trate is responsible to enforce God's law against public crime. These themes, as elementary as they may seem, have been my concern in the present study.[16]

Here you are getting the author's reason for undertaking the work. The author goes into more detail, qualifying his thesis and narrowing his objectives. Is there something missing in the field that he feels needs to be covered? Is there a new development in the field that should be part of the scholarly material? Does the author believe that a particular position has been so misinterpreted that a critical analysis is due? David Chilton, in *Productive Christians in an Age of Guilt-Manipulators*, believes that it was necessary to respond to the very popular, but seriously flawed book by Ronald J. Sider, *Rich Christians in an Age of Hunger*. Chilton writes in the preface to his third edition:

> This book is a response to Ronald Sider's *Rich Christians in an Age of Hunger* (1977). First published in 1981, *Productive Christians* went into a second, slightly revised edition in 1982. We had planned simply to keep the revised edition in print as long as there was sufficient demand; providentially, however, just as we were about to order another printing, Dr. Sider came out with a second edition of his own (1984), which differs at significant points from the first book (the type was also completely reset, so that the page numbers are different as well). The reprinting of *Productive Christians* thus presented a problem: Should it deal with the first or second edition of Sider's work? Sider's 1977 edition is, in my opinion, by far the strongest; the 1984 edition is considerably watered-down.

This edition of *Productive Christians*, therefore, is a response to Sider's *two* editions.[17] Both books, Bahnsen's *Theonomy in Christian Ethics* and Chilton's *Productive Christians*, do us a great service by their detailed prefaces.

8. Foreword

The foreword (not *forward*) is usually a statement by some distinguished person who strongly recommends the book. It's one long endorsement. Francis A. Schaeffer, author of nearly twenty-five books, and called the "Guru of the Fundamentalists" by *Newsweek*, wrote this about John Whitehead's *The Second American Revolution*:

John Whitehead has attacked and exposed an issue that has been festering, hidden beneath the surface, for far too long. The issue is that of church and state: Christian and religious freedom versus a secularist, humanistic elite, which increasingly controls our society. . . .

This is certainly the most important book I have read in a long, long time. Because of its lucid and well-written nature, as well as its profound depth, this book will appeal to layman, lawyer, minister, judge: all, alike. I recommend this book highly.[18]

The writer of the foreword brings a unique perspective to the book. Again, you should continue to compile the thrust of the book as you read these preliminary data.

9. Introduction

The introduction is essential to the text of any book. Unfortunately, many books do not carry an introduction. The whole ball of wax should be contained here. A fuller statement of everything you have read up to this point should be evident in the introduction. The author should be setting the scene and giving you the historical background of the subject. *The introduction is must reading.* It will save you a tremendous amount of time down the road if you solidify your understanding of the author's thesis through your reading and assimilation of the introduction.

10. Chapter Summaries

Chapter summaries should also be read before diving into the chapter. There's an old adage: Tell them what you're going to tell them; tell them; tell them what you just told them. The summaries will prepare you for your reading. You're getting a sneak preview of the material.

11. Skimming and Note-Taking

Skim through the book making *brief* notes, or at least check marks in the margins. This procedure is laying a track for your final reading. Reading some of the opening paragraphs of each chapter will give you a clearer idea of where the author is going. If something does not fit the thesis, make a note of this also. When test time comes, you will show your professor that you've read and understand the material and are able to interact with the author. You'll also show him you can *think*, a rare commodity these days. Transfer these brief notes to the front and back leaves of your book. For example, here are some notes that I made while I was skimming Paul Johnson's *Modern Times* (New York: Harper and Row, 1983).

PAGE
36 – Germany's economy ravaged by War reparations
37 – Oppression of own minorities
48 – Nietzsche – "Will to Power"/emergence of "gangster states-
    men"
51 – Lenin: replaced religion with "Will to Power"
52 – Lenin: viewed intellectual class as "uniquely privileged priest-
    hood," endowed with special gnosis (knowledge) and chosen
    by history

There is a tremendous amount of material you could take down in notes, but your reading should be *selective*. You're looking for material that relates to the course under study, a related course, or a paper you are preparing. Transfer these notes to the front and back leaves *after* you have finished reading the book. By this time you will know what is important. This is your own special review of the book for an exam and *your* handy index for writing papers.

12. Footnotes

One way to learn about other good books is by paying attention to footnotes. Of course, many books don't have footnotes. Footnotes at the bottom of the page will save you time having to flip to the back of the book to find the reference. Many books, so as not to appear too "scholarly" to the average reader will have endnotes at the end of the book or at the end of each chapter. A footnoted or endnoted book will help you with collateral reading. A particular footnote, while not germane to the author's present thesis, may help you. It might be the very key you're looking for to finish up a paper. Moreover, it will give you an idea of what books you might like to have for your own library. An author who footnotes has done the preliminary reading for you. He can save you time and money in the end. Much of my library is the result of following the trail of numerous footnotes.

13. Reading the Book

Now begin to read the book all the way through, underlining the important points and using the margin for any additional notes you might need to make. Keep a dictionary handy to look up words that are unfamiliar to you. Include a brief definition in the margin. Refer to your note card to remind yourself of the author's purpose when you run across anything that seems contradictory. Make a note of it.

14. Summing Up

Your reading analysis is not over when you finish the book. Go back and summarize each chapter in a few written sentences. Do this from memory if you can. If you can't, then go over your notes and underlining. Finally, summarize the book in a brief paragraph.

PROBLEM-ORIENTED READING

The best way to retain what you read is to approach your reading matter with a problem in mind. For example, you have a paper due in a sociology class. You've chosen a topic that will deal with the effects of population on economic growth. Where do you begin? Much of your reading will be discarded. Your task is to search out the material pertinent to your topic. In the end you will *remember* what you've read because you developed a hook on which to hang your new reading material. You went after a problem to solve. In this case, it was a paper on economic growth and population. You suspect that R. J. Rushdoony's book, *The Myth of Over-Population*,[19] will deal with the topic. In most cases, however, you will have to search for the needed material in books not directly related to your topic. Thomas Sowell's *The Economics and Politics of Race: An International Perspective* comes to your attention. You might not remember another thing in Sowell's book, but you will remember the material on population density and income levels. "The more general question of crowded cities has little to do with total population or 'over'-population, relative to the land area of a country. . . . [T]here is little or no relationship between poverty and population density."[20]

Problem-oriented reading is not always possible. You can create your own problems by formulating questions before you read. Ask yourself "filtering questions" such as:

- What significance does it have?
- Why is this so important?
- Who says so?
- Are there any other options, opinions, beliefs, or objections?
- Can I trust his statistics?
- Are his assertions true?
- Is his argument valid?
- Are his conclusions sound?
- Does the author discuss and reject other positions?
- If so, what are they, and on what grounds are they rejected?
- Why are these themes included but not others?
- Is he unfamiliar with these themes?
- Why doesn't he cite this or that author?
- Is he hiding certain contrary positions from his readers?

The most important reading skill is interaction with the reading material. Do not become a passive reader. Engage yourself. It will keep you alert and help you remember.

WHAT ABOUT SPEED READING?

A final word needs to be given on speed reading. There are a lot of courses out there that promise to increase your reading speed "four-fold." Maybe they can. But don't count on it.

Consider sprinting and jogging. You can't sprint a mile. You'll lose in the 100-meter dash if you decide to jog. There are different racing strategies for different races. This is common sense. Everyone knows the differences between the mile and the 100-meter dash. Reading is no different. Some material you can sprint through while other material needs a slower pace, a jog.

The same reading techniques cannot be used effectively for different kinds of books. You would not read a technical scientific journal in the same way as you would read a work in sociology. Most students do not understand this. The same techniques when applied to different reading materials will lead to misinformation, misinterpretation, and certainly rapid dropout in memory retention.

You must adjust your reading technique as you change the type of book you read. But, don't change your analytical techniques. Determining the philosophy of the book remains the same for all types of books. It might be more difficult to find with different kinds of books, but it is there.

CONCLUSION

Reading is probably the most important skill you will take to college. If you do not know how to read well, your entire college career is going to be a struggle. In fact, poor reading will keep you from getting that most prized possession—a college degree. Reading is like any other skill: The more you practice the better you get at it. Poor reading comes from little or no reading. Read at every opportunity. Push yourself to read material you really are not that interested in. If you can't (or won't) read, you will not be able to lead.

————— 13 —————
HOW TO WRITE AND RESEARCH

1. Always try to use the language so as to make quite clear what you mean and make sure y[ou]r sentence couldn't mean anything else.

2. Always prefer the plain direct word to the long, vague one. Don't *implement* promises, but *keep* them.

3. Never use abstract nouns when concrete ones will do. If you mean "More people died" don't say "Mortality rose."

4. In writing. Don't use adjectives which merely tell us how you want us to *feel* about the thing you are describing. I mean, instead of telling us a thing was "terrible," describe it so that we'll be terrified. Don't say it was "delightful"; make *us* say "delightful" when we've read the description. You see, all those words (horrifying, wonderful, hideous, exquisite) are only like saying to your readers "Please will you do my job for me."

5. Don't use words too big for the subject. Don't say "infinitely" when you mean "very"; otherwise you'll have no word left when you want to talk about something *really* infinite.[1]

WELL written books, whether good or bad in what they espouse, have changed the way people think and act. Shifts in worldviews have taken place through books. Of course, Christianity is the most obvious example of this. Western civilization would never have developed without the Bible. From literature, modern science, and education to law, medicine, and government, the Bible has been instrumental in transforming civilizations wherever it is believed and acted upon. Once people become new creatures in Christ (2 Corinthians 5:17), they want direction in their lives. Their question is, "How should we then live?" The Bible tells them. Consider the following quotations from some of our nation's presidents:[2]

> *John Quincy Adams*: The first and almost the only Book deserving of universal attention is the Bible.

> *Abraham Lincoln*: All the good from the Saviour of the world is communicated through this Book; but for the Book we could not know right from wrong. All the things desirable to man are contained in it.

> *Woodrow Wilson*: The Bible is the one supreme source of revelation of the meaning of life, the nature of God and spiritual nature and need of men. It is the only guide of life which really leads the spirit in the way of peace and salvation.

> *Andrew Jackson*: Go to the Scriptures . . . the joyful promises it contains will be balsam to all your troubles.

> *Calvin Coolidge*: The foundations of our society and our government rest so much on the teachings of the Bible that it would be difficult to support them if faith in these teachings would cease to be practically universal in our country.

But the Bible has not been alone in shaping the way people think and act. Other writings have been specifically designed to undermine the authority of Scripture. Darwin's *Origin of Species* (1859) turned the religious and scientific communities upside down. God as creator was slowly pushed out of the universe. Darwinian evolution has influenced every branch of learning, from the physical sciences to ethics. The philosophy set forth in Karl Marx's *Das Kapital* has been used to enslave half the world. *Mein Kampf* established the principles of nazism and turned the name of Adolf Hitler into the very embodiment of evil. Its doctrines sent the world to war and nearly eradicated the Jewish community in Europe. Mao Tse-tung's writings brought on a communist Cultural Revolution in China from 1966 to 1977. *The Collected Works of Mao Tse-tung* acted as the bible for the people. The Chinese people were to read, meditate upon, memorize, and live by Chairman Mao's sayings. Revolutions are built on the printed page.

Have you ever stopped to consider why revolutionaries first attempt to capture the radio and newspapers before taking over the Presidential palace? They know that he who controls the information channels can mold the minds, and ultimately the hearts, of the people.[3]

Ideas put to paper and acted upon with the highest of energy and uncompromising zeal can change the world. Even the worst of ideas have been used for this very purpose. If minds are going to be transformed and civilizations changed, then Christians must learn to write and write well. Writing is a sword, mightier than all the weapons of war because writing carries with it ideas that penetrate deeper than any bullet. Writing about the right things in the right way can serve as an antidote to the writings of skepticism and tyranny that have plundered the hearts and minds of generations of desperate people around the world.

There is another factor to consider in the area of writing. We cannot count on those who shape public opinion to be neutral in the way they handle the news, especially the Christian worldview. Presuppositions filter the facts. The Christian message, in the hands of a skeptic, comes out twisted and distorted. In fact, evidence indicates that there is a general bias against the Christian faith in what has been described as the "Media Elite."[4] Of course, there is nothing new in all this. The account of Jesus' resurrection was falsely reported by the "press," those who held a contrary opinion of Him.

> Some of the guard came into the city and reported to the chief priests all that had happened. And when they had assembled with the elders and counseled together, they gave a large sum of money to the soldiers, and said, "You are to say, 'His disciples came by night and stole Him away while we were asleep.' And if this should come to the governor's ear, we will win him over and keep you out of trouble." And they took the money and did as they had been instructed; and this story was widely spread among the Jews, and is to this day (Matthew 28:11-15).

While there isn't blatant bribery going on in the press corp today, there still is a bias against religion in general and Christianity in particular. One way to decrease the anti-Christian bias is through competitive reporting. We need Christian writers who have a fully developed Biblical worldview, who will work hard, develop the necessary journalistic skills, and then land jobs in media positions around the world. Your skills will get you hired, although your beliefs may get you fired. We cannot expect objective reporting from those who are hostile to the things of Christ. Franky Schaeffer writes of the media bias:

> In the United States today, and indeed in the whole world, one group more than any other forms public opinions: the media. The film industry, the television networks, newspapers, periodicals, and the people who run these enterprises have an immense amount of power, which is totally disproportionate to their numbers and, unhappily, to their moral perception and compassion.[5]

The forming of public opinion is going on around-the-clock. Christians need to have a voice in shaping that public opinion. Good writing is a tool to bring sanity back to the media. There are numerous positions open with newspapers, magazines, radio, and television. Begin by joining your school's newspaper.

THE ART OF READABLE WRITING

Writing is an art that can be mastered even by those who never thought they could write. I don't mean that you have the ability to turn out a best-selling novel or even an article good enough to be accepted by *Reader's Digest*, although you might. But you can learn to write well enough to be understood by the average man or woman. Getting your point across in a coherent and logical manner is the important thing. Style certainly counts for something. But readability is more important.

Now, don't say to yourself, "Well, I've never been a good writer. I'm one of those people who just doesn't have the knack." Put aside what you think about your writing ability. Go into this chapter with something of a positive attitude. Keep in mind that, like any other skill, writing takes practice. Skills are not cultivated in one sitting. It takes time to develop proficiency in any new skill. One reason for poor writing is that the skill is not practiced regularly. Starting a paper is like beginning a workout that you haven't done in six months. The muscles are stiff and you're out of breath after the first three minutes of vigorous exercise. The stiffness and cardiovascular inefficiency begin to disappear in time.

Like exercise, writing is not something that most students do on a daily basis. Your first attempts at turning out award-winning prose are probably stiff and halting. Frustration might follow with the belief that you are incompetent when it comes to writing. Then the "what's-the-use" attitude raises its ugly head. Writing then takes a back seat to other academic pursuits. This cycle confirms your initial belief that you are not a good writer.

The best way to improve your writing is to write. Write letters to the editor. Take an elective writing class while you're still in high school. Take a summer creative writing course at your local junior college. I recommend a year on the student newspaper; it will sharpen your skills, especially the skill of writing short, coherent sentences.

This chapter will show you the steps of turning out a paper. It is not designed to make you a good writer. Good writing comes with practice. If you do not exhibit good writing ability, don't give up, and don't let anyone tell you that you can't write. But before we discuss the mechanics of writing and how to put a paper together, let's look at the condition of writing in our schools.

The Demise of the Written Word

Poor writing is the result of an all around poor education and a sloppy mind that is not used to thinking logically. Writing is simply thinking on paper. If you have trouble thinking through issues in your head, then you will have trouble putting coherent thoughts to paper. In a word, poor writing is the result of an underdeveloped Biblical worldview. It's easy to conclude that the following is bad writing:

> It's obvious, in our modern world of today theirs a lot of impreciseness in expressing thoughts we have (eighteen-year-old college Freshman).

This is a college student. Sure, he may not be typical. But he did get into college. What can we expect when he graduates? Will he be limited in job advancement? What if he decides on a career that demands good writing? When will he ever develop the skill? The place to start is in high school. But even here there is disappointment:

> John F. Kenedy if he had not buen shat he would be presdent now, and in World War II he was a hero in the war, and he had a lat of naney and a nice fanily, and his wife was very nice, and when I die I would like to b buruid in a plac like that (seventeen-year-old high school student).

227

Certainly the spelling is atrocious. That's not too difficult to remedy. A good editor and proof reader can make the poorest speller look good. But the disjointed thinking is what stands out. What is going on in this student's mind? It's sad. These young people are not stupid. With a little training and a willingness to learn, they could become good writers.

Universities are getting stuck with these unskilled high school graduates, partly due to a lower birth rate. Fewer students mean greater competition among the many colleges and universities. They need the students to pay the bills. The entrance requirements have been lowered to try to keep the colleges full. The colleges have had to adjust to the inferior class of students. Consider the following, written in 1975:

> If your children are attending college, the chances are that when they graduate they will be unable to write ordinary, expository English with any real degree of structure and lucidity. If they are in high school and planning to attend college, the chances are less than even that they will be able to write English at the minimal college level when they get there.[6]

Officials at schools of law, journalism, and business are reporting that basic reading and writing skills are not part of the typical college graduate's academic portfolio. Even the best colleges have failed to turn out graduates with the needed skills for the corporate world. Businessmen complain that secretaries cannot spell and punctuate sentences accurately. Young executives cannot develop and write readable reports. Some of these graduates are coming from our nation's (once) prestigious schools, such as Harvard, Michigan State, and the University of California.

The students are not developing and honing their writing skills in high school. In most cases, schools are not teaching the needed skills. And more often than not, students are not interested when the material is taught. They don't see the need for it. Many colleges have developed remedial reading and writing courses for incoming freshmen who show gross deficiencies on their records. For example:

> At the University of California at Berkeley, where students come from the top 12.5 per cent of high-school graduates, nearly half of last year's freshmen demonstrated writing skills so poor that they were forced to enroll in remedial courses nicknamed "bonehead English." Officials at Michigan State University are so concerned about writing incompetence that they may soon re-

quire all undergraduates to pass a writing exam demonstrating "minimal literary skills" before they receive diplomas. The Georgia Board of Regents, distressed at the lack of writing skill demonstrated by graduates at the state's thirty-two colleges, already requires such a test – and demands remedial writing programs of those who cannot pass. At Temple University in Philadelphia, the proportion of freshmen failing an English placement exam has increased by more than 50 per cent since 1968. Harvard's freshman course in expository writing–the only class every Harvard student is required to take–has been expanded to such an extent in the past two years that some faculty members now call it a "pseudo-department."[7]

GETTING STARTED: WRITING TOOLS

While some of these tools will not be needed until the rewrite stage, it will be good to have them around before you lack the time, energy, and money to acquire them. They should be purchased *before* going to college. This way you can look for discounts. Check a used bookstore first. You can pick up some great bargains.

Style Manuals

Style manuals will help with your manuscript preparation by covering rules of composition, word usage, footnotes, bibliographies, quotations, abbreviations, punctuation, spelling, etc. Here's a list of some of the basic ones:

1. William Strunk, Jr. and E. B. White, *The Elements of Style* (3rd ed.; New York: Macmillan, 1979). This little book covers all the basics: elementary rules of usage, principles of composition, form, words and phrases commonly misused, and an approach to style. Its uniqueness and usefulness is in its brevity. The authors get right to the point.

2. Robert A. Webb, ed., *The Washington Post Deskbook on Style* (New York: McGraw-Hill Paperbacks, 1978). While this book has the newspaper field in mind, it's still extremely valuable. Since copy editors cover all fields, you're likely to find the most unusual grammatical problems covered.

3. *The Chicago Manual of Style* (13th ed.; Chicago, IL: University of Chicago Press, 1969). The style manual that covers it all; designed for authors, editors, and copywriters. It's rather expensive ($35.00). Used bookstores carry older editions that will serve your purposes.

4. Kate L. Turabian, *A Manual for Writers of Term Papers, Theses, and Dissertations* (5th ed.; Chicago, IL: University of Chicago Press, 1987). Probably the most popular and usable manual on the market. The advice and examples of style usage are based on *The Chicago Manual of Style*. Just ask for "Turabian" at the bookstore. Make sure it's the latest edition.

5. Kate L. Turabian, *Student's Guide for Writing College Papers* (3rd ed.; Chicago, IL: University of Chicago Press, 1976). This manual is designed for high school, junior college, or college students faced with writing their first long, documented paper. Sections dealing with writing style and reference works are included.

All these works are helpful (and there are many more like them). But check your college catalog for a preferred style manual and/or ask your professor what he or she prefers.

While the following books are not technically "style manuals," they are helpful for any writer. By the time we get out of college, the king's English has usually been slaughtered. One way to bring it back from the dead is to get *English Grammar for Language Students* by Frank X. Braun (distributed by Ulrich's Books, Inc., 549 E. University Avenue, Ann Arbor, Michigan 48104). If you're taking a foreign language (English included), the booklet (twenty-three pages) is a must.

What word to use when? *Say it right!* by Harry Shaw is a guide to everyday speaking and writing. It will help you in public speaking, whether delivering a lecture or leading a discussion group. One of its most helpful sections is how to avoid "Common Errors in Using Words" (pp. 78-246). What's the difference between "venal" and "venial," "affect" and "effect," and "imminent," "eminent," and "immanent"? When do you use "farther" and "further," "less" and "fewer"?

Grammatical rules have always been difficult to keep straight. *The Elements of Grammar* by Margaret Shertzer (New York: Macmillan, 1986) is helpful in getting through the morass of grammatical confusion. The back covers grammatical terms (parts of a sentence), points of grammar (formation of noun plurals, pronouns, verbs, adjectives, etc.), capitalization, punctuation (the period, comma, semicolon, colon, question mark, etc.), expressing numbers, spelling and choice of words, signs and symbols.

Dictionaries

Dictionaries of thirteen hundred to fifteen hundred pages are sufficient for the kind of work you'll be doing. You can consult dictionaries of
specialty fields for more detailed study (e.g., *Dictionary of Economics*, *The
Dictionary of Hymnology*, *The Encyclopedia of Philosophy*, *The Harper Dictionary of Modern Thought*, etc). The *Oxford English Dictionary* is the most
comprehensive general dictionary. It traces the history of every word
that has been in use in English since 1150, showing how, when, and in
what form words came into the language and what changes have occurred in their meanings, spellings, and usages. There are periodic sup-
plemental volumes that update the work since the major portion of the
set was completed in 1933. In 1971 a two-volume edition in tiny print
was made available. You must read it with a magnifying glass (supplied).
It costs far less than the thirteen-volume edition.

A dictionary that should be in every library is the *American Dictionary
of the English Language* by Noah Webster, published in 1828. It's a real
eye-opener to see how words have changed in meaning. For example,
look up the word "governor" in Noah Webster's dictionary and compare
his definition with any modern dictionary's definition. You can order a
facsimile reprint edition from the Foundation for American Christian
Education (FACE), P.O. Box 27035, San Francisco, CA 94127. It retails
for $30.00. I've seen it advertised for as little as $15.00.

I've already mentioned *Roget's International Thesaurus* and *The
Synonym Finder* (more than one million synonyms). *Webster's Dictionary of
Synonyms* is also quite good. My choice is *The Synonym Finder*, although it
does not have a list of antonyms (words with opposite meanings). When
your manuscript is ready to be typed, you'll want to review it for
repetitious words and dull, listless verbs.

Miscellaneous

An up-to-date almanac or yearbook would be helpful (*The World
Almanac and Book of Facts*, *Information Please Almanac*, etc.). You might
even want a current edition of *The Guinness Book of World Records* for a bit
of diversified interest. A comprehensive book on quotations and illustrations might prove to be helpful (e.g., *The Oxford Dictionary of Quotations*
and *Familiar Quotations* by John Bartlett). A dictionary on longer quotations can be used as quotable material. George Seldes' *The Great*

Thoughts is an up-to-date reference guide that covers everything from Abelard to Zola and Ancient Greece to contemporary America. Finally, a current atlas could save you a lot of guesswork.

There may be other items you'll need to tackle your writing assignments, but these will see you through the basics. There is one last item you might want to consider. More often than not you will find that you'll have to describe how something works. You could go through technical manuals and encyclopedias, but the description you'll find there will probably be too difficult to boil down for your reader. Try children's books.

If you want to write a medieval story and really want to know about armor, look up armor in the children's index. You'll find a book that will tell you each and every part of the knight's armor with beautiful illustrations. The children's library is great! That's where I learned how to start a train and how to blow up tracks. (From her novel, *The Man Who Loved Cat Dancing*, in which she describes the dynamiting of a train.)[8]

You will want to purchase those books and manuals that get used the most—certainly a good dictionary and style manual. The library will carry all that you need. Get familiar with where they are located. Note on your paper the items you need to check before you go to the library.

SCHEDULING

Not all papers will require the same amount of attention. You must learn to prioritize your writing assignments. The most important assignments will probably require the most effort. The length of your assigned papers will also determine which ones you will tackle first. Of course, if you have to turn in a five-page paper on some obscure assigned topic, you may find that it will take you as long to write as a twenty-page paper on a more familiar topic.

Ask the Right Questions

Ask yourself a number of questions before diving into a writing assignment:

- When is the paper due?
- Can I choose my own topic or will one be assigned?

- What's the purpose of the assignment?
- How long should the paper be?
- Will it need to be footnoted? If yes, how many sources will be required?
- Do I need a bibliography?
- Will my paper need to be typed?
- Can I turn in a Xerox copy of my typed paper? (This will allow you to use Liquid Paper on your original without corrected mistakes showing up on your professor's copy.)
- Must I turn in my chosen topic to get it approved? If so, by when?
- Must I turn in an outline and note cards with my completed paper?
- Is there a penalty for a late paper? What is it?

In most cases your professor will hand out a sheet with all the requirements listed. Don't be afraid to ask some questions if something is not covered.

Planning Ahead

Confirm the due date and establish times when each phase of the paper needs to be completed. Schedule some padding time as well. The following procedure is suggestive only. You may want to do it differently to fit your own style. Fill in the dates, moving from the day you get the assignment to the due date. When you finish mapping out what you have to do and when, transfer the dates to your semester calendar.

- Line up a typist by _____. (If you wait until the week you need your paper typed, you will be competing with all the procrastinators.)
- Choose your topic by _____.
- Research to narrow your topic by _____.
- Be willing to scrap your initial topic if it proves to be too obscure or too broad by _____.
- Compile all your research material by _____.
- Write first draft by _____.
- Wait 24 hours.
- Read first draft, making notations and adding new material to the draft by _____.
- Write your second draft by _____.

233

- Wait 24 hours.
- Read the paper aloud by _____.
- Make final adjustments (awkward sentences, transitional sentences, misspellings, poor punctuation, etc.) by _____.
- Write the final draft by _____.
- Proofread by _____.
- Type the final draft by _____.
- Proofread by _____.
- Type the bibliography by _____.
- Due date _____.

Some of these steps can be skipped, depending on the paper and your skill level. You can buy some time if you do your own typing. Some of the tasks can be consolidated. The point of all this is to plan for the unexpected. A comprehensive schedule like this will at least let you know where you are at all times. After you pull your first all-nighter, hopefully you will return to the life of planning, if you haven't flunked out!

Writing a good paper takes planning. The accumulation of facts and the positioning of those facts in a coherent composition is certainly achievable by even the moderately skilled student.

But if you want good grades, if you want your papers to stand out from the drivel that passes for writing these days, then you will have to write interesting and engaging papers. You can do this only when you get to the rhetoric stage of writing. The rhetoric stage is interaction with the written material. You are no longer presenting the opinions of other authors or the history of the topic; rather, you are assessing the evidence and coming to certain conclusions. Are the facts reliable? Has the topic been adequately covered in the past? Do the experts agree? Disagree? Why? What slant are you lending to the discussion? What are your conclusions? Why do you disagree (or agree) with your instructor's evaluation of the topic, if he has voiced an opinion? More about this later.

PLANNING YOUR PAPER

Choosing a Topic

Choose a topic that interests you, if the topic is not assigned. Your writing will probably be vague, aimless, dull, and sketchy if the material has to be dragged out of you. If you are wrapped up in your subject, you can expect your writing to have passion, especially if the topic relates to

a heart-held conviction.

Some of the most interesting topics are those that the revisionist historians have taken over. They have made their reinterpretation of history the standard explanation for what *really* happened. For example, John Brown is usually portrayed as a patriotic man who was against the dreadful concept of slavery. He has been elevated to sainthood by modern historians. Historian/biographer Otto Scott tells a different story. He alleges that John Brown and his band of abolitionists were the fathers of modern terrorism.

> Scott argues that Brown and his supporters were not making sympathetic or patriotic gestures by their guerrilla war in Kansas in 1856 or their Harper's Ferry raid in 1859. Rather, they were a group of senseless fanatics who revelled in the glories of dissension and whose mania, ego, and illiteracy were manipulated into a lunatic rage that managed to make a martyr out of John Brown. (From the dust jacket flap).[9]

Talk about a hot topic!
Consider these revisionist topics:
1. Was Galileo claiming that the Bible was in error when he asserted that the earth revolved around the sun?

> Cardinal Bellarmine stated the Church's position: "The doctrine attributed to Copernicus and championed by Galileo, that the earth moves around the sun . . . is contrary to the Holy Scriptures and therefore cannot be defended or held."[10] Galileo maintained that there was nothing in the "book of nature" that would contradict the Bible. Galileo wrote: "The Holy Bible can never speak untruth–whenever its true meaning is understood."[11] What's the real story? The church had actually adopted an Aristotelian cosmology which it forced on the Bible. Aristotle believed that the universe is finite, with the stationary earth at its center. All planetary objects revolved around the earth.

2. Did the ACLU use the "academic freedom" issue at the Scope's "Monkey Trial" in Dayton, Tennessee in 1925 to get evolution taught in order to give them time to work in the courts to disallow the teaching of creation altogether?

> The Tennessee law, repealed in 1967, read: "It shall be unlawful for any teacher in any of the universities, normals and all other

public schools of the state which are supported in whole or in part by the public school funds of the state, to teach any theory that denies the story of the divine creation of man as taught in the Bible, and to teach instead that man has descended from a lower state of animals." The attorney for John Scopes, the high school teacher who was on trial for teaching evolution, insisted that "It is bigotry for public schools to teach only one theory of origins."[12] Why was it bigotry in 1925 to mandate the teaching of only creation, while it's not bigotry today to mandate the teaching of only evolution?

After some research on your initial choice of a topic, you may find that you are no longer interested. This is why planning is necessary. Give yourself plenty of time to choose another topic. Some instructors require you to turn in your topic by a certain date. If you decide to narrow your topic or change your topic after you've turned one in, be sure you let your professor know.

Be sure your topic is neither too broad nor too narrow. When you start your research you may find that you will have to choose only an aspect of your broader topic. Don't be afraid to chop your topic down to a manageable size. Consider the John Brown topic. The "Abolition Movement" would be too broad. "John Brown at Harper's Ferry" may be too narrow. A broad topic forces you to cover too much ground with very little space for analysis. A narrow topic is usually too difficult to research. It simply takes too much time. You might find yourself scrapping the narrow topic after you've spent quite a bit of time in research, only to find that there's not enough research information available to do a good job. "John Brown and the Revisionist Historians" would not only be just right but *very* interesting. On Galileo you might want to discuss how an Aristotelian cosmology was adopted by the Church. You could discuss the non-neutrality factor in the creation-evolution debate. These topics would allow you to apply your presuppositional grid to the facts. This is the ideal. Moreover, they are very interesting for your professors.

Writing for Your Audience

Remember that you are writing for your professor, not your fellow students. (Of course, there may be times when a different audience is in view, including fellow students. Vary your audience direction appropriately.) Don't try to fool your professor with two dollar words and sentences with forty words or more. Clarity is what he's looking for. If you try to hide your ignorance with unclear writing, he'll spot it. Students are often tempted to fill up their papers with unnecessary words. Your prof requires a twenty-page paper and all you can crank out is fifteen pages. You hit on an idea. Instead of writing, for example, "All thinking is religious," you opt for, "The thinking of all individuals is tied to what some might describe as religious ideas rooted in faith-held presuppositions that circumvent the options normally attributed to religiously neutral thinking." Sounds impressive, but it's all unnecessary. As a matter of fact, a description of "All thinking is religious" with examples from science, psychology, history, education, and journalism will extend the length of your paper and make for far more interesting reading. Wordiness is worthless. Here's what a former professor has to say on the subject:

> [Students] try to impress the professor with their knowledge or the amount of energy they have spent writing the paper, but nearly all professors mark *down* for irrelevant remarks. We want to know your purpose and the way you try to achieve it, and padding confuses and irritates us. Later audiences (such as your bosses) will have even more damaging reactions: they will simply ignore your memos and reports [and eventually fire you].[13]

One key point to remember in writing is that the writer knows what he has written, or, at least, he *thinks* he knows what he has written. Do not assume that your prof will understand an obscure idea or poorly constructed sentence or poor transitional sentence. Assume nothing.

Purpose or Theme

"The single most important part of any essay is its purpose. *Everything* should be subordinate to that purpose; if an idea, a paragraph, a sentence, or even a word does not contribute to that purpose, it does not belong there."[14] Time must be spent on shaping, formulating, sculpting, honing, and narrowing the purpose of your paper. Write it out on a three by five card and keep it in front of you as you research and write. It will save you time in both areas. Put your thesis statement at the beginning of your working outline. Your "thesis" sentence may be required by your professor. If not, it's still a good idea to keep it in front of *your* mind as you write. Here are four things to include:

  1. Write a complete declarative sentence that sets forth your point of view.

2. Write a thesis statement that is open to argument by your reader, rather than a statement of personal preference or observation with which no one can disagree.

3. Write a thesis statement that is narrow in scope.

4. Spend some time on your thesis statement. A well-written and defined thesis statement will save you from meandering all over the research stacks in the library.

Your reader must be aware of your purpose when he starts reading the first few sentences. He should not have to hunt for it. If you have to come out and write, "My purpose is . . . ," then do it. There might be more creative ways to state a purpose, but this will do for now. Hopefully, it will not be so formal. You want to engage the reader's interest. When you revise your work, every new sentence, illustration, example, anecdote, or quotation must be aimed at the purpose. If something doesn't fit, cut it out. You'll lose your reader if you hook him with a dangling thought that doesn't fit your theme. He'll have to stop and think how it fits. If he has to do this too often, you're sunk.

Do an Outline

Before you do any serious writing, do an outline. You want to move the information point by point to a conclusion. Your outline serves as a road map for getting you there so you can write a good conclusion. Hopefully it will get your professor there as well. An outline is an exercise in logic. It's a way of cutting through your own confusion about the topic.

Your outline will vary with the subject matter. It might be historical progression, comparative analysis, or thematic. In some cases it might include all three.

There are three main sections to cover: introduction, body, and conclusion. Save the introduction and conclusion for last. Concentrate on the body of the paper.

Your outline will change as you do more research. What you thought should be emphasized as a main point has now become a sub-point under a new main point. At the beginning you may have very little to put down for your outline. Double or even triple-space your outline. This will leave you enough space for notes and bibliographical information.

Give yourself a wide left margin for notes as you do your research.

DOING THE RESEARCH

The best way to do research is to get familiar with the library. Can you find the following?:

☐ Card catalogs

☐ Indexes for periodicals, newspapers, and scholarly journals

☐ Volumes of Abstracts

☐ Periodicals

☐ Audio-visual materials: records, slides, filmstrips, microfilm, microfiche, audio and video tapes

☐ Access to computer data bases

☐ Reference books: encyclopedias, special collections, stacks, almanacs, atlases

☐ The librarian

• *Read the general literature*: In gathering information you will need to start with the general information that's available and move to the specialized material on the subject. During this period of research you will be getting a feel for the subject matter. You will notice repetition among the many sources.

A good place to start is with encyclopedias and the standard works in the field. An encyclopedia should only be used for *your* background information and *should never be quoted anywhere in your paper* unless the reference is so unusual and insightful that it cries out to be repeated. Make sure your professor knows this is why you are quoting such a source. On a freshman paper, however, leave out any reference to encyclopedias.

An invaluable guide to research materials is *The Basic Guide to Research Sources*. Its subtitle tells all: "How to Find What You Want Quickly and Easily in: Government and Private Sources, Books for Specialized Fields, Business, the Arts, the Sciences."[15] Included in the "Specialized Fields" section are the following broad topics: art, architecture, and the minor arts, business and economics, education, history, literature, mathematics, music and dance, mythology, philosophy, plays, poetry, political science, religion, sciences, social sciences, speeches, and sports and hobbies. It's an inexpensive paperback.

The United States Government, the largest printing concern in the world (naturally), can be a great help. If you have enough time to research your topic, you can ask your congressman to have The Congressional Research Service do some work for him, for you.

239

The Congressional Research Service works exclusively for the Congress, conducting research, analyzing legislation, and providing information at the request of Committees, Members and their staffs.

The Service makes such research available, without partisan bias, in many forms including studies, reports, compilations, digests, and background briefings. Upon request, the CRS assists Committees in analyzing legislative proposals and issues, and in assessing the possible effects of these proposals and their alternatives. The Service's senior specialists and subject analysts are also available for personal consultations in their respective fields of expertise.[16]

Periodicals are a good source of research material. You'll never find the needed articles without the *Reader's Guide to Periodical Literature*. All articles are indexed under subject and author (in some cases under title). A more specialized periodical index is the *International Index*. Whereas the *Reader's Guide* indexes over 100 American and Canadian popular magazines, the *International Index* lists over 250 American and foreign scholarly magazines, largely in the fields of language, literature, and history. There is a specialized index to the *New York Times*, the *New York Times Index*, of course.

The card catalog file under your subject is essential. Learn how to use it. *The Scholastic's A+ Guide to Research and Term Papers* has a chapter on research and note taking that will get you through the basics.[17]

Write letters to other universities, directing your letter to the appropriate department, and ask for a reading list on your topic. Or write to organizations that you feel might have specialized information. One neglected source of information is the personal interview. These can be done by phone or in person. Ask your professor if he knows of anyone in the city who might be able to help you on the subject. If he doesn't know, then go to the head of the department.

• *Play detective*: How do you find what you need in a five hundred-page book? Good question. Obviously you do not have the time to read it. If you have been led to the book by a footnote from another book, the footnoted material often has a certain page identified. The author has done the work for you. In most cases you will be led to the book through the card catalog file. Here you'll have to play Sherlock Holmes. The index is the first place to start. If you're looking for material on the First Amendment, be aware that the topic is broad. Check a number of index entries. For example, *The Separation Illusion* by John Whitehead deals with the First Amendment. You know a book-length treatment of the subject is going to be more comprehensive than your twenty-five-page paper. Turn to the index and look up First Amendment, Bible, Bill of Rights, Christianity, Church, God, Fourteenth Amendment, Government, Jefferson, Law, etc. With those books without indexes you will have to rely on the table of contents and some fast skimming.

One creative and non-systematic way to do research is the "lucky dipping" method. "Lucky dipping" research is pulling books off the shelves at random and looking in the index for references to your topic. You never know what you'll find. I would save this for last, a sort of icing on the cake.

• *Throughout the research phase you'll want to write down any idea that comes into your head*: "Just write down whatever crosses your mind, no matter how silly or irrelevant it seems. Your mind does *not* wander randomly; there is a method in its madness and a reason for every thought that enters it. If you let it go, and follow it wherever it goes, you will be astonished at the originality and creativity that you have buried inside of you. You will also end up with far more ideas than you need and solve that terrible problem of getting started."[18] Do not assume that you'll remember any of these ideas when it comes time to write the first draft. The following story is told of the renowned scientist Baron Alexander von Humboldt when he was exploring Mexico and making the first accurate map of that land.

> The native who guided him through the countryside around Mexico City did not see why the baron was considered a genius. The guide admitted the baron was a quick-moving hard worker. "The baron couldn't have a good memory," the guide said with a contemptuous shrug, "because he had to write down the names of villages and streams which everyone knew."[19]

Who's the really smart researcher? The one who knows his mind's limitations.

• *Nail down your topic and sharpen your purpose*: After your initial research, you will need to go back and revise your purpose if you think it needs it based on your research at this point.

• *Fill in your outline with more detail as you read*: Your main points and sub-points should be fleshed out. Complete bibliographic data should be noted at the appropriate places.

241

- *Gather your research material*: Make Xerox copies of the material you need, even if you have to copy one hundred pages of material. At ten cents a page that's only ten dollars. What you spend in money you'll make up in time. Every time you copy a quotation by hand mistakes will occur. When it comes time to write your first draft, cut out the quotations and glue them on note cards with the bibliographic information on the back. Label the material you think you'll use by marking off the pertinent information and placing an uppercase letter beside it (A, B, C, etc.) Go to your outline and plug in the information where it belongs. There's no need to write in your quotations. Put the quotations you think you'll use in the order they follow in your outline.

Be sure you put the bibliographic information on all your quotations. You'll have a rough time trying to find the information you're using if all you have is a Xerox copy. Someone may have checked the book out. Include the following:

Author (first and last name), title (underlined), where published (city and state), date originally published and latest publication date, page or pages where quotation appears. When it comes time to do your footnotes and bibliography, all the information will be gathered.

- *Make sure the information you've gathered is accurate and can be substantiated*: Is it necessary to find the original source for a quotation? It could be that the original source is apocryphal and all subsequent writers are copying one unreliable and unchecked source. For example, some have maintained that Charles Darwin repudiated his evolutionary theories, and on his deathbed embraced Christianity. In *The Central Significance of Culture*, Francis Nigel Lee cites as his source a book by H. Enoch, *Evolution or Creation?* (London: Evangelical Press, 1968), pp. 166-67. Enoch, in turn, cites a 1916 article in the *Bombay Guardian* (March 25, 1916). In 1916 Darwin had been dead for 34 years.[20] If your professor questions your sources, he may also question your conclusions. Don't give any excuse to reject your thesis and your paper's conclusions.

- *Specialized research manuals*: One of the most comprehensive books on research is *The Modern Researcher* by Jacques Barzun and Henry F. Graff. It goes beyond the "how to write" books and the usual "introduction to research" manuals. "This book does not profess to make good writers by rule and precept, but it does attempt to show how skillful expression is connected throughout with the technique of research and the art of thought."[21]

Ronald Gross' *The Independent Scholar's Handbook* (Reading, MA: Addison-Wesley Publishing Co., [1982] 1985), designed for the advanced and independent researcher, and Alden Todd's *Finding Facts Fast* (Berkeley, CA: Ten Speed Press, 1979), are helpful guides for those who want to go the extra mile to develop incomparable research papers. They are indispensible for the graduate student.

PUTTING IT ALL TOGETHER

Now, what do you do with all this great information that you've just collected? Don't expect to write a perfect paper your first time around. Give yourself enough time to deal adequately with all the steps.

Writing the First Draft

Pay little if any attention to style at the beginning. Your filled in outline has nearly completed your first draft. Have Xerox copies of the quotations you will use. Number them or letter them, leave a space where the quotation is to go in your draft, and make a notation in the blank space where the quotation is to go. This procedure will save you a great deal of time. The chances of misquoting are also reduced.

Do not worry about misspelling a word or whether you are using proper grammar. Just write your ideas. You've done your research. Once you start writing, the ideas should flow, maybe awkward and stilted at first, but as your mind searches for patterns the process will come more easily. You will stifle your creativity if you worry about style at this point. You can always go back to organize, polish, and revise the raw data. Writing the first draft will be difficult if you have not done much reading and thinking about your research material.

Readability

Have something to say, collect the data, think about it, organize it and then write. Embellishment causes confusion. Be specific. Be direct. Don't be afraid to use colloquial and conversational English. Don't make your paper read like a technical journal. Of course, if the paper requires technical jargon, statistics, and a specialized vocabulary then there's not much you can do. But even with this type of paper readability is important, probably even more so than with a typical research paper. As students climb the walls of ivy, their writing seems to get bogged down in the mire of convoluted thinking. You don't want to write in "bureau-cratese." Here are a couple of examples of how simple ideas can be made complicated. How do you tell factory workers during World War II to turn the lights out when they're not working and to cover the windows when they are? Here's how one bureaucrat wrote it:

> Such preparations shall be made as will completely obscure all Federal buildings and non-Federal buildings occupied by the Federal Government during an air raid for any period of time from visibility by reason of internal or external illumination. Such obscuration may be obtained either by black-out construction or by termination of the illumination.

President Franklin D. Roosevelt rewrote the memo and sent it back to the government worker:

> Tell them that in buildings where they have to keep the work going to put something over the windows; and, in buildings where they can let the work stop for a while, turn out the lights.[22]

George Orwell, best known for *Animal Farm*[23] and *1984*, in making his point on readability, turned this famous verse from Ecclesiastes 9:11

> I returned and saw under the sun, that the race is not to the swift, nor the battle to the strong, neither yet bread to the wise, nor yet riches to men of understanding, nor yet favor to men of skill; but time and chance happeneth to all.

into "modern bureaucratic fuzz":

> Objective consideration of contemporary phenomena compels the conclusion that success or failure in competitive activities exhibits no tendency to be commensurate with innate capacity, but that a considerable element of the unpredictable must invariably be taken into account.[24]

One way to check your paper's "readability factor" is to use Rudolf Flesch's "Readability Formula" found in his *The Art of Readable Writing*.[25] The entire book is valuable.

Rewriting

Interviewer: How much rewriting do you do?

Hemingway: It depends. I rewrote the ending of *Farewell to Arms*, the last page of it, thirty-nine times before I was satisfied.

Interviewer: Was there some technical problem there? What was it that had stumped you?

Hemingway: Getting the words right.[26]

The most difficult and yet most necessary task of a writer is to rewrite. For a student who is not used to such things, just the fact that the paper is researched and at least one draft is completed brings on a sense of accomplishment. The student who waits until the week (or even the night) before to write a paper never gets around to considering rewriting.

Most amateur writers assume that the "professionals" sit down at their typewriters and bang out page after page of material and send these pristine pure to their publishers. Don't you believe it. The mark of a good writer is that he takes time to rewrite. Of course, as your experience grows, the time needed to rewrite will decrease but will never be eliminated.

Here are a few things to keep in mind:

1. Go back to consider your main idea. While you may have included a great deal of material, all of it very interesting, some of it may have little or nothing to do with your thesis.

2. Put yourself in the place of the reader. Remember, your professor cannot read your mind.

3. Now reread the entire theme with the first two points in mind. Are there gaps in your writing? Will the reader ask, "How does this fit?" or "What does he mean by that?" Do not assume that your professor will know what you think you mean.

4. Check to see that you are making your case stronger as you read. Read it as a series of dominos falling. Is the reader being led point by point to a convincing conclusion?

5. Consider the parts in relation to the whole. Do the paragraphs follow logically? Paragraph C may belong after paragraph A, with B now following C. Don't rewrite entire paragraphs. Cut out the paragraph shifts and tape the pieces together.

6. There should be progression and logical thought within paragraphs. Does each paragraph begin with a strong topic sentence and do the sentences that follow "fit" the main theme of the topic sentence and the specific theme of the paper?

7. Sentences should be coherent. Do all the words work together giving meaning to what you want to say? Don't let thoughts "dangle," creating hooks that will divert the reader from your main theme.

8. Eliminate all unnecessary words. "That" is often overused. As you read, consider shortening sentences by dividing complex ones with a

245

period making two new sentences. "Along the lines of" can be substituted with "like." "For the purpose of" can be shortened to "for." "To" works just as well as "in order to."

9. Read the paper aloud and *listen* to it. You might want to record it and play it back. Have you gone overboard with your style? Have you substituted simplicity, clarity, and crispness with overwriting? Will something be misread by a hasty reader? Will you be misunderstood because you did not develop or support an idea well enough? Are there places where it just doesn't "sound" right?

10. Check spelling, grammar, and punctuation. Have your roommate or a classmate read your paper and have him or her check for the same points listed above.

11. Reread the final draft after you've made all the necessary adjustments. Be sure you included all the revisions and no new errors have resulted. Oftentimes a new sentence does not fit with what was written before and after it. Check for shifts in tense or person or mood. Transition is important. You don't want to lose your reader with unconnected thoughts.

What to Write Last

THE INTRODUCTION

You want to engage the reader's attention. You might try asking some thought-provoking question or stating a fact that can hardly be believed. Surprise your reader. Make him angry, happy, or sad.

> The most important sentence in any article is the first one. If it doesn't induce the reader to proceed to the second sentence, your article is dead. And if the second sentence doesn't induce him to continue to the third sentence, it's equally dead. Of such progression of sentences, each tugging the reader forward until he is safely hooked, a writer constructs that fateful unit: the "lead."[27]

The introduction is written last, or at least revised last, because it may change as the body of your paper changes. Additional insights may be added as you write and you want these reflected in the introduction. You could write a *preliminary* introduction to keep your paper in proper perspective.

Remember, you must communicate to a first-time reader of your paper what it took you weeks to research and to write. You must work to change the gears of your professor's mind. Your paper is one among many. He will assume, even before picking up your paper, that it's just another paper from some mediocre student who wrote it just to get it done. Getting your professor in a new frame of mind is of the utmost importance.

Teaching you to write an introduction is not my purpose. Since the introduction is so important, do a little research on the subject. You might even try sampling some newsletters and books to see how they begin their articles. Get a feel for the style.

THE CONCLUSION

Knowing when to stop writing is as important as knowing how to begin. First and last impressions are usually retained while the mushy middle grows dim with time. A conclusion is a hidden summary. "To summarize, therefore, the main points of my thesis. . . ." is a bore. Once you inform your reader that you are about to summarize, you've lost him. Your wind down should be gradual, bringing your reader to a certain conclusion without jostling him on the way. You want to surprise your reader that the end has come. Yet, the end should seem exactly right for him. The conclusion should not be a grind.

CONCLUSION

If there is one activity that most students do not get enough of in school, it's writing. Unfortunately, teaching a person to write has become a dissatisfying experience for most teachers. Many teachers and students are led to believe that writing is simply a gift: Either you have the gift of writing or you don't. While there are certainly gifted writers, this does not mean that all of us cannot gain some writing skills with practice. While few of us will ever grow up to write award-winning articles or books, all of us can gain a great deal of competency in the art and skill of writing. Writing is thinking with pen in hand.

14
TAKING EXAMS

> I'm really wired for this exam. I hope I know
> all this stuff. I stayed up all night studying. If
> I can just get past the first question, I'll be
> Okay—I'll relax. Here goes! What's the first
> one? "Name?" Name *who? Name what?* Good
> grief!! I'm losing it!! Oh . . . *My* name. Come
> on, Skyler, get a grip on it.[1]

DID you ever feel this way? I always tell students that one of the most important traits of a successful test-taker is *coolness under pressure*. Like the man tossed overboard, who drowns if he struggles too wildly, so it is with the student, especially freshmen who panic when they take a test. This chapter is designed to help you reduce the panic factor. Preparation is the key. Let's begin with the preliminaries: How to study for a test.

COMPOUND LEARNING

If you follow the tips in the chapter on "How to Study," you'll be way ahead when the week before exam time rolls around. There will be no need to cram, only review. Cramming may seem like a good idea, but the drop off in memory retention twenty-four hours later is dramatic. Only five minutes after you sit down to study something a significant amount of the new material is already being lost. Retention continues to suffer a speedy decline, and an hour later about two-thirds of all we tried so hard to remember has been forgotten. A day later, forgetting levels off at around ninety percent of loss and stays there, which means we end up retaining only some ten percent of the information we hoped to commit to memory. Of course, with planned memory techniques, this rapid downward curve can be averted.

While short-term memory retention might be profitable for tomorrow's test, the long-term benefits are almost nil. There is one thing you should keep in mind about memory: The more "memory hooks" you can develop to hang new data on the easier it will be to remember long-term. When you read a book or review your notes, you will be surprised how easily you are retaining the new information. You want to layer your study so that the first day's review overlaps with the next day's new material. There should not be a break in the knowledge flow.

Compound learning begins with your daily study time: the review of your notes, study of the outline you made of the material in your textbook, study of the questions in your textbook, collateral reading, and the formulation of your own notes. If you quickly review the previous day's studied material, you are involved in compound learning. A certain amount of material will be forgotten from the day before or two days before, but a significant amount will be remembered. If you quickly review all the material, you will reinforce what you remembered, and you will relearn much of what you have forgotten. Material which is studied like this needs very little review to restore it to the level of near one hundred percent retention. It follows from this that the more reviews you can do before an exam, the more easily you can recall the needed information at examination time. During the last week before the exam, a five day heavy concentration of compound learning will bring all the material into focus. By following this procedure, you can spend more time on your memory trouble spots. Moreover, you won't have to neglect your other courses.

In this final review period before exam day, you may be tempted to go back and reread all the material. If you've done your initial outlining and marking and have a good set of notes, there is really little need for rereading. Instead of covering hundreds of pages of text material you should study only the highlighted material. If you follow the daily review method, the most important material in your textbook should stand out. Your professor will give you further hints as to the most important data. You may have been mistaken on your initial reading. Make the necessary changes.

After going over each section of your notes, set them aside and try to recall what you've been studying. Then check how well you did against the notes. Don't read your notes passively. As you go through your notes, formulate questions that you think *might* be on the exam. Write them in the margin or on the back of your note pages. Formulate answers without looking at the notes. Create memory devices for yourself. Sometimes it helps to draw a diagram of the material. This will help you to see some abstract concepts.

These systematic review sessions will help you think through the material in a logical way so not only will you know the facts, but you will also understand how to fit them into a coherent whole. The crammer has no coherency to his learning. He hopes that at test time the facts will pour out in some logical fashion. The essay answers of a crammer are usually muddled and illogical.

Get a good night's sleep while your procrastinating friends are pulling all-nighters, drinking strong coffee, and taking showers at midnight to stay awake.

STUDYING FOR THE RIGHT TEST

Different types of tests require different study strategies. Short-answer, fill-in-the-blank, matching, and true-false tests require an emphasis on facts, the regurgitation of raw information. Essay tests require an understanding of the facts and the ability to formulate arguments in a logical way. You will need to know the facts; and you will also be required to integrate those facts in a coherent format. You won't be able to just "dump" the facts on the page and expect your instructor to figure out that you "know" the material.

Oral exams are very similar to the essay test. Here you must be able to think on your feet. The difficult element in the oral exam is that you won't be able to think with a pencil, a decided disadvantage. You will need to develop an outline in your head and then draw on your reservoir of knowledge on the spot. Unfortunately, there is no going back. Often-times you will be taking an oral exam with some other students from your class. Your answers will be compared with the others who are also being examined. If you're in a grouping with some really sharp students, your mediocre answers will stand out more than on a written essay test.

Multiple-choice tests often bring a sigh of relief. Their seemingly simple format (the answers are there; you just have to choose [guess?] the right one) can give you a false sense of security during your study time. Recognition of the facts is the most important thing to remember. If you're good at guessing, that is, eliminating the wrong answers, then this is your test.

What kind of test will it be? Ask your professor. Ask students from previous classes if he won't tell you. One way to figure out what he'll do is to look at past exams. Many times these are on file. Sororities and fraternities often keep files on all professors. Look at these tests for the *type* of exam he gives. They might give you a *feel* for his testing style.

Are his multiple-choice and true-false questions clear? On essay tests does he ask you to compare, contrast, defend, define, discuss, or summarize? I would stay away from studying the *content* of old exams to anticipate the same questions. They can lead you astray. I've known professors who asked nearly the same questions but with a word change here and there that completely changed the question's intent. Some students began reading and *assumed* it was the same question and wrote accordingly. You guessed it. They flunked.

Will there be a mixture of true-false, multiple-choice, and essay questions? Does he ask trivial things? Does he favor the facts? Were there any "trick" questions? Study accordingly.

OBJECTIVE EXAMS

Objective exams do not ask for opinion. Your professor is only interested in how well you know the facts. He is not interested in opinion or a discussion of the facts.

1. Pay attention to all the instructions; instructions that tell you *where* (e.g., on a separate answer sheet, on the test paper itself, etc.) and *how* (e.g., check a box, circle a number, etc.) to answer questions.

2. Quickly survey the whole test before answering any questions. This procedure will give you an idea of how much time you'll have to spend on the entire exam.

3. Answer the questions you know and do not labor over the difficult ones. You can always come back to those. If you spend too much time on the difficult questions, you may have to rush through the last part of the test where there may be a number of easy questions. It may be that time will run out before you even get to the last part of the.

4. Watch for qualifying words such as *usually, always, most, never, some,* etc. *Always* and *never* are usually real giveaways. Modifiers play a large role in true-false tests.

5. Don't sprint over the questions. This is no time for speed reading. Make sure you understand the question. There's a big difference between a *conservative* and a *conservationist,* a *liberal* and a *libertarian.*

6. Your first choice is *often but not always* the correct one. Change answers only reluctantly. Another question further along in the test may trigger something in your memory that necessitates a change in a previous question. Your first choice on true-false tests is usually your best shot.

7. Make sure your choices are marked clearly. If you are taking a true-false exam, and you are required to mark your answer with a T or

an F, don't try to fake-out your professor by scribbling your T in such a way that it could be either a T or an F. Write legibly.

Multiple-Choice Tests

These are the most popular tests. They're a lazy professor's test, second only behind true-false tests. You can take advantage of your prof's laziness with these effective strategies.

1. One effective technique to help you with multiple-choice tests is to try to answer the question before looking at the four or five options. Your studying was probably geared to handle factual material. You didn't study for multiple-choice questions. You hoped to learn the right answer, so why not go for the right answer without any help or confusion?

2. As a Christian you may have problems with some of the choices you're given. The correct answer may not be there. This is not the time to make a point by choosing "none of the above." Give the answer the professor wants. After you give what your prof wants make a note in the margin if you feel you want to make a statement. There's probably no use if it's machine graded. See him after the test or make an appointment with him.

3. Most tests ask for the *most correct* answer. In your own mind you may feel that there are two or even three correct answers. At this point you'll have to know something about your instructor. What did he emphasize in class? What are his biases. On "all the above" options make sure *all the options are correct*.

4. Go through a process of elimination when you are stumped. Start with those answers that are obviously wrong. Move on to the doubtful answers. Check your options again, look at the question again to make sure you understand it, then make your choice. Here are a few examples:

1. Football, basketball, and soccer are
   a. played best in the rain.
   b. the favorite American sports.
   c. team sports of the world.
   d. three team sports.

You can eliminate *a*. Football and basketball are favorite American sports, but you cannot say the same thing about soccer. Therefore, *b* can be eliminated. Choice *c* is true but too general. It's the best answer so far. The *most correct* choice is *d*.

2. Coffee, tea, and milk are
   a. beverages.
   b. stimulants.
   c. liquids.
   d. refreshing.

Choice *a* is correct, but you need to read on to see if there is a more correct answer. Coffee and tea are stimulants, but milk is not. Choice *b* is wrong. While choice *c* is true, choice *a* is *most true* when *compared* with *c*. Oil, sea water, and some poisons are also liquids. All beverages are liquids, but not all liquids are beverages. Refreshing is an adjective while the other choices are nouns. This does not settle the question but it should make you suspicious. Choice *d* is still too general when compared to *a*. Anyway, Mormons would not consider coffee and tea refreshing since they are not permitted to drink them.

• Look for qualifiers and absolutes. Questions that include *always*, *never*, *none*, or *all* are often incorrect. Again, it depends on the test material. In this relativistic world you can usually bet on it. But be careful. For most teachers, there is little in life that is *always* true or *always* false. Some of the most confusing questions are sprinkled with qualifiers, such as *seldom*, *generally*, and *tend to be*.

• Sometimes the answer does not grammatically line up with the question. You may find a singular verb in the question, but a plural noun as one of your options in the answer section. Three of the options may be nouns while a fourth option is an adjective. Be careful.

• Look for phrases in the questions that come right out of the textbook. This is the quickest way for a professor to make up a test. Take advantage of your professor's laziness.

• When all else fails, guess, but not until you go through a process of elimination.

• When there is a separate answer sheet make sure your numbered answers line up with your numbered questions. I would check this after the first ten questions. You could be in big trouble if you have only five minutes left and you find that you misnumbered question number four on your answer sheet.

True-False Tests

Like multiple-choice exams, true-false exams test your recognition, not your recall.

• Read the question carefully. Make note of clue words that *usually* call for a false answer. Be careful.

Positive Determiners	Negative Specific Determiners
all	none
every	not one
everybody	nobody
everyone	no one
always	never
all of the time	at no time
invariably	occasionally
will certainly	will certainly not
will definitely	will definitely not
will absolutely	will absolutely not
the best	the worst

Here are some examples:

1. July is always a summer month. T or F

False. July is not a summer month in the southern hemisphere.

2. The shortest route is the best route when you are in a hurry. T or F

False. The shortest route might be crowded with traffic, or might run through a body of water or under a mountain. Therefore, it might not be the best route to take when in a hurry.

3. Everybody eats at least one meal a day. T or F

False. Many people in the world starve to death from lack of food [usually due to Marxist policies]; others purposely fast for longer than a month [to make political statements].

4. There are no people who enjoy suffering. T or F

False. Masochists enjoy suffering.

5. All people say a "dirty" word now and then. T or F

False. There must be somebody somewhere who never said a "dirty" word—no matter how you define "dirty." Also, if *say* means "to speak," no person mute since birth has said a "dirty" word.

You can always find something to read into every question, making the question ask more than it was designed to ask. If you've checked over some previous tests by the same instructor, you will get some idea of his testing methodology. Is he a straight shooter or does he opt for hidden meanings? If you feel a question is poorly worded, ask your instructor for a clarification. Do this when you've gone through the entire exam.

Look out for double negatives. Statements that contain double negatives are more difficult to interpret than statements that contain no negatives. *When there are two negatives, cross out both negatives—the double negative.*

DOUBLE NEGATIVE	INTERPRETATION
*not un*healthy	healthy
*not in*direct	direct
*not im*perfect	perfect
*not il*legal	legal
*not ir*responsible	responsible
*not non*toxic	toxic
*not dis*agreeable	agreeable

Here are some examples:

1. A lie is a statement that is not incorrect. T or F.
Cross out *not* and *in*.
Answer: A lie is a statement that is correct. *False*.

2. A wealthy man is not without money. T or F.
Cross out *not* and *out* (a negative suffix).
Answer: A wealthy man is with money. *True*.

3. The totally mute are not unable to speak. T or F.
Cross out *not* and *un*.
Answer: The totally mute are able to speak. *False*.

Matching Questions

You won't find many matching questions on college tests. Some specialized course material might have them, however.

1. Determine if choices are used once or if a choice can be used for a number of matches. This makes things a little more difficult.

2. Some test strategists suggest that you read the column that has the longest phrases first and match the choices with the short-phrase column. They say you'll save time by only having to reread the short-term phrases. Unless you're really pressed for time this might not be of any real help.

3. Try to answer the match before looking to the matching column for an answer. This is similar to the technique outlined for the multiple-choice test.

4. Do the easy matches first. Matching tests are nothing more than composite multiple-choice tests.

THE ESSAY TEST AND ORAL EXAMS

The Essay Test

You will probably encounter more essay tests than any other kind. Of course, this will not be the case if your major is mathematics or engineering. You may be able to avoid an essay test if you get a lazy professor. Here are some suggestions for taking an essay test:

1. There is some debate over whether you should read the entire exam before proceeding with the first question. Of course, if you get to choose which questions you want to answer, it's mandatory that you read it through. Some "experts" say that reading all the questions, especially on an essay test, will rattle the student. You may be so overwhelmed with the material that you'll be defeated before you start. But, if you've done your homework, there's really nothing to fear. You might get a little rattled, but you'll gain your composure as you proceed. I suggest that you read it all the way through. You may give a partial answer for, say, question three in question two. If you knew what question three was about, you could save yourself a lot of time by dealing with the subject at the proper time.

2. Write out a rough time budget. Usually professors give different grading standards to each question. If question one is worth forty points and question two is worth twenty points and question three is a set of definitions each worth two points (there are ten for a total of twenty points) and the final question is worth twenty points, then the way you divide up your time will be determined by the point size of the questions. Instead of going in order, you should tackle question three last. In the margin of your test, if you're permitted to write on the test, write down how much time you think you'll need to answer each question. The time spent on each question should be determined by what each one is worth.

3. If you have a choice of questions, select and mark those questions you feel sure you can answer well. Don't be a prima donna and try to figure out what questions your professor really wants you to answer. *Pick the easiest ones.* This is no time to try to impress your professor. You may learn that he won't be grading them, so there's no way to impress him. Many college professors get their teaching assistants to help in the grading. There's no impressing them.

4. Read each question through *thoroughly*, and make sure you understand it. If you're having trouble with a question, go to your professor and get some clarification. Underline key words or phrases. Don't read anything into the question that you think *ought* to be there; you may find

257

yourself answering the wrong question, *your* question! This is probably the biggest fault of all students who take essay tests. They misunderstand or misinterpret the question and end up answering a completely different question. Here are some terms to keep in mind as you read the questions:

- *Compare*: Look for similarities and differences.
- *Contrast*: Set in opposition in order to bring out differences.
- *Criticize*: Give your opinion or judgment about the merit of theories or about the truth of facts, and back up your judgment by a discussion of the evidence.
- *Define*: Set down the precise meaning of a word or phrase. Show that the distinctions implied in the definition are necessary.
- *Describe*: Give a detailed or graphic account.
- *Discuss*: Investigate or examine by argument; sift and debate, giving reasons pro or con.
- *Evaluate*: Make an appraisal of the worth of something, in the light of its truth or utility; include to a lesser degree your personal opinion.
- *Explain*: To make plain, to interpret, and to account for.
- *Illustrate*: Use a figure or diagram to explain or clarify, *or* make clear by the use of concrete examples.
- *Interpret*: Expound the meaning of; make clear and explicit; usually giving your own judgment also.
- *Justify*: Show adequate grounds for decisions or conclusions.
- *Outline*: Give the main features or general principles of a subject, omitting minor details, and emphasizing structure and arrangement.
- *Relate*: (a) To narrate. More usually, in [oral] examinations; (b) Show things are connected to each other, and to what extent they are alike, or affect each other.
- *Review*: To make a survey of, examining the subject critically.
- *State*: Present in brief, clear form.
- *Summarize*: Give a concise account of the chief points or substance of a matter, omitting details and examples.
- *Trace*: Follow the development or history of a topic from some point of origin.

5. Make an outline of the main points you want to cover. This might take you a few minutes, but you will more than make up the time with this track. It will keep you from rambling. An illogical paper will probably lead your professor to quit reading before he gets to the end where your best material might be. If you ramble with your first answer, you

may color the quality of the other answers before your prof gets to them. The outline will keep you from getting excessive and will allow you to edit as you write.

6. You probably don't need an introductory paragraph. Get right to the point.

7. Your handwriting will lose some of its clarity during an essay test. You will probably get a few extra points just for neatness. Your practice of taking fast notes in class should have you warmed up for an essay test.

8. Answer all the questions. Even if you think you don't know the answer. Put something down. You'll get at least some points. You may get a total of eighty points on three questions but because you failed to answer one question worth twenty points, you can get nothing better than a low B (eighty percent).

9. Leave a few minutes for review. Remember the advice on doing a research paper—wait twenty-four hours before you turn it in so you can make any adjustments. What sounded good on Tuesday may sound muddled on Wednesday. Well, you don't have twenty-four hours to review your answers on an essay test but you should leave some time to check over all your answers. Are your verb tenses correct? Was a negative omitted, making nonsense of a sentence? Are your pages in the right order? Have you missed anything?

Oral Exams

Many of the techniques for the essay test apply here. Some professors give students the option of an oral exam or a written exam. If you can think on your feet and are a good speaker, take the oral exam.

1. Follow the procedures of developing a research paper if you are given a list of possible questions. Limit the scope of each possible question in formulating your study answer. Develop an outline that can be memorized. Present your oral answer from the memorized outline. Use a memory technique to help you learn it.

2. If you're given a time limit to present your answer, say two to three minutes, be sure you can present your topic within the specified time. This will mean practicing your presentation with a stop watch.

3. Be prepared for follow-up questions. Anticipate what a critic would say if he just heard your presentation. You might want to get a classmate to play devil's advocate.

4. Study with a group. Make sure some ground rules are laid down before you agree to such a study arrangement. All participants should come prepared. The purpose of a study group is to *refine* and *test* arguments, not to prepare them.

5. Use your normal speaking voice and vocabulary. Don't try to impress your professor by spouting off words you really don't understand. It will be very embarrassing if your professor stops you and asks what you mean by "existential encounter" after you say: "The existential encounter of supposed agrarian features of the back-to-nature movement has led many to believe that existence is indeed essential to essence." If you don't know what a word means, don't use it.

6. Be sure you can substantiate your facts. Be able to cite the references you use to support your conclusions. It would be good to bring a copy with you of everything you plan to use.

7. If you're permitted to jot down notes as your professor gives the question, don't be afraid to do so. This will help you formulate your answer while he is asking you the question, and it will keep you on track while you are answering the question. It will also save you from asking him to repeat the question half way through your muddled answer. You'll need to check with him ahead of time to see if he'll permit it.

8. Ask to have the question clarified if there are a number of possible angles to take. It's best to know this before you proceed. When you complete your answer, ask if it answers the question or if he would like more.

9. Concentrate on what you know best. If you know that there should be four main parts to your answer and you only know three of them well, put most of your energy into the three points. Save the one you know best for last. Hide your mediocre answer in the middle.

10. Don't panic if you don't know an answer. Some professors allow you to pass on one question if there is a group oral exam. There will be no chance to pass on another, however. If you believe the question is outside the scope of the course, say so. Be ready to substantiate your assertion, however. If two other students concur, you may win your case.

Test Day

1. Get all your needed materials together the night before. Make sure you have two of everything. You'll need at least two soft lead pencils and a small pencil sharpener for machine-graded tests. Be sure the erasers are not worn down. Your pens should be new. Don't write in colored ink. Blue and black are fine. Your professor might have a preference, however. A watch might be of some help. Many classrooms are equipped with clocks that hang on the back wall. This will present a problem if you are going to need every precious minute to finish your

exam. You don't want to be accused of cheating because some proctor sees you turning around every five minutes to see how much time you have to complete your exam.

2. Get to the examination room on time. I suggest that you get there early to get a good seat away from possible distractions. You've been going there long enough to know where the good seats are. This will mean staying away from windows with a view (a terrible distraction on a beautiful spring day) and doors. You may want to get a seat that is against the wall. This will eliminate distractions on at least one side of you. But the familiar may be the best: your own seat.

3. When you get the exam, read the instructions carefully and make note of any verbal instructions from the instructor or proctor or any notes left by either on a chalkboard.

4. *Put your name on the test papers where your answers will be written.* "You're kidding?" No, I'm not. There have been more than a few times when students turned in a paper with no name. It's awfully embarrassing when a college professor has to stand up in class and wave an exam with no name, and you have to be the one to claim it.

CONCLUSION

Preparation for any activity relieves an awful lot of tension. Knowing that you are prepared for almost anything will raise your confidence level as you sit down to take a test. While this chapter has not covered every contingency, most of the bases have been covered. You will have to adapt these techniques to your specific major. Remember, the best techniques are the ones that work for you.

APPENDIX

TABLE OF COMMONLY USED PREFIXES

Prefix	Meaning	Example
a	not	atheism, agnostic
ab	from	absent, abort
ad	to	adhere, advent
ante	before	anteroom, anterior
anti	against	antislavery, antinomian
apo	away from	apogee, apostasy
bene	well, good	beneficial, benefactor
bi	two	bicycle, bifocal, bicep
cent	hundred	century, centennial
circum	around	circumvent, circumcise
co	with, together	cooperate, conjoin
col	together, with	collaborator, collate
com	together, with	compose, compile
contra	against	contradict, contraband
de	down	descend, demean, debase
dec	ten	decade, decameter, decathlon
deci	tenth	decimal, decibel
di	two	diphthong, divide
dia	through, between	diameter, diapause
dis	not	dishonest, disavow
du	two	duet, duel, dualistic
dys	bad	dystrophy, dysfunction
e	out	eject, emit
epi	upon	epidemic, epicenter
eu	well, good	eulogy, euphoria, utopia
ex	out	exit, exam, exegesis
hept, sept	seven	heptagon, September
hex, sex	six	hexagon, sextet
hyper	over	hypersensitive, hyperbole
hypo	under	hypodermic, hypocrite

Prefix	Meaning	Example
il	not	illegal, illegitimate
im	not	immovable, immobile
in	not	inactive, innate
inter	between	international, interlude
ir	not	irregular, irrational
kilo	1000	kilocycle, kilogram
macro	large	macroscopic, macrocosm
mega	large	megaphone, megadose
meta	change	metaphor, metagalaxy
micro	small	microphone, microbiology
milli	1/1000	millimeter, milligram
mis	wrong	misspell, misshape, misinform
mono	one	monorail, monotheism, monistic
multi	many	multitude, multinational
novem	nine	November, novena
ob	against	objection, obviate
oct	eight	octopus, octagon
penta	five	pentagon, pentad, pentateuch
per	through	perforate, permeate
peri	around	perigee, periphery
poly	many	polygon, polytheist
post	after	postscript, postgraduate
pre	before	precede, prescribe
pro	forward	progress, promote
proto	first	prototype, protozoan
pseudo	false	pseudonym, pseudoscience
quad	four	quadruplet, quadrillion
quin	five	quintuplet, quintessence
re	back	refund, regain
re	again	readmit, reprint
retro	back	retroactive, retrorocket
semi	half	semicircle, semilethal
sub	under	submarine, subsidiary
super	over	supersede, superimpose
sym	together	symmetry, symphony
syn	together	synonym, synergy, synthesis
tetra	four	tetrameter, tetrad
trans	cross	transcontinental, transit
tri	three	triangle, tripod, trinity
ultra	beyond	ultraviolet, ultrasound
un	not	unsafe, unsound, unfit
uni	one	unicycle, united, universe

TABLE OF COMMONLY USED SUFFIXES

Suffix	Meaning	Example
able, ible	can be done	readable, credible
ancy, ency	state of	infancy, delinquency
al	relating to	natural, nocturnal
and, end	to be done	multiplicand, extend
ant, ent	person who	immigrant, resident
cule	small	minuscule, molecule
dom	state of	freedom, martyrdom
ectomy	surgical removal	vasectomy, mastectomy
ence	state, quality, condition of	dependence, essence
er	comparative degree	faster, wilder
er, or	person who	farmer, actor
ess	feminine ending	actress, tigress
et, ette	little, small	islet, kitchenette
ful	full of	skillful, vengeful
ful	enough to fill	cupful, headful
fy	make into	deify, edify
hood	state of	manhood, statehood
ian	related to	parisian, persian
ical	of the nature of	comical, hysterical
ine	like	canine
ine	feminine suffix	Josephine, feline
ish	to form adjectives	Turkish, foolish
ism	state of	hypnotism, Hinduism
ist	person who	biologist, chemist
less	without	witless, aimless
let	small	ringlet, omelet
ling	small	duckling, fledgling
logy	science of	zoology, theology
ly	in the manner of	fatherly, tenderly
ment	state of	amazement, excitement
ness	state of	sickness, messiness
oid	like, resembling	spheroid, android
or	person who	auditor, mentor
orium, arium	place for	natatorium, aquarium
ory	place where	laboratory, observatory
osis	abnormal condition	neurosis, psychosis
ship	state of	friendship, ownership
ule	little, small	molecule, tubule
ward, wards	direction	homeward, backward
wise	way	clockwise, otherwise

TABLE OF COMMONLY USED ROOTS

Root	Meaning	Example
agr	field, land	agriculture, agronomy
alt	high	altitude, altimeter
annu	year	anniversary, annum
aqua	water	aquarium, acuatint
aster, astro	star	asterisk, astronomy
aud	hear	audible, audio, auditory
auto	self	autonomy, automatic
baro	weight	barometer, barograph
bio	life	biography, biology
cide	kill	suicide, infanticide
crat	rule	democratic, autocrat
cred	believe	incredible, credal, creed
cycl	circle, wheel	cyclist, cyclical
demos	people	democracy
dent	tooth	dentist, dentalium
dic, dict	say	predict, edict
do	give	donate, donative
dorm	sleep	dormitory, dormant
duc	lead	conduct
enni	year	bicentennial, centennial
equ	equal	equality, equitable
fac	make, do	manufacture, facsimile
fer	carry, bear	transfer, confer
flec	bend	deflect, inflect
fract	break	fracture, fraction
frat	brother	fraternity, fraternize
fug	flee	fugitive
gen	race, birth	generation, genesis
geo	earth	geology, geocentric
gon	angle	trigonometry, pentagon
graph	write	autograph, polygraph
greg	herd	congregation, gregarious
homo	same	homonym, homogeneous
ign	fire	ignite, ignition
insul	island	insular, insulate
ject	throw	eject, interject
leg	law	legal, legislate
loc	place	location, locale
log	speech	dialogue, epilogue
magni	great	magnify, magnificent
man	hand	manual, manage

Root	Meaning	Example
mater, matri	mother	maternity, matriarchy
math	learning	mathematics
maxima	greatest	maximum, maximal
meter	measure	centimeter, altimeter
metro	mother	metropolis
migr	move	migrate, emigrate
min	small	minute, minimum
mnem	memory	amnesia
monstr	show	demonstrate, remonstrate
mort	death	immortal, mortuary
mot	move	motion, motivate
nom	law, arrangement	astronomy, pronomian
nov	new	novelty, novice
onym	name	synonym, homonym
ov	egg	ovary, ovum
path	feeling	sympathy, empathy
patri	father	patriotism, patrimony
ped	foot	pedestrian, pedometer
pend	hang	pendulum, pendant
phag	eat	esophagus, phagocyte
phil	love	philosophy, Philadelphia
phon	sound	phonics, phonograph
port	carry	import, deport
pter	wing	helicopter
rupt	to break	rupture, erupt
saur	lizard	dinosaur
sci	know	science, conscience
scope	to watch	telescope, microscope
scrib, script	write	inscribe, manuscript
sect	cut	dissect, intersect
somn	sleep	insomnia
son	sound	unison, sonic
soph	wise	philosopher, philosophy
soror	sister	sorority, sororal
spect	look	spectator, inspect
spir	breath	respiration, spirit
tang, tact	touch	tangible, tactile
tele	distant	televise, telephone
ten	hold	tenacious, tenable
tom	cut	anatomy, atom
tract	pull	tractor, extract
urb	city	suburb, urban

Root	Meaning	Example
ven	come	convention, convene
verb	word	verbal, verbose
vers	turn	reverse, inverse
vid	see	evidence, vivid
vir	man	virility
vis	see	visual, vision
viv	live	survive, vivacious
voc	call	vocal, vocation
volv	roll, turn	resolve, evolve

END NOTES

Chapter 1 – Preparing for Battle

1. From the comic strip "Funky Winkerbean" by Tom Batiuk, Field Enterprises, 1980.
2. Cornelius Van Til, *Apologetics* (Phillipsburg, NJ: Presbyterian and Reformed, 1976), p. 1.
3. Greg L. Bahnsen, "The Reformation of Christian Apologetics," *Foundations of Christian Scholarship*, Gary North, ed. (Vallecito, CA: Ross House Books, 1976), pp. 194-95.
4. *Ibid.*, p. 198.
5. "The *Council of the Areopagus* was a venerable commission of the ex-magistrates which took its name from the hill where it originally convened. In popular parlance its title was shortened to the 'the Areopagus,' and in the first century it had transferred its location to the Stoa Basileios (or 'Royal Portico') in the city marketplace – where the Platonic dialogues tell us that Euthyphro went to try his father for impiety and where Socrates had been tried for corrupting the youth with foreign deities. Apparently the Council convened on Mar's hill in Paul's day only for trying cases of homicide. That Paul 'stood in the midst of the Areopagus' (v. 22) and 'went out from their midst' (v. 33) is much easier understood in terms of his appearance before the Council than his standing on the hill (cf. Acts 4:7). . . . [The commission] exercised jurisdiction over matters of religion and morals." Greg L. Bahnsen, "The Encounter of Jerusalem with Athens" in *Ashland Theological Bulletin*, Ashland Theological Seminary, Ashland, Ohio (Spring, 1980), p. 16.
6. Richard L. Pratt, Jr., *Every Thought Captive: A Study Manual for the Defense of Christian Truth* (Phillipsburg, NJ: Presbyterian and Reformed, 1979), p. 87.
7. R. C. Sproul, *The Psychology of Atheism* (Minneapolis, MN: Bethany Fellowship, 1974), pp. 128-29.
8. Bahnsen, "The Encounter of Jerusalem with Athens," p. 11.
9. Robert McCauley, "The Business of the University," *Liberal Education*, 68:1 (1982), p. 28.
10. David Chilton, *Paradise Restored: A Biblical Theology of Dominion* (Ft. Worth, TX: Dominion Press, [1985] 1987), p. 4.
11. John J. Dunphy, "A Religion for a New Age," *The Humanist* (January/February 1983), p. 26. Quoted in John W. Whitehead, *The Stealing of America* (Westchester, IL: Crossway Books, 1983), p. 95. Emphasis supplied.
12. From a letter to the author, April 27, 1979.
13. Herbert Schlossberg, *Idols for Destruction: Christian Faith and its Confrontation with American Society* (Nashville, TN: Thomas Nelson, 1983).
14. Herman J. Muller, "One Hundred Years Without Darwin Are Enough," *The Humanist*, XIX (1959); reprinted in Philip Appleman, ed., *Darwin: A Norton Critical Edition*

(New York: Norton, 1970), p. 570; quoted by Gary North, *The Dominion Covenant: Genesis* (2nd ed.; Tyler, TX: Institute for Christian Economics, [1982] 1987), p. 245.

Chapter 2 – Worldviews in Conflict

1. Harry Blamires, *The Christian Mind* (London: S.C.P.K., 1963), p. 3.
2. Joseph Epstein, "A Case of Academic Freedom," *Commentary* (September 1986), pp. 40-41.
3. Herbert Schlossberg and Marvin Olasky, *Turning Point: A Christian Worldview Declaration* (Westchester, IL: Crossway Books, 1987), p. 47.
4. The First Amendment addresses religion this way: "Congress shall make no law respecting an establishment of religion or prohibiting the free exercise thereof; or abridging the freedom of speech, or of the press; or the right of the people peaceably to assemble, and to petition the Government for a redress of grievances." Notice that there is no mention of a "separation between church and state."
5. W. Andrew Hoffecker, "Preface: Perspective and Method in Building a World View," *Building a Christian World View: God, Man, and Knowledge* (Phillipsburg, NJ: Presbyterian and Reformed, 1986), pp. ix-x.
6. Schlossberg and Olasky, *Turning Point*, p. 71.
7. John M. Frame, *The Doctrine of the Knowledge of God* (Phillipsburg, NJ: Presbyterian and Reformed, 1987), pp. 45, 125.
8. John W. Whitehead, *The End of Man* (Westchester, IL: Crossway, 1986), p. 16.
9. R. J. Rushdoony, *The Institutes of Biblical Law* (Phillipsburg, NJ: Presbyterian and Reformed, 1973), p. 540.
10. Thomas V. Morris, *Francis Schaeffer's Apologetics: A Critique* (Chicago, IL: Moody Press, 1976), p. 108n.
11. Whittaker Chambers, *Witness* (New York: Random House, 1952), pp. 9f.
12. William L. Shirer, *The Rise and Fall of the Third Reich: A History of Nazi Germany* (New York: Simon and Schuster, 1960), p. 240.
13. William Shirer, *The Nightmare Years: 1930-1940* (Boston, MA: Little, Brown and Company, 1984), p. 156.
14. Donald D. Wall, "The Lutheran Response to the Hitler Regime in Germany," ed., Robert D. Linder, *God and Caesar: Case Studies in the Relationship Between Christianity and the State* (Longview, TX: The Conference on Faith and History, 1971), p. 88.
15. Shirer, *The Rise and Fall of the Third Reich*, pp. 248-49.
16. *Ibid.*, p. 249.
17. *Idem.*
18. Rheta Grimsley Johnson, "'People' vs. Fundamentalists," *The Marietta Daily Journal* (September 2, 1986), p. 4A.
19. A portion of a radio editorial heard over WGST Radio in Atlanta, Georgia on September 9, 1986.
20. "A Conversation With Francis Coppola," *U.S. News and World Report* (April 5, 1982), p. 68.
21. Alan N. Schoonmaker, *A Student's Survival Manual, or How to Get an Education Despite it All* (New York: Harper & Row, 1971), pp. 111-12.
22. Edmund W. Sinnott, *The Biology of the Spirit* (New York: The Viking Press, 1955), p. 7.
23. Whitehead, *The End of Man*, p. 144.
24. Charles B. Thaxton and Stephen C. Meyer, "Coming soon . . . human rights for bacteria?," *Houston Chronicle* (January 10, 1988), p. 4, section 6.

25. Lloyd Billingsley, *The Generation That Knew Not Josef: A Critique of Marxism and the Religious Left* (Portland, OR: Multnomah Press, 1985), p. 24.
26. *Idem.*

Chapter 3—The Christian Worldview

1. John Calvin, *Institutes of the Christian Religion*, John T. McNeill, ed. (Philadelphia, PA: Westminster Press, 1960), Book I, chapter 2, section 1.
2. The Trinity is a difficult concept. It is not the purpose of this book to discuss the finer points of theology. This short definition defines the doctrine, although it does not fully explain it: "Within the one essence of the Godhead we have to distinguish three 'persons' who are neither three gods on the one side, nor three parts or modes of God on the other, but coequally and coeternally God." Geoffrey W. Bromiley, "The Trinity," *Baker's Dictionary of Theology* (Grand Rapids, MI: Baker Book House, 1960), p. 531.
3. "God and Biblical Language," *God's Inerrant Word: An International Symposium on the Trustworthiness of Scripture*, John Warwick Montgomery, ed. (Minneapolis, MN: Bethany Fellowship, 1974), p. 173.
4. Conde Pallen, *Crucible Island* (New York, 1919), quoted in Thomas Molnar, *Utopia: The Perennial Heresy* (New York: Sheed and Ward, 1967), p. 186.
5. Francis Schaeffer, *The Complete Works of Francis A. Schaeffer: A Christian Worldview*, 5 vols.: *He Is There and He Is Not Silent* (Westchester, IL: Crossway Books, 1984), vol. 1, pp. 274-352.
6. James W. Sire, *The Universe Next Door: A Basic World View Catalog* (Downers Grove, IL: InterVarsity Press, 1976), pp. 35-36.
7. *Ibid.*, p. 37.
8. *Ibid.*, p. 49.
9. See John Eidsmoe, *Christianity and the Constitution* (Grand Rapids, MI: Baker Book House, 1987), pp. 39-45. "Deism, while it existed in America and was accepted by a few leading Americans (Thomas Paine, Ethan Allen, and possibly James Wilson), was (1) less influential than Christianity and (2) fundamentally compatible with Christianity in its view of law and government" (p. 45).
10. Carl Sagan, *Cosmos* (New York: Ballantine Books, [1980] 1985), p. 1.
11. Carl F. Ellis, Jr., *Beyond Liberation: The Gospel in the Black American Experience* (Downers Grove, IL: InterVarsity Press, 1983), p. 17.
12. Paul Kurtz, ed., *The Humanist Manifesto I and II* (Buffalo, NY: Prometheus Books, 1973), p. 16.
13. Arlie J. Hoover, *Dear Agnos: A Defense of Christianity* (Grand Rapids, MI: Baker Book House, 1976), p. 106.
14. *Life and Letters of Charles Darwin*, Frances Darwin, ed. (New York: Johnson Reprint [reprint]), vol. 1, p. 285. Quoted in *ibid.*, pp. 106-107.
15. Robert A. Morey, *Death and the Afterlife* (Minneapolis, MN: Bethany House, 1984), p. 191.
16. Kurtz, ed., *Humanist Manifesto I and II*, p. 16.
17. *Ibid.*, p. 14.
18. Joseph Fletcher and John Warwick Montgomery, *Situation Ethics: True or False?: A Dialogue Between Joseph Fletcher and John Warwick Montgomery* (Minneapolis, MN: Bethany Fellowship, 1972), p. 15.
19. "Students Defend Abortion For 'High' Social Reasons," *The Rutherford Institute*, Vol. 1, No. 2 (January/February 1984), p. 8.
20. Friedrich Engels, *Anti-Dühring* (1934). Quoted in Francis Nigel Lee, *Communist*

Eschatology: A Christian Philosophical Analysis of the Post-Capitalistic Views of Marx, Engels and Lenin (Nutley, NJ: The Craig Press, 1974), p. 322.

21. Sidney Abbott and Barbara Love, *Sappho Was a Right-On Woman: A Liberated View of Lesbianism* (New York: Stein and Day, 1972).

22. Adolf Hitler at Buckenburg, October 7, 1933; cf. *The Speeches of Adolf Hitler*, 1929-39, N. H. Baynes, ed. (2 vols., Oxford, 1942), vol. 1, pp. 871-72. Quoted in Leonard Peikoff, *The Ominous Parallels: The End of Freedom in America* (New York: Stein and Day, 1982), p. 3.

23. The Bible does not talk about rights. See Gary DeMar, *God and Government: The Restoration of the Republic* (Atlanta, GA: American Vision, 1986), pp. 212-43.

24. This use should not be confused with caring for the environment.

25. Rousas J. Rushdoony, *Salvation and Godly Rule* (Vallecito, CA: Ross House Books, 1983), p. 66.

26. Allan Bloom, *The Closing of the American Mind: How Higher Education Has Failed Democracy and Impoverished the Souls of Today's Students* (New York: Simon and Shuster, 1987), p. 25.

27. David Brock, "A Philosopher Hurls Down a Stinging Moral Gauntlet," *Insight* (May 11, 1987), p. 10.

28. It is true that language (as a social tool) is not used completely in the same way as in the 1780s. The issue, however, is whether the *sense* or *intent* of the words from the 1780s can be ascertained and understood effectively today.

29. John W. Whitehead, *The Second American Revolution* (Westchester, IL: Crossway Books, [1982] 1985), p. 46.

30. Os Guinness, *The Dust of Death: A Critique of the Establishment and the Counter Culture and a Proposal for a Third Way* (Downers Grove, IL: InterVarsity Press, 1973), p. 338.

Chapter 4 – Shopping for a God

1. John W. Whitehead, *The End of Man* (Westchester, IL: Crossway Books, 1986), p. 15.

2. Herbert Schlossberg, *Idols for Destruction: Christian Faith and Its Confrontation with American Society* (Nashville, TN: Thomas Nelson Publishers, 1983), p. 6.

3. "Are American Families Finding New Strength in Spirituality?" *Better Homes and Gardens* (January 1988), p. 19. The editor of *Better Homes and Gardens*, David Jordan, was surprised by the response of the magazine's readership. He writes:

   I must admit that when our managing editor, Kate Greer, urged me to let her publish the questionnaire "Are American Families Finding New Strength in Spirituality?" in our September issue last year, I wasn't all that enthusiastic. . . .

   But now, the results are in, and I'm amazed. . . . I have to comment on two things: the size of the response (eighty thousand replies when we expected thirty thousand), and the fact that more than fifty percent of you said you thought spirituality is gaining influence on family life in America. These statistics illuminate a significant shift in the spiritual life of many of us (p. 15).

4. *Ibid.*, p. 25.

5. *Idem.*

6. Allan Bloom, *The Closing of the American Mind: How Higher Education Has Failed Democracy and Impoverished the Souls of Today's Students* (New York: Simon and Schuster, 1987), p. 26.

7. Douglas Groothuis, "The Smorgasbord Mentality," *Eternity* (May 1985), p. 32.

8. See Gary DeMar, *Ruler of the Nations* (Atlanta, GA: American Vision, 1987), pp.

22-23 and *God and Government: A Biblical and Historical Study* (Atlanta, GA: American Vision, 1982), pp. 82-83 for a definition of "democracy" and its inherent instability.

9. Groothuis, "The Smorgasbord Mentality," p. 33.

10. While Mormons may accept the Bible as authoritative, they also maintain that *The Book of Mormon, The Pearl of Great Price, Doctrine and Covenants*, and the continuing authority of the church apostles are equally trustworthy and authoritative.

11. Quoted in John Allan, *Shopping for a God: Fringe Religions Today* (Grand Rapids, MI: Baker Book House, 1987), p. 10.

12. C. S. Lewis, *They Asked for a Paper* (London: Geoffrey Bles, 1962), pp. 164f.

13. John Frame, *The Doctrine of the Knowledge of God* (Phillipsburg, NJ: Presbyterian and Reformed, 1987), p. 258.

14. Thomas Sowell, *Knowledge and Decisions* (New York: Basic Books, 1980), p. 3.

15. J. P. Moreland, *Scaling the Secular City: A Defense of Christianity* (Grand Rapids, MI: Baker Book House, 1987), p. 190. The short story *Twelve Angry Men*, and later a movie starring Henry Fonda, depicts this process quite well.

16. "Modern irrationalism has not in the least encroached upon the domain of the intellect as the natural man thinks of it. Irrationalism has merely taken possession of that which the intellect, by its own admission, cannot in any case control. Irrationalism has a secret treaty with rationalism by which the former cedes to the latter so much of its territory as the latter can at any given time find the forces to control." Cornelius Van Til, *The Defense of the Faith* (rev. ed.; Philadelphia, PA: Presbyterian and Reformed, 1963), pp. 125-26.

17. Michael Denton, *Evolution: A Theory in Crisis* (Bethesda, MD: Adler & Adler, 1986), p. 255.

18. Edmund H. Harvey, ed., *Reader's Digest Book of Facts* (Pleasantville, NY: The Reader's Digest Association, Inc., 1987), pp. 388f.

19. Carl Sagan, *Cosmos* (New York: Ballantine Books, [1980] 1985), p. 1.

20. *Idem.*

21. *Ibid.*, pp. 241-42.

22. *Idem.*

23. *Ibid.*, p. 286.

24. *Ibid.*, p. 200.

25. *Idem.*

26. *Idem.*

27. *Ibid.*, p. 212.

28. Herman J. Muller, "One Hundred Years Without Darwinism Are Enough," *The Humanist*, XIX (1959); reprinted in Philip Appelman, ed., *Darwin: A Norton Critical Edition* (New York: Norton, 1970), p. 570.

29. Schlossberg, *Idols for Destruction*, p. 84.

30. Carl Sagan, *Broca's Brain: Reflections on the Romance of Science* (New York: Random House, 1979), p. 286.

Chapter 5 – Leaping into the Void

1. Aldous Huxley, *Science, Liberty, and Peace* (New York: Harper, 1946), p. 291.

2. Herbert Schlossberg, *Idols for Destruction: Christian Faith and its Confrontation with American Society* (Nashville, TN: Thomas Nelson, 1983), p. 2.

3. *Idem.*

4. John R. Robbins, "The Scientist as Evangelist," *Trinity Review* (The Trinity Foundation, P.O. Box 169, Jefferson, MD 21755, January-February 1986), p. 3.

5. R. L. Meek, ed., *Marx and Engels on Malthus* (New York: International Publishers, 1954), p. 171. Quoted in Michael Pitman, *Adam and Evolution* (London, England: Rider & Company, 1984), p. 24.

6. *Idem.*

7. John Jefferson Davis, *Foundations of Evangelical Theology* (Grand Rapids, MI: Baker Book House, 1984), p. 127.

8. Francis A. Schaeffer, *The Complete Works of Francis Schaeffer: A Christian Worldview*, 5 vols.: *Escape From Reason* (Westchester, IL: Crossway Books, 1984), vol. 1, pp. 237-38.

9. Pat Means, *The Mystical Maze* (San Bernardino, CA: Campus Crusade for Christ, 1976), p. 39.

10. James W. Sire, *The Universe Next Door: A Basic World View Catalog* (Downers Grove, IL: InterVarsity Press, 1976), p. 133.

11. Pagan creation myths abound with this notion. According to one Babylonian account, Marduk, the great stone god, "killed the dragon Tiamat and split her body in half. The upper half was made into the sky, and the lower half the earth." John J. Davis, *Paradise to Prison: Studies in Genesis* (Grand Rapids, MI: Baker Book House, 1975), p. 69.

12. Douglas R. Groothuis, *Unmasking the New Age: Is There a New Religious Movement Trying to Transform Society?* (Downers Grove, IL: InterVarsity Press, 1986), p. 18.

13. Means, *The Mystical Maze*, p. 21.

14. Groothuis, *Unmasking the New Age*, p. 21.

15. *Idem.*

16. "The universe was conceived as a 'great chain of Being,' starting with the completely real being, the One, or God, or the Idea of the Good, whose very nature overflowed into lesser realms of being, such as the world of Ideas, human beings, animals, inanimate objects, down to matter, 'the last faint shadow of reality. . . .'

    "In this theory, the aim of human existence was seen as an attempt to move up the ladder of existence, to become more real. To accomplish this, men were to direct their interests and attention to what was above them on the 'great chain of Being.' By philosophizing they could liberate themselves from the sense world, and become more and more part of the intelligible world. The more one could understand, the more one would become like what one understood. Ultimately, if successful, one would reach the culmination of the 'journey of the mind of God,' by a mystical union with the One. Thus the final end of seeking to understand the nature of reality would be to become absorbed by what is most real, and to lose all of one's individuality which merely represents lesser degrees of reality. Through philosophizing, through art, and through mystic experience of unity with the One, [an individual found] the path to human salvation, and of liberation from the lesser reality of sensory and material worlds." Avrum Stroll and Richard H. Popkin, *Introduction to Philosophy* (2nd ed.; New York: Holt, Rhinehart and Winston, 1972), pp. 100-101.

17. Ray Sutton, *That You May Prosper: Dominion By Covenant* (Tyler, TX: Dominion Press, 1987), p. 37.

18. For an insightful analysis and critique of Cayce's views see: Gary North, *Unholy Spirits: Occultism and New Age Humanism* (Ft. Worth, TX: Dominion Press, 1986), pp. 193-225. Cayce was an avid Bible student. It is reported that he tried to read through the Bible once each year. He tried to reconcile his occultism with the Bible and failed, ignoring Hebrews 9:26-27. See Phillip J. Swihart, *Reincarnation, Edgar Cayce & the Bible* (Downers Grove, IL: InterVarsity Press, 1975).

19. John Snyder, *Reincarnation vs. Resurrection* (Chicago, IL: Moody Press, 1984), p. 19.

20. Naisbitt, *Megatrends: Ten New Directions Transforming Our Lives* (New York: Warner Books, 1982). Marilyn Ferguson, author of *The Aquarian Conspiracy*, writes of *Megatrends*: "In such turbulent times, we prize those among us who see clearly. John Naisbitt offers a dramatic, convincing view on the changes already under way. This is a book for everyone who wants a sense of the near future."

21. John Naisbitt and Patricia Aburdene, *Re-inventing the Corporation* (New York; Warner Books, 1985), p. 252.

22. New York: Dell, 1979.

23. New York: Simon and Schuster, 1982.

24. Los Angeles, CA: J. P. Tarcher, Inc., 1980.

25. North, *Unholy Spirits*, p. 6.

26. Schaeffer, *The Complete Works of Francis A. Schaeffer*, 5 vols.: *Pollution and the Death of Man: The Christian View of Ecology*, vol. 5, pp. 3-76.

27. "New Age Harmonies," *Time* (December 7, 1987), p. 72.

28. Os Guinness, *The Dust of Death: A Critique of the Establishment and the Counter Culture—and a Proposal for a Third Way* (Downers Grove, IL: InterVarsity Press, 1973), p. 209.

29. *Idem.*

30. *Idem.*

31. For helpful and balanced treatments of the New Age movement see: Gary DeMar and Peter J. Leithart, *The Reduction of Christianity: Dave Hunt's Theology of Cultural Surrender* (Ft. Worth, TX: Dominion Press, 1988); Karen Hoyt, ed., *The New Age Rage: A Probing Analysis of The Newest Religious Craze* (Old Tappan, NJ: Fleming H. Revell Company, 1987); Douglas R. Groothuis, *Unmasking the New Age: Is There a New Religious Movement Trying to Transform Society?* (Downers Grove, IL: InterVarsity Press, 1986).

32. Stephen H. Balch and Herbert I. London, "The Tenured Left," *Commentary* (October 1986), pp. 44-45.

33. Quoted in *ibid.*, p. 45.

34. Quoted in *ibid.*

35. Karl Marx, "Contribution to the Critique of Hegel's Philosophy of Right, in *Early Writings*, trans. and ed. by T. B. Bottomore (New York: McGraw-Hill, 1963), pp. 43-44.

36. Klaus Bockmuehl, *The Challenge of Marxism: A Christian Response* (Downers Grove, IL: InterVarsity Press, 1980), p. 52.

37. Quoted in *ibid.*, p. 91.

38. Emilio A. Núñez C., *Liberation Theology*, trans. by Paul E. Sywulka (Chicago, IL: Moody Press, 1985), p. 47.

39. *Ibid.*, p. 205.

40. *Ibid.*, pp. 235-36.

41. *Ibid.*, p. 236.

42. *Ibid.*, p. 273.

43. Harold O. J. Brown, "What Is Liberation Theology?" in *Liberation Theology*, Ronald Nash, ed. (Milford, MI: Mott Media, 1984), p. 11.

44. D. G. Myers, "MLA Malaise," *The American Spectator*, (March 1988), p. 33.

45. James L. Sauer, "Letter From Philadelphia," *Chronicles* (February 1988), pp. 40-41.

46. Phyllis Zagano, "In Whose Image?—Feminist Theology at the Crossroads," *This World* (Fall 1986), pp. 81, 83-84.

47. Jeffrey B. Russell, *A History of Witchcraft* (London: Thames and Hudson, 1980), p. 156.

48. Quoted in Mary Pride, *The Way Home: Beyond Feminism, Back to Reality* (Westchester, IL: Crossway, 1985), p. 5.

49. George Gilder, *Men and Marriage* (Gretna, LA: Pelican, 1986), pp. 103-104.
50. Quoted in Mary Pride, *The Way Home*, p. 12.
51. Allan Bloom, *The Closing of the American Mind: How Higher Education Has Failed Democracy and Impoverished the Souls of Today's Students* (New York: Simon and Schuster, 1987).
52. Quoted in Bernard D. N. Grebanier, *English Literature*, 2 vols. (Woodbury, NY: Baron's Educational Series), vol. 2, p. 627.
53. Bloom, *Closing of the American Mind*, p. 256.
54. David Cohen, "Behaviorism," in *The Oxford Companion to the Mind*, Richard L. Gregory, ed. (New York: Oxford University Press, 1987), p. 71.
55. B. F. Skinner, "Skinner on Behaviorism," in *ibid.*, p. 75.
56. *Ibid.*
57. Vincent Bugliosi, *Helter Skelter: The True Story of the Manson Murders* (New York: W. W. Norton & Company, 1974), p. 389.
58. *Ibid.*, p. 224.

Chapter 6—Spiritual Counterfeits

1. Murray N. Rothbard, *The Sociology of the Ayn Rand Cult* (Port Townsend, WA: Liberty Publishing, 1987), p. 1.
2. J. K. Van Baalen, "The Unpaid Bills of the Church," in *Chaos of Cults* (4th ed.; Grand Rapids, MI: Eerdmans, 1962), pp. 390-98.
3. Mary Baker Eddy, *Christian Science Journal*, January 1901. Quoted in Josh McDowell and Don Stewart, *Handbook of Today's Religions* (San Bernardino, CA: Here's Life Publishers, 1983), p. 123.
4. Quoted in *ibid.*, p. 37.
5. Herbert W. Armstrong, *The Autobiography of Herbert W. Armstrong* (Pasadena, CA: Ambassador College Press, 1967), p. 298-99. Quoted in McDowell and Stewart, *Handbook of Today's Religions*, p. 114.
6. Vincent Bugliosi, *Helter Skelter: The True Story of the Manson Murders* (New York: W. W. Norton and Company, 1974), p. 428. As a follow-up, the prosecuting attorney asked these two questions:

   Q. "Even commit murder?" I asked instantly.
   A. "I'd do anything for God."
   Q. "Including murder?" I pressed.
   A. "That's right. If I believed it was right" (p. 429).

7. Mary Baker Eddy, *Science and Health with Key to the Scriptures* (Boston, MA: The First Church of Christ, Scientist, 1971), p. 480.
8. William Sanford LaSor, *The Truth About Armageddon: What the Bible Says About the End Times* (Grand Rapids, MI: Baker Book House, 1982), p. 103, Note *a*. For a balanced treatment of what Christians should expect in terms of the "end times," the reader is encouraged to study Gary DeMar and Peter J. Leithart, *The Reduction of Christianity: Dave Hunt's Theology of Cultural Surrender* (Ft. Worth, TX: Dominion Press, 1988).

Chapter 7—The Occult Explosion

1. C. S. Lewis, *The Screwtape Letters* (New York: Macmillan, [1942] 1946), p. 9.
2. "Theologian Protests 'Witchcraft at Indiana University,'" *Christian News* (May 18, 1987), p. 1.

3. "Cobb Teen Charged in 'Ritual Murder' of Girl, 15," *The Marietta Daily Journal* (January 29, 1988), p. 7A.

4. Dirk Kinnane Roelofsma, "Battling Satanism a Haunting Task," *Insight* (January 11, 1988), p. 49.

5. *Idem.*

6. Gary North, *Unholy Spirits: Occultism and New Age Humanism* (Ft. Worth, TX: Dominion Press, 1986), pp. 65-66.

7. It's ironic that Roman Polanski directed *Rosemary's Baby.* Sharon Tate, the victim of Charles Manson's murdering occult-worshipping "Family," was pregnant at the time of her slaughter. She was married to Roman Polanski. Sharon Tate's movie debut was *Eye of the Devil* (1965), in which she "played a country girl with bewitching powers." In the film, David Niven "became the victim of a hooded cult which practiced ritual sacrifice." Vincent Bugliosi, *Helter Skelter: The True Story of the Manson Murders* (New York: W. W. Norton, 1974), p. 27. In 1967 Sharon Tate appeared in another Polanski Production, *The Fearless Vampire Killers.* "A victim of the vampire early in the picture, in the last scene she bites her lover, Polanski, creating still another monster" (p. 28).

8. Robert S. Wheeler, *The Children of Darkness: Some Heretical Reflections on the Kid Cult* (New Rochelle, NY: Arlington House, 1973), p. 31.

9. James Sire, *The Universe Next Door: A Basic World View Catalog* (Downers Grove, IL: InterVarsity Press, 1976), p. 142.

10. Gary DeMar and Peter J. Leithart, *The Reduction of Christianity: Dave Hunt's Theology of Cultural Surrender* (Ft. Worth, TX: Dominion Press, 1988).

11. Os Guinness, *The Dust of Death: A Critique of the Establishment and the Counter Culture—and a Proposal for a Third Way* (Downers Grove, IL: InterVarsity Press, 1973), p. 277.

12. Cornelius Van Til, *The Defense of the Faith* (3rd. ed.; Phillipsburg, NJ: Presbyterian and Reformed, 1967), p. 8.

13. Jeffrey B. Russell, *A History of Witchcraft: Sorcerers, Heretics and Pagans* (London: Thames and Hudson, 1980), pp. 174-75.

14. Quoted in Chris Morgan and David Langford, *Facts and Fallacies: A Book of Definitive Mistakes and Misguided Predictions* (Ontario, Canada: John Wiley & Sons Canada Limited, 1981), p. 110.

15. Guinness, *The Dust of Death*, p. 280.

16. Peter Leithart and George Grant, *A Christian Response to Dungeons & Dragons: The Catechism of the Occult* (Ft. Worth, TX: Dominion Press, 1987), p. 7.

17. Robert A. Morey, *Horoscopes and the Christian* (Minneapolis, MN: Bethany House, 1981).

18. Robert Somerlott, *"Here, Mr. Splitfoot": An Informal Exploration into Modern Occultism* (New York: Viking, 1971), p. 4.

19. Leithart and Grant, *A Christian Response to Dungeons & Dragons*, p. 4.

20. Quoted in *ibid.*, p. 7.

21. Josh McDowell and Don Stewart, *Handbook of Today's Religions* (San Bernardino, CA: Here's Life Publishers, 1983), p. 150.

22. Gary North, *Unholy Spirits*, p. 65.

23. Quoted in John M. Leighty, "Biblical Satan is Lukewarm Topic in Today's Modern World," *The Marietta Daily Journal* (January 29, 1988), p. 5B.

24. James Randi, *Flim-Flam: Psychics, ESP, Unicorns and other Delusions* (Buffalo, NY: Prometheus Books, [1982] 1987), pp. 248-49. See his chapter on "Medical Humbugs," pp. 173-95. For a Christian critique of the paranormal, see Danny Korem and Paul Meier, *The Fakers: Exploding the Myths of the Supernatural* (Grand Rapids, MI: Baker Book House, [1980] 1981).

25. Korem and Meier, *The Fakers*, p. 17. Korem illustrates his point by convincing a student at Tulane University that he, Korem, has supernatural powers and that he is a visitor from the planet Pluto.

26. Milbourne Christopher, *Houdini: The Untold Story* (New York: Pocket Books, [1969] 1975), p. 215.

27. Quoted in Loraine Boettner, *Immortality* (Philadelphia, PA: Presbyterian and Reformed, 1956), p. 156.

Chapter 8 – Keeping Your Faith Alive

1. Dave Lambert, quoted in "Helping 'Adult' Teens Face the Eighties," *Christianity Today* (February 19, 1988), p. 50.

2. For two very fine studies see: R. C. Sproul, *The Holiness of God* (Wheaton, IL: Tyndale House Publishers, 1985) and Jerry Bridges, *The Pursuit of Holiness* (Colorado Springs, CO: Navpress, 1978).

3. A very good book is available that will answer most of your questions regarding what it means to be a Christian: John Blanchard, *Right With God* (Chicago, IL: Moody Press, 1971).

4. Tyler, TX: Geneva Press, 1983.

5. David Chilton, "The Case of the Missing Blueprints," *The Journal of Christian Reconstruction*, Symposium on Social Action, Gary North, ed. (Vallecito, CA: A Chalcedon Ministry Publication, Summer, 1981), pp. 132-54.

6. R. C. Sproul, *Knowing Scripture* (Downers Grove, IL: InterVarsity Press, 1977); T. Norton Sterrett, *How to Understand Your Bible* (rev. ed.; Downers Grove, IL: InterVarsity Press, 1974); Leland Ryken, *How to Read the Bible as Literature* (Grand Rapids, MI: Academie Books/Zondervan Publishing House, 1984); Henry A. Vickler, *Hermeneutics: Principles and Processes of Biblical Interpretation* (Grand Rapids, MI: Baker Book House, 1981). For a more philosophically advanced discussion of Biblical interpretation, see John M. Frame, *The Doctrine of the Knowledge of God* (Phillipsburg, NJ: Presbyterian and Reformed, 1987).

7. Grand Rapids, MI: Zondervan, 1969.

8. Second edition; Wheaton, IL: Tyndale House, 1982.

9. "The first chapter of Genesis repeats this phrase, 'and God saw that it was good,' five times (verses 10, 12, 18, 21, 25), in addition to the final summation in verse 31. God's creative acts were evaluated by God and found to be good. They reflected His own goodness and the absolute correspondence among His plan, His standards of judgment, His fiat word, and results of His word, the creation. The creation was good precisely because it was solely the product of God's sovereign word. God therefore imputed positive value to His creation, for He created it perfect. It was completely in conformity to His decree. The doctrine of *imputation* lies at the heart of the doctrine of *creation*. The creation was good because God created it good and because God said it was good. It was good *objectively* because of its inherent conformity to God's decree. It was good *subjectively* because God announced its perfection, indicating its conformity to His standards." Gary North, *The Dominion Covenant: Genesis* (2nd ed.; Tyler, TX: Institute for Christian Economics, [1982] 1987), p. 37.

10. See David Chilton, *Paradise Restored* (Ft. Worth, TX: Dominion Press, 1985).

Chapter 9 – Getting Ready for College

1. Carol Innerst, "Freshmen: A Study in Unreadiness," *Insight* (January 19, 1987), p. 58.

2. *Idem.*

3. Cited in "Opening the American Mind," *U.S. News & World Report Guide: America's Best Colleges* (Washington, D.C.: U.S. News & World Report, 1987), p. 6.

4. John Stickney, "The Class of 2000 Just Entered the Second Grade," *Money*, November 1985, p. 111.

5. Quoted in William C. Ringenberg, *The Christian College: A History of Protestant Higher Education in America* (Grand Rapids, MI: Eerdmans, 1984), p. 17.

6. Quoted in *ibid.*, p. 38.

7. Quoted in *idem*.

8. Harry S. Stout, *The New England Soul: Preaching and Religious Culture in Colonial New England* (New York: Oxford University Press, 1986).

9. Franklin B. Dexter, *Biographical Sketches of the Graduates of Yale College with Annals of the College History, 1745-1763* (New York, 1896), vol. 2, p. 2. Quoted in Sol Gordon, ed., *Education in The United States: A Documentary History*, 5 vols. (New York: Random House, 1974), vol. 2, p. 675.

10. American Vision is in the process of developing a course on "critical thinking" to supplement this manual.

11. Quoted in Henry M. Morris, *Men of Science — Men of God: Great Scientists who Believed the Bible* (San Diego, CA: Creation Life Publishers, 1982), pp. 34-35.

12. E. D. Hirsch, Jr., *Cultural Literacy: What Every American Needs to Know* (Boston, MA: Houghton Mifflin, 1987), p. xiii.

13. Jeffrey Breshears, "Our Students' Minds are a Cultural Disaster," *The Atlanta Journal/Constitution*, (January 10, 1988), p. 1C. The answers: (1) The four Beatles: John Lennon, Paul McCartney, George Harrison, and Ringo Starr; (2) the nine justices: Chief Justice William H. Renquist, Associate Justices William J. Brennan, Jr., Byron R. White, Thurgood Marshall, Harry A. Blackmun, John Paul Stevens, Sandra Day O'Connor, Antonin Scalia, and Anthony Kennedy; (3) Georgia's two senators: Sam Nunn and Wyche Fowler; (4) U.S. population: between 220-240 million.

14. "Getting Smart About IQ," *U.S. News & World Report*, (November 23, 1987), p. 53.

15. William Adams Simonds, *Edison: His Life, His Work, His Genius* (New York: Bobbs-Merrill, 1934), p. 42.

16. Matthew Josephson, *Edison: A Biography* (New York: McGraw-Hill, 1959), p. 33.

17. Quoted in *ibid.*, p. 34.

18. "Getting Smart About IQ," p. 54.

19. *Ibid.*, pp. 54-55. Answers: 1. None. Unlisted numbers do not appear in the telephone book. 2. The man is a minister. The critical word in the problem is "married." The man married the various women, but he did not himself become married to them. 3. The President. The death of the Vice President has no effect upon who is President. 4. AFFECTION 5. YELLOW 6. SMOOTH 7. FEATHERY 8. SNAKE 9. Part to a whole. 10. Equivalent. 11. Antonyms. 12. Synonyms. 13. Completion: New Orleans is a city. 14. Negation. 15. Antonyms.

20. Perry W. Buffington, "Strokes of Genius," *Sky* (February 1987), p. 121.

21. Milo progressed in strength by regularly lifting a calf as it grew to a bull.

22. Emmaus, PA: Rodale Press, 1978. You might want to get a combined work like *Funk & Wagnalls Standard Handbook of Synonyms, Antonyms, and Prepositions*. James C. Fernald (New York: Funk & Wagnalls, 1947).

23. Milo O. Frank, *How to Get Your Point Across in Thirty Seconds or Less* (New York: Pocket Books, 1986).

Chapter 10 – How to Study

1. Jeremy Rifkin, *Entropy: A New World View* (New York: Viking Press, 1980), p. 164.
2. Charles B. Thaxton and Stephen C. Meyer, "Coming soon . . . human rights for bacteria?," *Houston Chronicle* (January 10, 1988), p. 4, section 6.
3. Alan N. Schoonmaker, *A Student's Survival Manual, or How to Get An Education Despite it All* (New York: Harper & Row, 1971), p. 220.

Chapter 11 – Memory Mechanics

1. David M. Roth, *Roth Memory Course* (New York: The Sun Dial Press, 1918), p. 1.
2. Joan Minninger, *Total Recall: How to Boost Your Memory Power* (Emmaus, PA: Rodale Press, 1984), p. 2.
3. *Idem.*
4. "Memory," *Newsweek* (September 29, 1986), p. 48.
5. *Idem.*
6. Please, if you're studying to be a doctor, drop the mnemonic device by the time you get to the operating room.
7. Please, do not associate this with the New Age movement. We all visualize or picture things in our minds. There's nothing evil about it. The New Age movement takes a normal function of the mind and perverts it so that the mind is used as a vehicle for holistic healing. See Douglas R. Groothuis, *Unmasking the New Age* (Downers Grove IL: InterVarsity Press, 1986), p. 61.
8. Roth, *Roth Memory Course*, p. 2.
9. There are a number of books that might prove helpful: Harry Lorayne and Jerry Lucas, *The Memory Book* (New York: Ballantine Books, 1973) and Joan Minninger, *Total Recall: How to Boost Your Memory Power* (Emmaus, PA: Rodale Press, 1984). Check out your local bookstore. You'll find some older works in used bookstores that are out of print but are just as good.
10. "Memory," *Newsweek*, p. 54.
11. Existence actually begins at conception. But for this memory exercise, I am using existence in a slightly different way.
12. William H. Armstrong and M. Willard Lampe II, *Study Tips: How to Study Effectively and Get Better Grades* (New York: Barron's Educational Series, [1975] 1983), pp. 47-48.

Chapter 12 – How to Read

1. John Morley, *Aspects of Modern Study*, p. 71. Quoted by F. M. McMurry, *How to Study and Teaching How to Study* (Cambridge, MA: The Riverside Press, 1909), p. 31.
2. Kathryn Stechert, "Illiteracy in America: The Shocking Silent Crisis," *Better Homes and Gardens* (November, 1985), p. 27.
3. Rudolf Flesch, *Why Johnny Can't Read* (New York: Harper & Row, 1955).
4. Rudolf Flesch, *Why Johnny Still Can't Read* (San Francisco, CA: Harper & Row, 1981), p. 161.
5. Quentin Schultze, *Television: Manna From Hollywood?* (Grand Rapids, MI: Zondervan, 1986), p. 7.
6. *Insight* (May 11, 1987), p. 10.

7. Mortimer Adler, *How to Read a Book* (New York: Simon and Schuster, 1940), p. 248.
8. Thomas A. Morris, *Francis Schaeffer's Apologetics: A Critique* (Chicago, IL: Moody Press, 1976), p. 108n.
9. One very helpful way to find the worldview of an author is to check the biographical information supplied in *Contemporary Authors: A Bio-Bibliographical Guide to Current Writers in Fiction, General Fiction, General Non-Fiction, Poetry, Journalism, Drama, Motion Pictures, Television and Other Fields.* This massive set comes with a "Cumulative Index for Volumes" 1-106. At the end of some of the biographies, a brief but accurate "philosophy" of the author is given.
10. Alvin Toffler, *Future Shock* (New York: Bantam, 1971), p. 155.
11. *Ibid.*, pp. 336-37.
12. Francis A. Schaeffer, *A Christian Manifesto* (Westchester, IL: Crossway Books, 1981), p. 17.
13. Rousas J. Rushdoony, *The One and the Many: Studies in the Philosophy of Order and Ultimacy* (Nutley, NJ: The Craig Press, 1971).
14. See Franky Schaeffer, *A Time for Anger: The Myth of Neutrality* (Westchester,IL: Crossway Books, 1982) and Cal Thomas, *Book Burning* (Westchester IL: Crossway Books, 1983).
15. *The Chicago Manual of Style* (13th ed.; Chicago, IL: University of Chicago, 1982), pp. 19-20.
16. Greg L. Bahnsen, *Theonomy in Christian Ethics* (2nd ed.; Phillipsburg, NJ: Presbyterian and Reformed, 1984), p. xxix.
17. David Chilton, *Productive Christians in an Age of Guilt-Manipulators* (3rd ed.; Tyler, TX: Institute for Christian Economics, 1985), p. xi.
18. John W. Whitehead, *The Second American Revolution* (Westchester, IL: Crossway Books, [1982] 1985), p. 13.
19. Rousas John Rushdoony, *The Myth of Over Population* (Fairfax, VA: Thoburn Press, 1975).
20. Thomas Sowell, *The Economics and Politics of Race: An International Perspective* (New York: William Morrow, 1985), p. 210.

Chapter 13 – How to Write and Research

1. C. S. Lewis, "*Yours Ever,* C. S. Lewis," *Eternity* (July/August, 1985), p. 24.
2. Nancy Leigh DeMoss, ed., *The Rebirth of America* (Philadelphia, PA: Arthur S. DeMoss Foundation, 1986), p. 37.
3. Cal Thomas, *Book Burning* (Westchester, IL: Crossway Books, 1983), p. 114.
4. S. Robert Lichter, Stanley Rothman, Linda S. Lichter, *The Media Elite: America's New Powerbrokers* (Bethesda, MD: Adler & Adler, 1986).
5. Franky Schaeffer, *A Time For Anger: The Myth of Neutrality* (Westchester, IL: Crossway Books, 1982), p. 26.
6. Merrill Sheils, "Why Johnny Can't Write," *Newsweek* (December 8, 1975), p. 58.
7. *Ibid.*, p. 59.
8. Marilyn Durham, *Writer's Digest,* March 1973. Quoted by Robert J. Hastings, *How I Write: A Manual for Beginning Writers* (Nashville, TN: Broadman Press, 1973), p. 84.
9. Otto J. Scott, *The Secret Six: John Brown and the Abolitionist Movement* (New York: Times Books, 1979).
10. Charles E. Hummel, *The Galileo Connection: Resolving Conflicts Between Science and the Bible* (Downers Grove, IL: InterVarsity Press, 1986), p. 103.

11. Quoted in *ibid.*, p. 105.
12. R. O'Bannon, "Creation, Evolution, and Public Education," #5 Dayton Symposium on Tennessee's Evolution Laws, May 18, 1974; quoted by Wendell R. Bird, "Freedom of Religion and Science Instruction in Public Schools," *Yale Law Review,* Vol. 87, No. 3 (January 1978), p. 561.
13. Alan N. Schoonmaker, *A Student's Survival Manual; or How to Get an Education Despite it All* (New York: Harper & Row, 1971), p. 239.
14. *Ibid.*, p. 239.
15. New York: The New American Library, 1975.
16. Taken from the inside front cover of Merete Gerli, *How to Find Information About Your Subject: A Guide to Reference Materials in Local Libraries* (Washington, D.C.: Congressional Research Service, The Library of Congress, September 25, 1980, Report No. D-102). This is a gold mine of research information. Ask your congressman for a copy. He'll be glad to send you one. He may think you'll vote for him in the next election.
17. Louise Colligan, *Scholastic's A+ Guide to Research and Term Papers* (New York: Scholastic Inc., 1981), pp. 27-45.
18. Schoonmaker, *A Student's Survival Manual*, p. 237.
19. Donald A. and Eleanor C. Laird, *Techniques for Efficient Remembering* (New York: McGraw-Hill, 1960), p. 11.
20. Gary North, *The Dominion Covenant: Genesis* (2nd ed.; Tyler, TX: Institute for Christian Economics, [1982] 1987), p. 18n.
21. (4th ed.; San Diego, CA: Harcourt Brace Jovanovich, 1985), p. ix.
22. Hastings, *How I Write*, p. 49.
23. A friend of mine went into a used book store looking for a copy of *Animal Farm.* When he asked the store clerk where he could find a copy, she asked him if it was about animals and told him that if it was, he would find it in the pet section.
24. William Zinsser, *On Writing Well: An Informal Guide to Writing Nonfiction* (3rd ed.; New York: Harper & Row, 1985), p. 146.
25. Flesch, *The Art of Readable Writing*, pp. 247-51.
26. Quoted in John R. Trimble, *Writing With Style: Conversations on the Art of Writing* (Englewood Cliffs, NJ: Prentice-Hall, 1975), p. 95.
27. William Zinsser, *On Writing Well*, p. 65.

Chapter 14 – Taking Exams

1. "Shoe," *The Atlanta Journal/Constitution*, June 6, 1985.

DAILY SCHEDULE

*Date*_____

IMPORTANT REMINDERS:

6	
7	
8	
9	
10	
11	
12	
1	
2	
3	
4	
5	
6	
7	
8	
9	
10	
11	

WEEKLY SCHEDULE

*Date*_____

TIME	MONDAY	TUESDAY	WEDNESDAY	THURSDAY	FRIDAY	SATURDAY	SUNDAY

LONG-TERM SCHEDULE

DATE	JANUARY:		DATE	JULY:	
DATE	FEBRUARY:		DATE	AUGUST:	
DATE	MARCH:		DATE	SEPTEMBER:	
DATE	APRIL:		DATE	OCTOBER:	
DATE	MAY:		DATE	NOVEMBER:	
DATE	JUNE:		DATE	DECEMBER:	

COLOPHON

The typeface for the text of this book is *Caslon 540*. It is a modern design based on the famous fonts that the great pioneer of English typefounding, William Caslon, cut more than two hundred years ago. Caslon was born in 1692 at Cradley in Worcestershire, and turned to letter-founding after being apprenticed to an engraver of ornamental gunlocks and barrels. There was nothing startlingly new about his designs; he took as his models the best Dutch types of the seventeenth century, particularly those of Van Dijck. Retaining the old style forms of the Dutch types, he added more contrast in forms. The fact that he started a great era of British typography was due less to his originality than to his competence and ability at engraving and casting types at a time when letter-founding in England was at a very low ebb. His famous typeface in both the roman and italic first appeared in 1722. Since that time it has never gone out of style, although it has been recut and modified many times for more modern typesetting systems.

Editing by George Grant
Copy editing by Lynn Hawley
Illustrations by Dan Riedel, The Graphics Guild
357 Lawn Avenue, Sellersville, Pennsylvania 18960
Cover design by Kent Puckett Associates, Atlanta, Georgia
Typography by Thoburn Press, Tyler, Texas
Printed and bound by R. R. Donnelley & Sons Company
Harrisonburg, Virginia
Cover printing by Weber Graphics, Chicago, Illinois